D1109538

PETER N. STEARNS

is Professor of History and Chairman, New Brunswick Department of History, Rutgers University. He is managing editor of the *Journal of Social History*, author of *European Society in Upheaval*, and editor of *A Century for Debate, 1789–1914: Problems in the Interpretation of European History*.

THE IMPACT
OF THE
INDUSTRIAL
REVOLUTION

Protest
and
Alienation

Edited by

PETER N. STEARNS

PRENTICE-HALL, INC.   *Englewood Cliffs, N. J.*

A SPECTRUM BOOK

330.94
S

ISBN: C   0–13–451765–2
P   0–13–451757–1

Library of Congress Catalog Card Number 79–178764

Printed in the United States of America

10 9 8 7 6 5 4 3 2 1

Prentice-Hall International, Inc. (*London*)
Prentice-Hall of Australia, Pty. Ltd. (*Sydney*)
Prentice-Hall of Canada, Ltd. (*Toronto*)
Prentice-Hall of India Private Limited (*New Delhi*)
Prentice-Hall of Japan, Inc. (*Tokyo*)

CONTENTS

v

MAJOR SOCIAL CLASSES

INTRODUCTION

The Industrial Revolution dominates the history of nineteenth-century Europe. Indeed, few developments in the whole of human history rival its importance in changing every aspect of man's life, from place of residence to basic outlook. Yet the types of people most involved in industrialization did not leave clear or convenient records of their activities. Nineteenth-century writers bequeathed masses of materials to the historian, but they were not kind enough to arrange them in order of importance. We can be easily overwhelmed with the details of diplomatic negotiations or the writings of political theorists. Hence, most historians of the century, unlike students of earlier periods, who have been more interested in developments beneath the surface of events if only because they lack such voluminous documents, have concentrated on political and intellectual history.

The result is that we have only the haziest notion of what happened to people who crowded into the cities and who worked in the new offices and factories. Unresolved questions abound and new ones constantly crop up as historians delve into the workings of society. What happened, for example, to family structure under the impact of industrialization? Many people, including contemporary observers, thought that family ties loosened. It certainly seems logical to assume that traditional extended families, with links among all living generations and a wide range of relatives, separated as people moved to the cities and became more individualistic and more isolated. Evidence now indicates, however, that these broad extended families not only survived but were strengthened as people sought to adjust to the rapid change in their way of life. Certainly no assertion that industrialization weakened the family can be accepted at face value. Men began to marry younger. Affection for children probably increased. The family changed greatly, but we are only beginning to learn how.[1]

Problems of this sort must be solved, for they help us understand ourselves. It is extremely difficult to interpret the nature and functions of the family in modern society, but if we know the evolution of the family under the impact of industrialization, the interpretation will be considerably advanced. If family ties have long been loosening, studying the process will illuminate the situation of the family today. But if, as now seems probable, the emotional importance of the family increased, our approach to the sociology of the modern family must change. Observers of the contemporary family, from scholarly sociologists to magazine writers, have not been able to avoid references to history; generalizations about industrialization breaking up the traditional family are common. This is another reason why serious historical study is essential. We can discover whether there is an enduring trend which industrialization set in motion, and we can find out what factors operating today, such as rising geographic mobility or increasing longevity, did to the family in the past.

The obvious point is that we live in an industrial society and, in the history of industrialization, we have a record of a century and a half through which we can hope to find out what industrial society is. Not all features of earlier stages of industrialization correspond to the present, of course, for change has been constant. But most features of contemporary society can be found at least in embryo form from the beginnings of the Industrial Revolution without forcing the historical record. A study of the basic social processes produced by industrialization is essential to an understanding of the shape of the present. The field is extensive and the range of topics immense, precisely because most historians have been preoccupied with details of thought and politics, which were undoubtedly affected by industrialization but not central to it. When we can refer to histories that discuss the growth of leisure time and its meaning, whether pleasurable or unsettling, to people accustomed to work, or that trace and assess the sense of depersonalization felt in large units of employment—then our useful knowledge will be truly increased. Whether useful knowledge improves the quality of life in industrial society may be open to question, of course. We could benefit from some historical study of this issue too.

1 For the conventional view on the extended family see Philippe Ariès, *Centuries of Childhood: a social history of family life* (New York, 1962). Various revisions are suggested in Peter Laslett, "The Comparative History of Household and Family," *Journal of Social History* (Autumn 1970), and David Hunt, *Parents and Children in History: The Psychology of Family Life in Early Modern France* (New York, 1970).

The most basic theme in the social history of industrialization is reaction to change.[2] We know that the Industrial Revolution brought immense change in daily lives, and that industrial economies continue such change indefinitely. Was the initial change imposed and painful? If so, when did people become accustomed to it, and to what degree? Or were accommodations made at least by some groups early on, and, if so, on what bases? What sorts of people does industrial society alienate, under what conditions, and what does alienation mean? Answers to these questions are crucial to study of family history, or to the history of protest, or to virtually any significant topic in the social history of industrialization, because they constitute the human meaning of the whole process.

To answer such questions we must determine the outlook of ordinary men in the past. Naturally, this returns us to the problem of sources. The businessman who spent fifteen hours a day overseeing a spinning mill in Lille did not write neat little essays about his belief in progress. The worker who took a job for a giant Ruhr mining concern did not draw up a report on "my feelings concerning corporate management." The social historian, interested in large groups of people who left few direct records, must search for his sources. He must manipulate large quantities of material to determine what ideas and behavior are representative of the group he is studying. Rarely is there a single striking document, such as can be found in the history of politics. Often the bulk of the evidence is indirect—written about a group by others. Because of this, interpretations are inevitably open to question.

This book of readings has two purposes. It illustrates some gut reactions to nineteenth-century industrial change, from people daily involved in the process. It suggests some of the types of sources available for the social history of industrialization and the problems and pleasures in analyzing them.

Some vital sources are not represented. There is no reason to reproduce statistics on population or wages or strikes, though these play a major role in social history. Nor need the reader be burdened with typical wills or marriage documents, though these reveal much about the quality of life in the past. The sources are descriptive and therefore more interesting in themselves than some of the materials that social historians use. Even so, they are not sources of the sort usually produced in anthologies for political or intellectual history. None of them is really very important. Several of them could be lost without

2 Two general studies of the social history of industrialization are Barrington Moore, *Social Origins of Dictatorship and Democracy; Lord and Peasant in the Making of the Modern World* (Boston, 1966); and Peter N. Stearns, *European Society in Upheaval* (New York, 1967).

great harm to our historical understanding. Very few were written by people worth knowing much about as individuals. These are documents important as types, expressing thoughts to some degree representative of large groups of people.

No book of readings can convey more than a small portion of the materials it seeks to illustrate. In a book of readings in social history, this problem is particularly acute. The usefulness of sources in social history lies in their accumulated mass. Evaluation of any single document depends on comparison with many others. I believe that the following documents illustrate important and widespread reactions to industrialization. The reader may kindly assume that this belief is correct, but he cannot prove it from the materials in the collection. This is only an introduction to types of sources and topics.

The materials in this collection are not filled with great or complex ideas. Their complexity lies in evaluating what they imply about the outlook of ordinary people. Not everyone will feel them compelling. I am convinced that some people who are sincerely interested in history—students and professional historians alike—cannot empathize with the problems of social history. They require great men, great ideas, great events. I regret this, because I think such people miss the real substance of history and cannot really grasp what is great. An idea is historically important not because it excites intellectuals a century later (though it may be philosophically important because of this), but because it managed to spread widely in society or some portion of society; to assess this requires a social-historical dimension. But this does not change the fact that many will be most entranced by the exciting idea itself.

Because social history deals largely with ordinary people, it is not surprising that its sources are often prosaic. What makes them fascinating is the questions that can be asked of them, and the importance of the types of people from whom they stem. Many of the documents in this collection, for example, revolve around the belief in progress. When did major groups of people come to believe in progress, and why, and what kind of progress did they believe in? All this is far more difficult to trace and evaluate than the intellectual history of the idea of progress. Finding answers to these questions is far more important and it enlivens many obscure events and sources.

The idea of progress was not natural to the common man, whose life in pre-industrial society focused on maintaining existing standards and traditions. The idea was acquired, often slowly and sometimes painfully, during industrialization itself. In the latter part of the twentieth century, some ecologists and others find that the idea was too well learned—that industrial societies expect a harmful kind of progress. In studying the history of progress we may be able to determine whether, and how, the idea can be quickly altered or unlearned. Sources in social history raise several general problems of interpretation. The interest in common people means an interest in people who did not write for the historical record. We must try to decide who best represents the views of a social group. Who best conveys the outlook of workers—an unusually well-read miner or a bourgeois observer with experience in the factory? Is a union leader better aware of the nature of industrial protest than a group of young strikers? The documents in this collection have been chosen because of their diversity of origin. Many of them undeniably point in contradictory directions. The social historian must determine what ideas or conditions are most typical and why.

Sources describing material conditions or behavior in protest speak rather directly about topics in which social historians are interested. But when we reach more fundamental topics concerning ideas and outlook, we must raise questions which most of the documents did not intend to answer. We must make the author of a pamphlet on tariffs, for example, tell us what he thought about industrialization and progress. Again, what is intended is an introduction to the ways social historians must use most of their qualitative sources.

The documents in this volume are drawn mainly from Britain, France, and Germany, three countries that industrialized fairly extensively within the nineteenth century. But even these three countries raise a final pervasive interpretive problem. If we know something about German workers, can we apply it to workers elsewhere? How different were French and British businessmen? [3] The process of industrialization was not precisely the same in all three countries. Cultural traditions varied significantly. My own view is that industrialization created similar forces and problems in all three countries and that basic social concepts can be developed applicably to all three. But this is certainly open to question. Historians have generally emphasized national distinctiveness. It is plausible to decide that some of the contradictions in, for example, middle-class outlook reflect basic national differences. Anyone interested in society must be aware of a comparative dimension, which is not to say that comparative problems are easily resolved.

The sources in this book are grouped around two themes. Both have been studied by a number of historians so that problems of analysis are fairly clear. Other themes, such as the evolution of the family, are at least as important but are still so undeveloped for the

3 For two efforts at comparative social-economic history, see Charles P. Kindleberger, *Economic Growth in France and Britain, 1851–1950* (Cambridge, Mass., 1964); Peter N. Stearns, "National Character and European Labor History," *Journal of Social History* (Winter 1970).

industrial period that even good descriptive source material is scarce. This is in no sense even a preliminary introduction to all the topics involved in studying the social impact of industrialization. And even the themes selected remain open-ended. We know the questions but not all the answers.

Examining protest is the most obvious means of evaluating the key issue of adaptation or resistance to industrial change. Did industrialization increase or diminish the sorts of grievances that impelled people to violence? Historians are now distinguishing between pre-industrial and industrial protest, but they have yet to arrive at a satisfactory definition of the latter.[4] The nineteenth century obviously produced a variety of protest doctrines, such as socialism and anarchism. These are not reprinted here, in part because they are easily available elsewhere, and in part because the social historian must treat even protest ideas and organizations with some care. We need information from actual or potential protesters themselves before we can know the impact of doctrines and the organizations they spawned. We may discover that we can read Marx to know what nineteenth-century workers wanted, but we cannot assume this in advance.

Protest has its own forms and meanings. It also constitutes the most direct insight into the broader conditions and aspirations of many inarticulate social groups. Therefore, it leads logically into the second and more diffuse section of this book, the outlook of leading industrial classes. Most people did not protest often. Some never protested, even if they were aggrieved, because their values did not permit this. Protest itself rarely expressed more than a portion of the ideas of the protesters themselves about social and economic change. Hence, the excursion into a different type of documentation.

The middle and working classes were the groups most directly involved with industrialization, and their reactions to the process differed considerably. It is hardly surprising that differences in income, education, and ownership and non-ownership of property prevent sweeping generalizations about the impact of industrialization across the whole of society. But, in studying key divisions in social structure, the social historian must not assume that conventional units are always applicable, at least as they are conventionally used. We cannot simply define classes by income or property ownership. We cannot even define real or potential class conflict with an assurance that each conflicting group had genuine internal coherence. The social historian must seek shared values and life styles as the basis of his definition of social structure, for this is what his inquiry is all about. In the section

4 See Charles Tilly, "Collective Violence in European Perspective," in Hugh Davis Graham and Ted Robert Gurr, eds., *Violence in America: Historical and Comparative Perspectives* (New York, 1969).

on social outlook, the documents illustrate some of the divisions between middle and working classes. They also show great diversity in the response to industrialization within each class. They suggest the need for a somewhat more complex rendering of industrial class structure.[5]

Social history is a rather new field of inquiry, though, like all fields, it has an abundance of antecedents. Social historians are uncovering new types of documents. They are asking new questions, even about established historical themes such as industrialization. This book raises more questions about handling sources and about the social impact of industrialization than can be answered from the materials in it. This reflects the nature and the challenge of social history itself.

5 See Ralf Dahrendorf, *Class and Class Conflict in Industrial Society* (Stanford, 1959).

PROTEST

EARLY
INDUSTRIAL PROTEST

The two or three decades before a country began to industrialize, or as it just began, were usually wracked by protest from the lower classes. In this sense, the late eighteenth and early nineteenth centuries in France and Britain are comparable to the mid-nineteenth century in Germany and the end of the century in Italy and Russia. Artisans in the cities, manufacturing workers laboring at home in the countryside, and peasants with medium-sized landholdings who depended on the traditional village agricultural system typically conducted most of the protest.[1] They were oppressed by the rising population which increased competition for jobs and land. The first stages of modernization also infringed upon their position. Governments, needing money to finance industry (among other things), increased taxes, and more commercial, capitalistic practices were introduced even before major technological change.

There was a great deal to protest against. There was no need for a revolution in expectations to serve as the basis for agitation and there was little sign that such a revolution had occurred. This is one of the things that makes early industrial protest in Europe so fascinating, because it runs counter to modern notions of protest, even as they are applied to agricultural peoples today. There are many reasons why the lower classes in the contemporary "third world" might develop new expectations, but if the European experience is any guide, it is more likely that they are disturbed by change than that they are try-

[1] See E. J. Hobsbawm, *Primitive Rebels: Studies in Archaic Forms of Social Movement in the Nineteenth and Twentieth Centuries* (New York, 1957).

ing to take advantage of it. The question is, of course, the extent to which the European experience does apply.[2]

In Europe, artisans found their masters treating them more like paid labor than like colleagues. Their traditional protective organizations, the guilds, declined or were abolished by the capitalistic middle classes. Guilds had long given artisans a means of preventing innovations in manufacturing techniques and of limiting the numbers of entrants to their trades. Now they were deprived of this just as population increases threatened them with unprecedented competition.[3]

The protest that arose was far more intense than was common in pre-industrial society, but it used established forms for the most part. Its method was the riot, which could occasionally turn into revolution if middle-class elements used it for their own purposes. Its goals were traditional, though the protesters often idealized the past they invoked. Stop change, turn back the clock, return to the pure village and the pure guild—this was the common message. There was often a strong religious flavor as well. At the same time, major protests invariably occurred after a year or more of economic crisis, during which crops failed, food prices soared, and unemployment spread. It is not always easy to distinguish motives, to determine whether there were grievances against the whole economic structure, or whether immediate issues predominated.

Sources for early industrial protest are inevitably scattered and most of them are short. Many violent riots passed without a recorded statement from any of the participants. One must beware of self-appointed spokesmen, usually from the middle classes, who purported to express general popular grievances. They may or may not have done so accurately. In revolutions we know that middle-class leaders did not stress the issues that were of real concern to the common people, even when they were genuine democrats in principle. Did individual radicals, like William Cobbett in Britain for example, reach more genuinely into the minds of this audience? If so, we have a vast amount of source material.

When we find direct statements from lower-class protesters our problems are not over. Early industrial protest involved a good bit of ritual and, often, religious imagery. Issues that we imagine were basic to protest were often not phrased very directly. The causes of grievance

2 For the "revolution in expectations" approach, which often draws inaccurately on the European past whatever its merits in dealing with the "third world," see Ronald G. Ridker, "Discontent and Economic Growth," *Economic Development and Cultural Change* (1962).

3 Theodore Hamerow, *Restoration, Revolution, Reaction: Economics and Politics in Germany, 1815–1871* (Princeton, 1958); P. A. Noyes, *Organization and Revolution: Working-Class Associations in the German Revolution of 1848–1849* (Princeton, 1966).

were not always fully defined. Peasants, for example, frequently turned against aristocratic landlords. They had ample reason to do so but the reasons were not new; the new problems, which actually caused the protest to burst forth when it did, were less personalized, stemming above all from rapid population growth. But the peasants rarely showed any awareness of this. The historian must engage in the uncomfortable task of reading into the situation more than those directly involved were able to express.

Lower-class protest also used certain concepts in a way that differs markedly from modern usage. Until recently, it was common to claim that early industrial protest was nonpolitical, and it is true that it did not raise questions about the structure and control of government. But in terms of the politics that affected the common people, the power relationships that governed them, their protest could be highly political. The lower classes were aware, in their own way, not only of local political relationships, with manorial lords for example, but of the central state as well. Hence, they often attacked agents of the government. Beyond this, lower-class protesters displayed a sense of rights, which one historian has called a belief in "natural justice." They thought that governments had certain definite obligations toward them. In truth, it is possible that the belief in the nature of government obligations has not changed completely, even as modern political consciousness develops, for in the early nineteenth century we already see demands for government intervention against high prices and unemployment. But in all this we have to read into sources more than they explicitly state. The question is, of course, whether in our enthusiasm to point out the rationality and good sense of the protesters we do not read too much.

Most forms of early industrial protest were small-scale. Indeed, one element in the definition of the phenomenon is that it is localized, based on village or neighborhood ties more than on modern class ties. Most historians assume that early industrial protest represents grievances that were far more widespread than the sheer size of the protest can indicate. We can certainly hypothesize that the dispersion of the population in a largely rural setting, the possibilities of repression, and the inertia caused by poverty and exhausting work inhibited outright protest but that the protest that did occur expressed both general suffering and the sentiments of the lower classes. The question is whether the sources give us any basis for this belief.

Early industrial protest, if only because it was local and badly organized, took an amazing variety of specific forms. The selections that follow take us from peasant rioting through Luddism to early trade union organization. We must ask whether the generalizations about the nature of early industrial protest cover this diversity. My own belief is that largely they do, but that we cannot ignore early signs of more "modern" forms. The lower classes were not monolithic during this period of rapid social change. Certain elements could forge ahead more rapidly than most.

Early industrial protests were not blind expressions of rage. Rioters did not strike out indiscriminately. They thought they knew who their enemies were and they believed in their rights. The sources they have left us clearly reveal their sense of purpose.

AGRICULTURAL WORKERS

Most rural protest left little trace. Two of the excerpts that follow have the merit of coming from agricultural workers directly, though in different situations. For the most part, one must judge peasant protest by behavior rather than by words; what they attacked tells what they opposed. Hence, outside accounts, as in Russia in 1905, can be revealing, but they suggest rather than state peasant intentions.

In 1830, a riot spread through much of rural England.[1] Agricultural laborers, dependent on their wages and oppressed by population growth and the expansion of large estates through enclosure, attacked a new evil: harvesting machines. They destroyed many machines and other property—they did not attack persons, and many of their farmer-employers sympathized with them. When they expressed grievances they talked, understandably enough, in terms of material deprivation, for the previous years had seen poor harvests. But they seldom spoke for the record. The first passage resulted when the principal landowner of Ringmer in Sussex, Lord Gage, realizing that disorder was imminent, convened his laborers on the village green. No one—of the 150 men present—came forward, but someone tossed a letter at the landlord.

In 1893, peasants in Sicily rioted in the Fasci rebellion. They had some leadership from urban socialists and they described an egalitarian community as a *fascio*. The peasants were driven by rising population, by the evils of a sharecropping system in which ownership rested with large landlords while the peasant workers retained at most half their produce, and by the rising taxes of an industrializing Italian state. Two years of drastically-falling agricultural prices preceded the uprising, in which lands were seized and tax collectors attacked. The second passage is from an interview by a northern journalist during the uprising; the speaker is a peasant woman from Piana dei Greci (in the province of Palermo).

The third passage comes from an aristocrat who was pillaged in a riot in Russia, in the Poltava Guberniya, in 1902. Russian peasants also reacted to population pressure and the presence of large estates, in addition to dues payable to the government for redemption of manorial obligations abolished in 1861.[2]

1 George Rudé and E. J. Hobsbawm, *Captain Swing* (New York, 1969).
2 See Geroid T. Robinson, *Rural Russia under the Old Regime* (New York, 1932).

The three passages invite comparisons on several points. The peasants' pragmatic reaction to material hardship must be weighed against their sense of their rights. There is little question that both were involved in serious peasant protest, but it is not easy to decide which was more important. The peasant idea of justice as expressed in protest had another odd aspect, found in urban protest as well but to a lesser degree. Peasants, even during rebellion, managed to express their deference to their landlords and, in the Russian case, to the czar as well. Some grasp of this ambiguity is essential to an understanding of peasant outlook. Rather obviously, peasants accepted some kind of social hierarchy even as they fought its then-present manifestations.

While all three of these short passages reflect something of the common nature of peasant protest, differences should not be minimized. While the Italian and Russian peasants were protesting against remnants of the manorial system, the English laborers were dealing with the inroads of mechanization. In most ways, however, the Sicilian passage is most distinctive, for it goes farthest in its definition of justice. The unusual influence of urban socialists may have played a role here, but we must also be aware that the peasant world was not unchanging, that peasants could evolve toward more modern types of protest. The question here is how far the Sicilian peasants had moved from traditional peasant modes.[3]

A Rural Riot in England

We the labourers of Ringmer and surrounding villages, having for a long period suffered the greatest privations and endured the most debasing treatment with the greatest resignation and forbearance, in the hope that time and circumstances would bring about an amelioration of our condition, till, worn out by hope deferred and disappointed in our fond expectations, we have taken this method of assembling ourselves in one general body, for the purpose of making known our grievances, and in a peaceable, quiet, and orderly manner, to ask redress; and we would rather appeal to the good sense of the magistracy, instead of inflaming the passions of our fellow labourers, and ask those gentlemen who have done us the favour of meeting us this day whether 7d. a day is sufficient for a working man, hale and hearty, to keep up the strength necessary to the execution of the labour he has to do? We ask also, is 9s. a week sufficient for a married man with a family, to provide the common necessaries of life! Have we no reason to complain that we have been obliged for so long a period to go to

From *J. L. and Barbara Hammond*, The Village Labourer (*London, 1932*), *pp. 227–28. Reprinted by permission of the publisher, Longmans, Green and Company.*
3 For a study of genuinely modern peasant protest—in a situation far different from the nineteenth-century rural world—see Gordon Wright, *Rural Revolution in France* (Stanford, 1964).

our daily toil with only potatoes in our satchels, and the only beverage to assuage our thirst the cold spring; and on retiring to our cottages to be welcomed by the meagre and half-famished offspring of our toil-worn bodies? All we ask, then, is that our wages may be advanced to such a degree as will enable us to provide for ourselves and families without being driven to the overseer, who, by the bye, is a stranger amongst us, and as in most instances where permanent overseers are appointed, are men callous to the ties of nature, lost to every feeling of humanity, and deaf to the voice of reason. We say we want wages sufficient to support us, without being driven to the overseer to experience his petty tyranny and dictation. We therefore ask for married men 2s.3d. per day to the first of March, and from that period to the first of October 2s.6d. a day; for single men 1s.9d. a day to the first of March, and 2s. from that time to the first of October. We also request that the permanent overseers of the neighbouring parishes may be directly discharged, particularly Finch, the governor of Ringmer poor house and overseer of the parish, that in case we are obliged through misfortune or affliction, to seek parochial relief we may apply to one of our neighbouring farmers or tradesmen who would naturally feel some sympathy for our situation and who would be much better acquainted with our characters and claims. This is what we ask at your hands—this is what we expect, and we sincerely trust this is what we shall not be under the painful necessity of demanding.

The Fasci Rebellion

We want everybody to work, as we work. There should no longer be either rich or poor. All should have bread for themselves and for their children. We should all be equal. I have five small children and only one little room, where we have to eat and sleep and do everything, while so many lords (*signori*) have ten or twelve rooms, entire palaces.

—And so you want to divide the lands and the houses?

—No. It will be enough to put all in common and to share with justice what is produced.

—And aren't you afraid, if you got this collectivism, some people with confused heads or some swindlers might not come to the fore?

—No. Because there ought to be fraternity, and if anyone failed to be brotherly, there would be punishment.

From Adolfo Rossi, L'Agitazione in Sicilia (*Milan, 1894*), *pp. 69ff, reprinted and translated in E. J. Hobsbawm, Primitive Rebels. Studies in Archaic Forms of Social Movement in the nineteenth and twentieth Centuries (New York, 1965), p. 183. Reprinted by permission of the author and the publisher, Manchester University Press.*

—How do you stand with your priests?

—Jesus was a true Socialist and he wanted precisely what the Fasci are asking for, but the priests do not represent him well, especially when they are usurers. When the Fascio was founded our priests were against it and in the confessional they said that the Socialists are excommunicated. But we answered that they were mistaken, and in June we protested against the war they made upon the Fascio, none of us went to the procession of the Corpus Domini. This was the first time such a thing ever happened.

—Do you admit people convicted of crimes to the Fascio?

—Yes. But there are only three or four out of thousands and we have accepted them to make them better men, because if they have stolen a bit of grain they have only done so out of poverty. Our president has said that the object of the Fascio is to give men all the conditions for no longer committing crimes. Among us the few criminals feel that they still belong to the human family, they are thankful that we have accepted them as brothers in spite of their guilt and they will do anything not to commit crimes again. If the people were also to chase them away, they would commit more crimes. Society should thank us for taking them into the Fascio. We are for mercy, as Christ was.

A Rural Riot in Russia

Our whole village took part in the pillage of C's estate. It was done so quickly that by noon it was all over. The peasants returned home full of joy and songs. We were then at table. But hardly had we swallowed the first spoonful of soup when (I received a) note . . . saying we should be plundered at three o'clock. . . . The fatal moment had not yet arrived when my bailiff came to announce the approach of the peasants . . .

"Why have you come?" I asked them.

"To demand corn, to make you give us your corn," said several voices simultaneously.

"That is to say, you have come to plunder?"

"If you like, to plunder," said a young lad in the crowd, who had hitherto remained silent.

I could not refrain from recalling how I had treated them for so long.

From Istorischeski Vyestnik (April, 1908), reprinted and translated in R. Labry, Autour du Moujik (Paris, 1923), reprinted and translated in Hobsbawm, Primitive Rebels, p. 186. Reprinted by permission of the author and the publisher, Manchester University Press.

"But what are we to do?" several voices answered me. 'We aren't doing this in our name, but in the name of the Tsar.'

"It is the Tsar's order," said one voice in the crowd.

"A general has distributed this order of the Tsar throughout the districts," said another.

I should observe that at the beginning of the agitation there was a persistent rumour among the people that a general from Petersburg had arrived, an emissary of the Tsar, with the mission to proclaim to the people a manifesto written "in letters of gold" . . . There were stories that false police-sergeants were going round the villages distributing so-called "decrees" to the people. The peasant is prone to believe what serves his own interests. Thus he accepted these stories about an alleged general. None of my neighbours had seen him: but this or that other man had seen him, and this was sufficient for all to believe in the reality of such impostors and of their missions.

"Anyway, *barin*," my neighbours added, "if you will not give anything to your peasants, strangers will come to take it. So long as they know you have been plundered, they won't come. We shan't harm you. But as for the others, who knows what they may do?"

POLITICAL APPEALS

The unrest among the lower classes during the early industrial revolution invited political agitators to seek new support for their causes. Various middle-class reformers, angry at conservative government policies and eager to broaden the suffrage, took this course in Britain from 1815 until the repeal of the Corn Laws. William Cobbett was the most important radical to seek popular support.[1] He lectured and wrote tirelessly. He understood some of the economic grievances of the lower classes and constantly sought to politicize them. The question is, how open to persuasion of this sort the lower classes were. Cobbett was asking for a new kind of political consciousness that would involve direct representation in government and a belief that government was the prime source for the solution of the problems of the poor. It is not clear that this sort of political consciousness spread quickly. Therefore, we must be wary of using sources provided by articulate "outsiders" to understand the nature of lower-class protest.[2] We must ask if actual

1 See John W. Osborne, *William Cobbett, His Thought and His Times* (New Brunswick, N.J., 1966).

2 A masterful study of English workers, E. P. Thompson, *The Making of the English Working Class* (New York, 1964), depends heavily on the idea that political radicals can be taken as spokesmen for the workers generally. Against this, see the social analysis of Chartism, the most massive political movement stemming from the lower classes in early industial Britain, in Asa Briggs, *Chartist Portraits* (London, 1959).

lower-class protesters indicated and widely used the methods he advocated. Compare this passage to subsequent illustrations of British lower-class protest in the same years. Compare it to the plea by agricultural laborers in 1830; Cobbett spoke widely in the rural areas involved in the Captain Swing uprising, in terms similar to those he used in 1816. Some officials actually blamed the uprising on him, but, while some substantial farmers took his advice and petitioned the government, most of the laborer-rioters seemed unaware of the possibilities of a modern political process. I believe, then, that Cobbett and people like him were not representative of lower-class protest, but many historians would disagree.

The passage raises some interesting issues about Cobbett himself. He was not a genuine democrat. This being so, one might wonder about his motives in trying to appeal to the lower classes. Beware the middle-class radical, even bearing gifts.

William Cobbett

. . . The real strength, and all the sources of the country ever have sprung . . . from the *labour* of its people. . . . With the correct idea of your own worth in your minds, with what indignation must you hear yourselves called the Populace, the Mob, the Swinish Multitude. . . .

The times in which we live are full of peril. . . . As to the *cause* of our present miseries, it is the *enormous amount of the taxes* which the government compels us to pay for the support of its army, its placemen, its pensioners etc. and for the payment of the interest of its debt . . . the tax gatherers do not, indeed, come to *you* and demand money of you: but, there are few articles which you use, in the purchase of which you do not pay a tax. . . .

The weight of the Poor rate, which must increase while the present system continues, alarms the Corrupt, who plainly see, that what is paid to relieve you *they* cannot have. Some of them hint at your *early* marriages as a great evil, and a Clergyman named Malthus, has seriously proposed measures for checking you in this respect . . . while labourers and journeymen . . . are actually paying taxes for the support of these lords' and ladies' children, these cruel and insolent men propose that they shall have no relief and that their children ought to be *checked* . . .

The remedy . . . consists wholly and solely of such a *reform* in the Commons' or People's House of Parliament, as shall give to every

From an "address to journeymen and labourers", in 1816, printed in Cobbett's Weekly Political Register [*November 2, 1816*]. *Cobbett claimed that the effect of his Address on workers was "prodigious"; over 200,000 copies were sold within the month.*

payer of *direct taxes* a vote at elections, and as shall cause the members to be *elected annually*. . . .

. . . You should neglect no opportunity of doing all that is within your power to give support to the cause of Reform. *Petition* is the channel of your sentiments . . . you ought to attend at every public meeting within your reach. You ought to read to, and assist each other in coming at a competent knowledge of all public matters. . . . I exhort you to proceed in a peaceable and lawful manner, but at the same time, to proceed with zeal and resolution in the attainment of this object. . . .

VIOLENCE OF THE "COMPAGNONNAGES"

Here is the other extreme of early industrial protest, at least as typical if not as important as political protest. This is, on the face of things, blind violence, without political overtones or any clear purpose at all. The *compagnonnages* were groupings of journeymen, particularly in the construction industry, which dated from the Middle Ages. At times, they provided mutual aid for their members, but their main functions were ritualistic and social. Why did they remain attractive well into the industrial age? Why did they inspire violence? We are told [1] not to dismiss violent protest as irrational or purposeless, but can we apply this lesson here? We must try to grasp the importance of ritual and tradition for early industrial protest; consider, in this regard, the suggestive names of the two groups in Bordeaux. We must also ask if violence of this sort reflected, however obliquely, concern over the security of employment that undoubtedly mounted as more and more workers poured into the cities.

The *compagnonnages* retarded working-class unity and more "modern" labor organizations in France (and similar groups did the same in other countries). This means they must have fulfilled some genuine needs, perhaps emotional more than material, of their members. So, if we are to understand early industrial protest, we must try to grasp what these needs were.

A Battle among Construction Workers

The bridge works employ a great number of stonecutters. These workers are divided among themselves into two groups known variously as the wayfarers and the foreigners, the good fellows and the gluttons, the wolves and the dogs. A great hatred prevails between these two

From the Prefect of the Gironde to the Minister of the Interior, January 24, 1820. In Archives nationales (France) F⁷9786.20 Translated by the editor.

1 See George Rudé, *The Crowd in History, 1730–1848* (New York, 1964).

groups. Although both have been employed without distinction on the bridge, their animosity had not burst forth, thanks to the prudence and firmness of the supervisers. But on the 22nd, some disorders took place in the Bastide district, in which the worksite is located for the bridge on which these workers labor. The 23rd, a Sunday, the disorders resumed and the workers attacked each other with furor. The Mayor could not manage to get them to stop and was obliged to requisition the Bordeaux gendarmerie. Two workers, arrested and conducted toward the jail, were taken away by their companions from a troop too weak to resist an impetuous attack. Several seriously wounded men were taken to the hospital.

This morning, at 11 o'clock, a troop of 30 to 40 stonecutters from the "good fellows" group entered the port and assailed other workers from the rival group. A bitter battle began, which the engineer's efforts could not prevent and which ended only when the vanquished bled. It is impossible to imagine the rage and barbarity of these men who, armed with iron bars, stones, hatchets, beat to the ground those unfortunates who fell under their first blows. A fanaticism as terrible as it was absurd animated them. Four men were injured.

The gendarmerie and a detachment of the garrison hastened up and chased these miserable men, who ran off in all directions when they saw them. . . .

I have often had occasion to discuss these journeymen and the excesses which they commit. I think these men demand attention from the government. Grouped in organizations to which they are attached by an absurdly fanatic sentiment, they could become terrible instruments in the hands of political factions. Their audacity increases daily, because their number is rising rapidly now that military conscription no longer harvests them. The law assures them virtual impunity if they commit crimes and unity which prevails among them deprives the courts of any witnesses from their number, while the fear they inspire inhibits outside witnesses. I think there is reason to examine seriously the measures to take not to dissolve an association which managed to survive the Revolution, but to regulate it and to contain those who form it.

ECONOMIC PROTEST

Here is yet a third form of protest, again a common one in the early decades of industrialization. The goals were strictly economic, the method nonviolent. One might indeed question whether "protest" is a good word to describe craftsmen's efforts to limit entry to their trades. The efforts were illegal; they violated laws against workers' associations. They clearly attacked the principles of the industrial order, which required freedom to manipulate workers, in the name of older, guild-like principles of job security. This is why they fit the general pattern of early industrial protest. At the same time, the motives helped create craft unions, which survive and flourish to the present day. The fact is that many artisans learned early how to beat the system. Even during the first shocks of industrialization they may have outnumbered those who were driven to despair and who produced far flashier, but usually short-lived, protest.

This account came from master artisans in Thiers and reflects their biasses as employers. Historians must often extrapolate the nature of protest from accounts by the "other side." Here, the workers were distorting a law passed by Napoleon, which required each paper worker to pay a fee of five francs for his apprenticeship to each worker in his shop and further small fees for each subsequent advancement.

Agitation among Paper Workers

The paper workers, taking advantage of this law which they interpret and carry out in their own way, distinguish, among the apprentices, those who are sons of paper workers from those who are not. As to the first, they ask of them or their parents only the small payments set by the regulations. But as to the apprentices who are not sons of paper workers and whom they designate with the name *peasants,* they demand of them or their parents, in addition to the traditional payments, a sum of 150 francs, which they levy in each case. Thus whether the apprentice is, as often happens, made a journeyman or a more specialized worker after six months, a year, or two years, they nevertheless demand 150 francs for the right of apprenticeship.

What makes this an intolerable abuse is, first, that the workers insist on this sum of 150 francs without regard to the sums the apprentice has already paid in the different factories where he has worked. Secondly, the students or apprentices, drawn from the poorest classes of society, and most often from the orphanages, have to renounce a trade for which they have fruitlessly sacrificed several years of their life. Finally the money is spent on debaucheries or orgies which result in the shops being deserted for several days, to the great detriment of the manufacturer and the scandal of the general public. . . . The master manufacturers cannot intervene in favor of the apprentice without exposing themselves to the interdiction of their factories or at least to the desertion of their shops, and the apprentice cannot complain lest he expose himself to the hatred and pestering of those on whom

From a report by the Chambre Consultative des Manufactures, Arts, et Métiers of Thiers, to the Minister of Interior, March 9, 1815. In Archives nationales (France) F¹²194. Translated by the editor.

he will depend. The payment for apprenticeship ordinarily belongs to the master, as just compensation for the damage he may incur due to the inexperience and clumsiness of a beginner; by what right do the workers, who do not supply the materials, claim a 150 franc retribution? The master manufacturers never ask anything for the costs of apprenticeship; why should the workers be more demanding? . . .

LUDDISM

ENGLISH LUDDISM

Attacks on machinery were not new, but they increased in importance during the first half of the nineteenth century. The Luddite riots, which began in Britain, derived their name from the rioters' claim that they followed a leader, Ned Ludd, though he was a product of their imagination. The rioters concentrated on breaking new machinery and they often stated their reasons for their attacks. Most of the rioters were artisans or rural domestic workers in the textile industry. The actual number of the rioters was small, but there is ample indication that they operated in an environment of widespread public sympathy.[1] As industrialization advanced, Luddism faded. The wave of riots had ended in Britain by 1820, in France by 1835. But the motives that inspired the riots may not have faded so quickly.

The first reports, written by employers and government officials, deal with an early Luddite outbreak in Wiltshire. This is the kind of indirect source that must be used for most early industrial protest, because the protesters left no records of their own. But the sources are inadequate in many ways They do not provide a full description of the protest, since the outsiders who wrote them simply did not know how the protest was organized. They concentrate on visible, illegal actions, leaving motives unclear. These reports from a local "establishment" may well have exaggerated the national conspiracy angle—a common temptation throughout the history of protest. If the reports are correct, the protesters must have been capable already of sophisticated organization. In matters of this sort, the problems of evaluating sources, prosaic in themselves, go right to the heart of the interpretation of early industrial agitation.

Aside from their organizing ability, there are two major questions about the Luddites. First, it is not clear whether most of them were really hostile to machinery or whether they used their attacks to dramatize demands for higher pay and other improvements. Most Luddite attacks occurred in years

1 On British Luddism, see E. J. Hobsbawm, *Labouring Men* (New York, 1964) and Frank Darvall, *Popular Disturbances and Public Order in Regency England* (London, 1934). Above all, compare the account in E. P. Thompson, *Making of the English Working Class*, with the soberer treatment in Malcolm I. Thomis, *The Luddites: Machine-Breakers in Regency England* (Hamden, Conn., 1970). On French Luddism, Frank Manuel, "The Luddite Movement in France," *Journal of Modern History* (June, 1938).

of deep economic depression. There is no doubt that machines were attacked in some areas that were left alone in others—indeed, Luddites in
certain regions destroyed machines that had been in use for centuries. In
other words, we must ask how much deep aversion to modern industrialization Luddism reflects. Careful study of the Luddite sources ought to give
some suggestions here, if not positive answers. Less easy to deal with is the
extent of Luddite sentiment. Outright Luddite attacks involved few people.
They may however have expressed anxieties that were far more widespread.
This is a classic problem in the history of protest, modern as well as traditional. In the case of Luddism, the problem is complicated by the possibility
that the Luddites won approval from social groups far removed from their
own class, from businessmen and professional people frightened by change
as well as from other workers. Luddite sources give little direct evidence on
this point. Nor do they answer the related question of why formal Luddism
ended so quickly. The social historian must develop a feeling for this period
that goes beyond any specific set of sources if he is to deal with basic problems of this sort.

Luddism in Wiltshire

In addition to the many outrages lately committed in this town, I
am sorry to be under the necessity of informing your lordship that
this morning between 12 and 1 o'clock a rick of oats worth about £20,
belonging to Mr. Peter Warren, clothier of this town, was maliciously
set on fire and entirely consumed. A dog kennel at some distance therefrom, the property of the said Mr. Warren and others, was at the same
time also set on fire and partly consumed.

That there is no doubt but this daring outrage was committed by
some of the workmen usually employed in the woollen manufactory,
who now and have for many weeks past refused to work on account of
some machines being introduced which they consider as obnoxious,
although the same have been used for many years in other parts of
the kingdom.

They have at present no visible means of any livelihood, and there
is good reason to think they are supported and encouraged by contributions from many of the innkeepers and other inhabitants of the
place. It is thought some strong declaration on the part of Government
of the illegality of this practice, addressed to the neighbouring magistrates with orders that it may be printed and posted up in different
places, would be of great service.

*All of these documents come from Home Office 42/65. The first is
a letter from Matthew Davies to Lord Pelham, June 15, 1802; the second from John Jones, junior (a Wiltshire Justice of the Peace) to
Lord Pelham, July 20, 1802; the last from John Jones, senior, to John
Kind, July 26, 1802.*

They have secret combinations to support each other, which [it] is impossible to get good proof of without an accomplice will discover it . . .

An Employer's Complaint

. . . I solicit your Lordship to inform me if I shall be justified in endeavouring to seize a committee of 13 persons, with the papers and books belonging to the shearmen of Trowbridge, of which I have this morning obtained some intelligence, and I expect more momentarily.

It is reported these men are now soliciting a subscription throughout the country to support those refusing to work but upon their own terms, and that many persons have in consequence countenanced them by giving money. I learn the Committee issue pass tickets to their members.

I am compelled to inform your Lordship the threats which the workmen in my mill have received from these shearmen (or cloth workers) induce them daily to leave it, and I dread to be forced thereby to stop the whole works.

A Report and a Petition

. . . This day a deputation of seven men from the Society of these people waited on my son at his house in Wolley, nr. Bradford, and he having previous notice of their intention, requested Mr. Bush, a magistrate living at Bradford, and Mr. Hobhouse, M.P., living in our neighborhood, with two other gentlemen and myself to attend, and we were all there, the result of which, taken down in writing, I have the honour to transmit to you as well as a copy of an anonymous letter sent to Mr. Hobhouse, and also a pass ticket given by this Society to their members, which entitles them to a certain pecuniary donation when they are out of employ, and serves as a token of their being known to be one of their Society . . .

Mills are destroyed weekly all over the country, and ricks of hay almost nightly. A great number of these people reside in Leeds in Yorkshire, and carry on a regular correspondence with those here, and not only that, they have frequent deputations passing from the different Counties where they are employed. . . .

[Enclosure]

26 July, 1802—A deputation of seven shearmen, vix. Samuel Jones, John Mead, James Mead, Henry King, Benjamin Pitman, William Sheppard and Thomas Tuck, came to Mr. Jones's house at Woolley.

When he offered them to employ all the men at this time out of work
belonging to the parish of Bradford (stated by him at thirty) and always
to give a preference to the employment of men of the said parish
rather than use the frames for the cutting or shearing of cloth whilst
any such men should want work, and added that in future no gigging[1]
or shearing shall be done for hire by him on account of other manufacturers, which offer they rejected in behalf of the body of shearmen who
deputed them, and declared it was the resolution of the shearmen
thoughout England, Scotland, and Ireland not to work after machinery,
in the presence of the following gentlemen who were with Mr. Jones—
Benjamin Hobhouse, Esq., M.P., Thomas Bush, Esq., Acting Magistrate in Bradford, John Jones, senior, Thomas Tugwell, and John
Hunt.

Note. Samuel Jones declared he would rather be hanged than rec-
ommend the shearmen to accept Mr. Jones's offer, or to work after
machinery.

FRENCH LUDDISM

French Luddism was less severe than British but it produced a more ample documentation. French police procedures were more centralized and
better established; they resulted in fuller reports. The account of the attack on the shearing machine describes the riot rather thoroughly. It also
offers the sort of information about participants that delights social historians of disorder, since the professions of those arrested give some clue
about the broader patterns of participation in protest. Note that cloth
shearers are not alone involved. Again there is indication of broader public sympathy. The participation of women may be particularly significant
because women are usually more reluctant than men to join in violent protest; their involvement may thus indicate that the level of grievance was unusually intense. Note also the suggestion of previous preparation and leadership.

The poster text that follows, collected by the police, gives direct insight
into the French Luddites' motives. The statement of motives should be compared with the actions of protest. Which is a more reliable guide to the
intensity of grievance? The tone of respect is characteristic of early industrial protest. Does it denote genuine deference to social "betters"? The gov-

The report is in Archives nationales (France) F⁷9786.24. The plac-
ards are in F⁷9786.24. The first two posters are from Lodéve; the third
is a petition to the mayor of Vienne and deals with the same machine
over which the riot described in the police report occurred. All posters
date from 1819. Translations by the editor.

1 Gig mills were machines for raising the fibers in a piece of woolen cloth, in
order to form a nap on the surface which was later shorn off to give the cloth a
smooth, soft appearance. This latter process was done by shearmen who manipulated
heavy shears. Shearing machines were being introduced to replace this manual labor.

ernment does not appear as a hostile force in these petitions, and indeed the government was not entirely happy with the employers' policies, which they termed "unimaginative" in the account which accompanied the report on the posters. The government was nonetheless adamant in its defense of order. The rioters' willingness to petition and their clever use of arguments that might appeal to the government may suggest a political sophistication that settles some of the doubts raised about the representativeness of political agitators. But it can also be argued that this is a different kind of awareness of the government.

Luddism in Vienne

We, king's attorney in the court of first instance at Vienne, department of the Isère, acting on the information which we have just received this day February 26, 1819, that the new cloth-shearing machine belonging to Messrs. Gentin and Odoard had just reached the bank of the Gère river near the building intended to house it when a numerous band of workers hastened toward the spot crying *"Down with the shearing machine"*; that some rifle shots were heard, and in general everything about this meeting of workers announced the will and the intent to pillage by force a piece of property, we immediately went to the place where the mayor and the police commissioner agreed to authorize us to use armed force and to state the nature of any crimes and their perpetrators, and to hear with us the declarations of any persons who had information to give us.

Having arrived near the shop of Messrs. Odoard and Gentin, on the right bank of the river, we saw in the stream, at a distance of about fifteen feet, a carriage without horses, its shafts in the air, loaded with four or five crates, one of which was obviously broken, and at three or four paces off in the water, an instrument of iron or some other metal of the same size as the crate, in terms of its length. Various calvary posts and policemen, on foot and mounted, placed at various distances on the two banks of the Gère and on the hills, guarded all the paths and roads; the windows which gave onto the river were partially closed.

M. Desprémenil, lieutenant-colonel of the dragoons, the commander on the spot, declared to us that some minutes before our arrival, when the armed force had not yet managed to disperse the gathering on the right bank, many individuals in short vests whom he did not know but whom he presumed to be workers, hurled themselves into the water and rushed the carriage, armed with wooden clubs and an iron instrument called a cloth-shearer, that they broke the first crate which fell to their hands and threw into the water one of the instruments which it contained, that they were going to continue when Messrs. d'Augereauville, adjutant-major of the dragoons of the Gironde, de Verville, commandant of the gendarmerie, and successively the soldiers, dragoons and police managed to free it and put the assailants to flight, in spite of a hail of stones from the windows and the two banks of the Gère. The windows nearest the spot where we were were particularly pointed out to us—those of a Mr. Tachet. Mr. d'Augereauville, who came up at that moment, designated the same windows and showed us his cheek, which had been bloodied by a stone. The following people then came up: Clément, commissioner of police; Chassin, policeman;

Guillot, clerk in the Gentin and Odoard company; . . . Charreton, manufacturer with the Becourdau company; Charreton junior, grocer; the two Rousset sons, one a cloth manufacturer and the other a spinner in his brother's company, and Bizet junior, who gave us the following information.

Edlon Montal (Jean or Pierre) of Grenoble or Beaurepaire, who did his apprenticeship as cloth-shearer with Bomières in Vienne and worked in the New Way, is the man who provided half the strength to break the crates.

Pontet called Simon, worker for Messrs. Donnat and Boussut, was at the head of the workers and carried a club to break the machine. He was one of the first to climb on the carriage with one Hubert Richard, who works for Jean-François Ozier, cloth-shearer in Vienne.

Jacques Ruffe, shearer for his cousin Dufieux, was on the carriage, breaking and throwing the crates into the water.

Imbert Claude shearer for the Darrieux shop, in the New Way, was also on the carriage, along with Labre, an itinerant, and Jean-Pierre Plasson, who works for Dufieux.

The daughter of Claude Tonnerieux, butcher, threw stones at the dragoons and incited the workers with her shouts: *"Break it, smash it, be bold,* etc." Another woman, Lacroix, who has only one eye, shouted similar things.

Marguerite Dupont, spinner for Mr. Frémy, called the lieutenant-colonel of dragoons a brigand.

Pierre Dejean de Saint-Priest, a shearer who works for Velay Pourret, strolled through the shops during the day yesterday inviting the shearers to meet on this spot.

Jacques Boullé, a glass worker, was noticed shouting among the first workers who came down the Saint-Martin bridge.

Basset, weaver, said, *"Let's get the machine"* and Rousset, an itinerant, expressed himself thus: *"We'll get Gentin* (one of the owners of the machine). *It's not the machine we ought to wreck."* One of the Linossier sons, called Flandre, was seen at the entry of the stair which winds down to the river, inciting his comrades by saying *"Come on then, let's go down."*

Jean-Baptiste Gros, who works for Ozier the elder, threw a stone which hit his cousin who is in the dragoons.

A woman named Garauda shouted *"We must break the shearer."*

A woman named Mange and one of her sisters also drew attention by their shouts and remarks.

Not being able to obtain further information, we asked Mr. Clément, police commissioner, to bring to us all those he could round up later, and using the authority which article 40 of the Criminal Code provides we issued a warrant for the arrest of these nineteen individuals named above and charged the commandant of the gendarmerie to carry this out and make sure that, when arrested, each individual is placed in jail, to be left to our disposition and that of the trial judge. . . .

A Poster Appeal

Gentlemen, we are beside ourselves because of the inhumanity and hardness of your hearts, your scorn toward the poor workers who have helped you make your fortune. Seeing that we are abandoned by you, gentlemen, this alone has forced us to do what we don't want to do. We have no intention of attacking your fortunes, but if you don't arrange to give us work we can't avoid attacking you and the machines; so you have eight days to reflect. If at the end of these eight days you don't take your wool out of the machines in order to give work to four or five hundred people who are at your doors and whom you don't deign to look at, don't be surprised if you see a storm descend upon you and the machines—so much do we the poor workers suffer for ourselves and for our poor children.

We hope that you'll wish to spare us this effort which is otherwise inevitable.

An Appeal to the Government

You, gentlemen, who are endowed with supreme powers, please in your normal goodness be willing to conciliate those gentlemen, the manufacturers, in order not to cover us with shame for an effort to which misery forces us.

Please deign to induce the gentlemen to take this into consideration. You alone can do everything with regard to these gentlemen on whom our fate depends.

A Petition

They are at this moment working at the construction of a machine called the *Grande Tondeuse*.[1] In a short time it is supposed to be put into activity in this city under the supervision of Messrs. Gentin and Odoard and Company. It is different from all those which are already in use. It offers the *pernicious* means of shearing, glossing and brushing 1,000 ells of cloth in three hours, while being directed by only four men. Consequently, it is going to deprive a very great number of shearmen of work and our shops will be closed. You feel in advance, as an enlightened administrator, all the evil which these establishments are going to cause to all persons employed in the preparation of cloth and we are going to develop the reasons for you. As follows:

1. This new establishment will be beneficial only to the owners and will cause the closing of all the shops of the master-shearmen, who, not knowing what to do with their materials, will be ruined in one fell swoop.
2. There will result from this a general elimination of all the shearmen, fathers of families and others, the majority of whom are already very old and, not being able to take up other work, will be exposed to very great need. How then are they going to live, they and their families?
3. Finally, the government is going to find itself deprived of the income from all taxes of any kind from sixty master-shearmen who, no longer being able to exercise their profession, owe nothing to the state.

STRIKES

Strikes were not the most common form of early industrial protest, but they did occur. Indeed they can be found scattered through several centuries before the rise of the factory system. A significant wave of strikes burst forth in Britain in 1818 and continued sporadically over a decade. Factory

All three documents are from Home Office 42/193. The first is a letter from Messrs. King and Sculthorpe to Viscount Sidmouth, August 23, 1819; the second from the Duke of Newcastle to same, August 29, 1819; the third from H. Enfield to same.

1 A shearing machine.

workers were involved, but artisans and other non-mechanized workers took the leading role.

These reports on agitation by stocking knitters in Nottingham and Leicestershire in 1819 make interesting points about both the form and the motives of the protest. What is basically involved is indeed a refusal to work—a strike—but it is overlaid by suggestions of Luddism. It is, in other words, a strike before the notion of striking was well developed, when strikes were still illegal and therefore long before strikes could be entered into lightheartedly. Strikes require organization, and organization was difficult when unions were illegal and workers were scattered about the countryside. Aspects of these strikes, therefore, confirm the generalizations about the form of early industrial protest.

The motives of the strike must also be compared to the model of early industrial protest. They invite comparison with the Luddite documents, to determine which kind of protest reveals the most intense grievance and the most basic resistance to industrialization. The tone and substance of the argument about wages should also be compared to those in later industrial strikes. Most early industrial protest, it should be recalled, appealed to past rights and standards. Workers who might vigorously resist a deterioration in their standards of living could find it difficult to ask for an unprecedented improvement. Hence, the manner in which these workers talked about their wages should be carefully examined to determine whether they were asking for a raise or whether they might even have been capable of arguing for a raise in the modern manner.

A Strike Begins

Mr. John Sills, one of the principal manufacturers of hosiery in this town, has lately received an anonymous threatening letter . . .[1]

Some weeks ago the framework-knitters of Hinckley, in common with those of other parts of the County, resolved not to work for less than certain prices which were agreed upon in 1817, and the inhabitants at large, considering their demands reasonable, agreed to support them by parochial relief altogether rather than compel them to work for reduced prices, and then make up what they might require out of the poor rates.

The hosiers made no objection to a general advance of wages, but, as a partial advance would operate to the prejudice of individuals, they would not give the higher prices till all the hosiers of the County agreed to do the same.

Mr. Sills is principally concerned in manufacturing cotton hose, and, the Leicestershire manufacture being worsted hose, he said that, as to worsted goods, he would adopt the regulations of the Leicester

1 "Be careful of you shal hav a bit of cold led." A reward of £100 was offered for the arrest of the writer.

hosiers, but that as to cotton goods he would not, because if he did he should not be able to bring his goods into the market in competition with the manufacturers of cotton hosiery in Nottinghamshire and Derbyshire. It is supposed that this determination of Mr. Sills may have gained him enemies amongst the framework-knitters, who do not consider the peculiar injury which he would sustain by acceding to their demands. . . .

Report on the Strike

The stockingers in this County have in a body struck work. They have hitherto subsisted on a subscription fund, but that is now exhausted, and they have tried me for money, which I have declined. Their wretchedness is extreme. Their Treasurer told me two days ago that the fund had amounted to £250, from which 600 men have been supported for a fortnight. They were earning, the lowest say, 5s[hillings], the highest 9s. a week before they struck, by working 12 hours a day. This honest maintenance, though low, they have exchanged for their present miserable pittance, which is, from this fund, 3s. a man per week, if with a wife, 1s., and for as many children as he may have, 3d. a head. Hitherto all has been peaceably conducted, but the men parade in very large bodies, and make a display of their poverty. It is also said that they have drilled. They certainly *always* parade in parties of threes or fives, keeping step and under command, and they have *hinted* to me that it will be well to afford them means of subsistence, as hungry men know no law, and they cannot answer for what may be the consequence when their fund is exhausted, and they pinched with want.

I enclose for your Lordship's information their Address to me and my answer. I shall be sorry to irritate, but, at the same time, no encouragement must be given. The storm will break sooner or later, therefore, if it is to be, better now than later. At the same time I will endeavour to act with moderation and prudence mixed with determined firmness.

I find I can learn no truth here, therefore tomorrow I go to Nottingham and shall make a thorough private investigation of everything. I shall then, I hope, be able to form some judgment and to act upon some plan; first of all I must look to security which at present, I am told, is very defective . . .

P.S. I have been told to-day that to-morrow is to be a grand day with the stockingers at Nottingham, as they mean in a body to return their frames to the hosiers. Your Lordship must not be surprised if his Majesty's Lieutenant returns with a broken head.

[Enclosure]

*To His Grace the Duke of Newcastle (Lord Lieutenant),
the Nobility, Gentry, and Clergy of the County of Nottingham
The humble Address and Petition of the
Two-needle Framework-knitters*

We think we should be wanting in duty to ourselves and families, were we not, with all due respect and humility, to call your serious attention to those heart-rending woes and severe privations under which ourselves and families are now groaning, and to justify ourselves in sending forth the present Address, we beg leave to state that from the various and low prices given by our employers, we have not, after working from 14 to 16 hours per day, been able to earn more than from 4s to 7s per week to maintain our wives and families upon, to pay *taxes, house-rent Etc.,* which has driven us to the necessity of applying for *parochial aid,* which after all, has not in many instances left us sufficient to supply the calls of Nature, even with the most parsimonious economy; and though we have substituted meal and water, or potatoes and salt, for that more wholesome food an Englishman's table used to abound with, we have repeatedly retired after a hard day's labour, and been under the necessity of putting our children supperless to bed, to stifle the cries of hunger; nor think we would give this picture too high a colouring, when we can most solemnly declare that for the last eighteen months we have scarcely known what it was to be free from the pangs of hunger.

Think what must be our feelings when our little ones cling around our knees for bread, which we are unable to give them! Our partners in life, the poignancy of whose grief may be conceived, but cannot be described, looking on the pale and meagre form of her husband; her child, perhaps, at her breast, feebly sucking for that nourishment which Nature almost refuses to bestow!! This is a state of misery, wretchedness itself cannot depict; we hope, then, it will not be deemed too much to require from our employers a reasonable regulation and advancement in our prices, which they acknowledge they are willing to give, could it be adopted generally: all we ask and desire of them is an adequate remuneration for our labour.

We trust and hope we live amongst a Christian people not forgetful of that glorious precept of our Divine Master, "to love one another, to feed the hungry, clothe the naked, to pour in oil and wine, and bind up the wounds" of those lacerated hearts with feelings of sympathy; and we confidently rely on the generous, humane, and benevolent exertions which, in your wisdom, you may think proper to adopt, for the extricating of us from that climax of human misery in which we are at present involved.

Sincerely hoping this well-meant call will not remain unanswered, but that we may live in the most grateful remembrance of your assistance, we subscribe ourselves on behalf of the trade.

Walter Miller,
Thomas Sands,
Samuel Brentnall.

Strike Tactics and Results

Committee Room, Ball, Coal-Pit Lane.

Nottingham, 1 September, 1819

The magistrates direct me to report to your Lordship that yesterday the framework-knitters brought in many of the stocking frames and deposited them in the streets at the doors of their masters. Men harnessed together in ropes drew the frames upon drags, great crowds being collected by these proceedings, evidently tending to endanger the public peace, the magistrates, who were all in attendance throughout the day at the Police Office, issued a handbill prohibiting all persons from joining therein. The magistrates hope that this admonition will preserve quiet—if not, they are prepared to enforce the observance of good order.

The behaviour of the workmen themselves is, with the exception of this outrageous furtherance of their combination,[1] peaceable. Whether it will continue so, or what will be the termination of this distressing state of things, remains to be known. Many of the manufacturers have *"come in"* to the prices asked . . .

TRADE UNIONS

Trade unions were illegal everywhere in Europe in the early decades of industrialization. Forming them was a gesture of protest that could have political as well as economic implications. Certainly the woolcombers' statement echoes many of the themes of pre-industrial protest: the desire to protect job security, the apparent deference to social superiors, the religious references, and so on. Once again we see artisans (woolcombing was not mechanized until the 1840s) trying to resurrect many aspects of the old guilds,

Published in 1812, following a Congress in Coventry which was composed of delegates of several different local societies from "various parts of the Kingdom." In Home Office 102/22.

1 Their illegal association.

particularly by limiting entry to their trade and protecting apprenticeship and customary skill. Yet this was a genuine trade union as well, formed by men who knew they were employees and who sought to bargain with their employers. The line between traditional and modern is not easy to draw in trade union history.[1] Similarly, the implications of early trade unions for class consciousness are often ambiguous. The following document suggests some awareness of the employer class and of worker solidarity—both of which have a modern ring—but its craft focus and deferential approach are really the antithesis of class sentiment.

Trade unions occupy an ambiguous place in the history of protest. Early craft unions such as the woolcombers' are no exception. There were more unambiguously radical unions, such as the Owenite-socialist General Union formed in Britain in the 1830s, but they usually lasted only a short time. The union tends to create a carefully-elaborated organization and to develop some funds, both of which may restrain leaders and members from all-out protest. The woolcombers certainly reflect the impulse to work out every organizational detail. At the same time they suggest measures, such as a union shop, which may seem very radical for their time. Hence, the nature of the benefits workers intended to derive from their union require attention. The most basic question is whether they regarded their union as an agency of protest or simply as a means of working more effectively within the existing system. Certainly, in the long run unions have best served the latter purpose, but this does not mean that initial trade unionists, in the throes of early industrial pressures, intended them for this purpose.

The Woolcombers' Prospectus

READ, AND THEN JUDGE!!

Gentlemen,

The Congress, deeply impressed with a sense of the importance and necessity of an union upon a firm and liberal basis, between all the woolcombers in Great Britain, are desirous that the same may be communicated to every individual woolcomber, who is now in society, or whom societies may think proper to receive, consistent to the following articles.—Considering that union in itself is so essential, not only to the peace, but also to the prosperity of any community, society, or firm. The principle of union has the sanction also of divine authority, being inculcated in the sacred pages of holy writ; it is there said, "can two walk together except they be agreed," and as by walking together, we must understand, all the transactions and connections of men, (both civil and religious) in their social intercourse one with another; and, if

---

1 For early British union history, see G. D. H. Cole, *Short History of the English Working Class Movement* (Vol. I, London, 1927).

unity is so essential to the peace and good understanding of two only, how much more so ten, twenty, a society, community, or nation!!

Brethren, while the principal inhabitants and trades of the nation are uniting and exerting all their power and influence in the establishment of various institutions, for the avowed purpose of promoting the peace, prosperity, and happiness of the people; shall we as a body, still be divided; shall we still continue to tear and devour one another, by working against each other to the injury of the whole; shall we still continue to be wanderers in the land, as sheep having no shepherd, no control, no head, nothing to which we can refer, no place to which we can fly for shelter or security in time of peril or disaster; but still continue to expose ourselves to be torn, devoured, annihilated by the wild ungovernable passions of pride, malice, tyranny, and oppression? "Tell it not in Gath, publish it not in the streets of Askelon," suffer it not to be said in the nation, that at a time like the present, when all that can be lawfully obtained, is necessary, the woolcombers refuse to be united.—But brethren, we are persuaded better things of you, although we thus speak, things which accompany unity, peace, and concord.

There never was to our knowledge, any well-regulated articles, which took into their cognizance so many particulars, and on such an extended and liberal plan, as these now presented for your candid consideration, in which, we have endeavoured to consider every general circumstance, and particular usage in the trade, and adopt such measures as appeared to us, best calculated to promote a good understanding, and prevent infringements.—If any of the following articles in their execution, should fail, every society is humbly invited to point out such failures, and propose any amendments.—If we have exceeded our limits, we hope every society or individual will attribute it to our zeal for the public good.

Signed in behalf of the congress,
Daniel Lord.
Samuel Perry.
John Hewes.

Article I

The eldest son of any woolcomber, who is received by the trade as a fair man, shall be received by the trade as fair, provided he commences working at woolcombing trade, at not exceeding fifteen years of age, and continues till he is twenty-one, under the tuition of his father, or any other person properly appointed.

2. Second sons of woolcombers apprenticed to their father, are not

to be received, except their father employs them upon wool that is his own property.

3. That no other person shall be received into the United Societies of Woolcombers, or permitted to work at the trade, or receive any benefit therefrom, but such as have served a lawful apprenticeship of seven years, to a master or mistress, who, during their apprenticeship, employ them upon wool that is their own property, except those who are brought up under the first article.

4. If a youth learns the business under either of the preceding articles, and does not continue his full time in it, but engages in his Majesty's service, and continues therein, till the term of his apprenticeship is expired, he shall be received by the trade as a fair man.

5. No master or mistress to be permitted to have more than two apprentices at any time, who may board them either in or out of their own house, as may best suit their convenience.

6. Every woolcomber who is a member of any society in Great Britain, at the date of these articles, shall be received by the United Societies as a fair man; and every man who has a right to the trade, who does not belong to any society, shall be permitted and invited to join the nearest society to him, without any extent of limits, and free of any expence, provided he join within three months from the date of these articles.

7. In order thoroughly to unite the trade, and maintain its privileges, there shall be one general acting society; and the congress has appointed Warwick to be the general acting society. . . .

13. The eldest sons of woolcombers who are brought up to the business under their father, or any other person properly appointed, shall allow one halfpenny to every stranger, from the time of his first commencement at the business, till he is twenty-one, and if the father is obliged to travel, the son shall be entitled to the same relief of one halfpenny from every man, and nothing more.

14. That no society shall be allowed to give less than six-pence as a club benefit, to every stranger that crosses them with an union blank. If any society be not large enough to allow six-pence, they shall join the nearest society to them. . . .

18. If any man offer himself to become a member of any of our United Societies, after three months from the date of these articles, and the society to whom he offers himself approve of his right, they shall be at full liberty to take him in; and if he draws his blank before he has paid three succeeding months deficiencies, he shall pay the sum of one pound, to be forthwith forwarded to the acting society, for general expences, and the expence of sending to and from the acting society, for the certificate of his enrolment.

19. To render the woolcombing business more respectable, and pre-

vent as much as possible the disgrace of cutting. If any man who is enrolled, gets work within the limits of any United Society, without a blank, the society in whose limits he is, shall ask him where he was enrolled, and what society he belonged to last, and the society where he then is, shall be bound to send immediately to the society he came from, informing them that they have such a member, and who came without a blank, and whether the man was muffled at a disadvantage or cut; the society he came from shall send an account of all just debts due to master, society, shopmates, or lodgings, and the society where he is then a member, shall remit the whole of the debt, within one month from the receipt of the account, in order that the debts may stand against the man in that society where he is then a member. Although a strict compliance with this article will necessarily require some sacrifices to be made by the societies where it may occur; yet we are persuaded, if strictly adhered to, it will effectually remove the necessity of it; for men who are disposed to cut, will know the difficulty they have to get work, because every society will be reluctant to receive a man without a blank, and that they will not thereby get rid of their debts.

20. If any man presumes to send to a person for a dozen of wool, or any man obtains a dozen of wool in any way that is not according to the general rules of the woolcombing trade, he shall not be permitted to enjoy it; but if the society within whose limits he obtains the dozen of wool, shall after investigation, permit him to continue in it, he shall forfeit and pay the sum of one pound, to be forthwith sent to the acting society for general expences.

21. If any society in Great-Britain, shall think proper to become one of the United Societies after the fourteenth day of November next, when the articles and enrolments will be printed, they shall send a list of all their member's names, (both christian and sur-name and from what county they come) alphabetically arranged, and also what club benefit they allow to the acting society, and the acting society shall return them certificates to be given out with each of their blanks.

22. If any society, or shop, labour under burdens of any kind, from which they cannot extricate themselves by petition, or remonstrance, and they think proper to leave their employ, as the only effectual means of removing them, they shall give a fair and full statement of all their grievances to three of the nearest societies to them, and the societies to whom they write shall consider their case as soon as possible, and return them an answer whether they think they had better continue in their employ or not; and if the majority of the societies to whom they write, are of an opinion that they had better leave, they shall immediately send all the answers received from the societies consulted on the business to the acting society, together with a clear and full state-

ment of the number of wives and children who are dependent on their father's for support, and the acting society shall immediately send to every district society, and from thence to every society in union, on their behalf, and every society shall send their contributions to the district society, and from thence to the acting Society.

23. The relief to wives and children belonging to men who may leave their employ agreeable to the twenty-second article, and who are dependent on their father's for support, shall be two shillings and sixpence each per week as long as the necessity of the case may require.

24. If any society in union, acts derogatory to these articles and regulations, or neglects to comply with them in a regular manner, the said society may be reported by an individual, or more, or by any adjoining society, to the acting society, who shall be bound to give the case a clear, full, and impartial investigation, and if the society who is indicted should be convicted, the acting society shall be empowered to levy a fine on them, of not less than one, or more than five pounds, which sum shall be sent within one month to the acting society, towards general expences, and if the fine is not paid, their blanks shall not be suffered to pass, and the acting society shall inform every society in union of the circumstance.

25. When the acting society are in possession of all the societies who join in union, they will immediately divide the societies into districts, in order to facilitate communication, and one society in each district to be denominated the district society, and all general communications to be sent to the district society, and from thence to every society within its district, and all contributions for general expences, and for the relief of societies in union, when in distress, to be sent to the district society, and from thence to the acting society, and all annual enrolments to be sent to the district society in like manner, and from thence to the acting society.

26. The acting society shall provide proper books to keep a regular and just account of all receipts and disbursements on public accounts, and of all enrolments and certificates granted, of which several particulars after being audited by proper persons, there shall be a faithful report given annually with the enrolments, &c.

27. As a check against the acting society, every district society when appointed, shall provide proper books, in which to keep a regular and just account of all monies received from every society within their district, for general use, and of all remittances to the acting society.

28. If a district society is accused of irregularities or neglect of compliance, or breach of trust, by any society, or by the acting society, there shall be a clear, full, and impartial investigation of all the charges alledged against them, by three of the nearest societies in the district, or by delegates from them, and if found guilty, a fine shall be

levied on them, of not less than two, or more than five pounds, to be forthwith forwarded to the acting society for general expences and public uses, or their blanks shall not be suffered to pass.

29. If the general acting society is judged to be partial, irregular, or unfaithful in the discharge of the various important public concerns confided to its trust, they shall be subject to investigation, by delegates from five of the largest societies in union, and if proved to be guilty of any breach of public trust, shall be fined a sum not less than five, or more than ten pounds, which sum shall be paid before any of their blanks shall be suffered to pass, and the reasonable expences of investigation to be paid out of the fine, and overplus to go for general expences and public uses.

30. If any man who is enrolled, learns, or attempts to learn any man, woman or boy, so as thereby to bring them to the trade in an illegal manner, shall have his, or their names sent to the acting society, and from thence to every society in union, and if he should be found with an union blank, at any time after such public notice, any society will be justified in breaking it, and shall give information thereof to the general acting society, what society the blank was issued from, and the society that issued the blank shall be subject to a fine, levied on them by the acting society, of not less than one, or more than five pounds, to be forthwith remitted to the acting society for general expenses and public uses, before any of their blanks shall be suffered to pass again.

31. If any man, or shop of men, suffer any man or men who are not enrolled or regularly entered, to turn in upon, and work with them, without the knowledge and consent of the society whereunto they belong, such man, or men, so offending, by passive submission, to such a breach, shall be subject to a fine levied on them, by the majority of the members of the Society within whose limits it may occur, if only one man, not less than one, and if a shop of men, not more than five pounds, to go to the acting society for general expences and public uses. . . .

34. In order to strengthen the union between the members of society, let no young man, or any member who does not already belong to another sick society, be permitted to join any, but such as are purely amongst their own business. That is, let there be provision made for sickness in every United Society, and all the members who do not actually belong to a sick society already, whose articles forbid them to join in it.

35. If any dispute should arise, between any two or more of our United Societies, and the dispute be of such a nature as not to come within the cognizance of any of these articles, and they cannot settle it between themselves, each society shall give a clear and full statement

of the causes of difference, or points in dispute, to one, two, or three of the nearest societies to them, and the society or societies which may be consulted on the business, shall be by the joint consent of the contending parties, or one by each, and a third by both, and the decision of the societies consulted on the business shall be final; and if any society refuses to submit to such decision, because it is against them, their blanks shall not pass.

36. Every several United Society shall be at full liberty to appoint their own monthly, or other meetings, and payments and forfeits for non-attendance at meetings, or neglect of payments shall belong to the society where they are fortfeited to be disposed of as the society may think proper.

37. If any man upbraid his shopmate, or any member of society, or stranger, of his country or anything relating thereto, or use any other abusive language, so as thereby to cause disgust, the same shall be reported to the first committee or body meeting, or on the regular meeting night, when an impartial investigation of the charges shall take place, and if the accused is found guilty, he or they shall be fined according to the enormity of the offence, and such fine to go towards the deficiencies of the society.

38. If any man is disposed to leave his employ, and finishes up his work, and pays all just debts to master and shopmate, so as to leave them in every respect in an honourable way, he shall not be under any necessity of explaining his reasons.

39. If any member of our United Societies, should at any time be guilty of any criminal misdemeanour against the laws of the land, it is hereby enjoined upon every member of society, to aid and assist the civil powers, in endeavouring to bring such offenders to public justice.

40. If any master who is situated at a remote distance from those districts where woolcombers are more numerous, and employs men who are enrolled, and in union, should at any time be in want of men and cannot procure them, the men who may work for such a master, shall immediately communicate the same to the acting society, who shall make the same known to those districts where men are more numerous, and endeavour to obtain a regular supply of good workmen.

This Article is intended to stand as a check against, and to remove the cause of any Master introducing non-associates, or unfair Men. . . .

44. If any stranger crosses any shop or society, and refuses to take a dozen of wool when there is one for him, the stranger so refusing shall not be entitled to the benefit of either shop or club, but if any shop or society make a pretext of there being work, because they will not give the benefit when there actually is none, they shall be subject to a fine, upon full proof, of not less then one, or more than two

pounds, to be levied on them by the acting society, and the fine to be forthwith sent to the acting society for general expences and public uses.

N.B. No Irishmen to be admitted to society, after the date of these Articles.

Form of an Address,

To any master, or firm, who has employed men who have been divided.

Sir, or Gentlemen,

We humbly hope you will have the goodness, in your clemency, to pardon us, in thus presuming to address you, nor attribute it to any undue respect to either your person or property, but for the avowed purpose of informing you, that there has taken place a general union amongst woolcombers throughout Great Britain, and that any master who employs such men, and such only, as are regularly enrolled and in union, agreeable to, both the wholesome laws of the land, and the woolcombing trade, may be ensured of having a regular supply of men who are capable of working well at the business, and their property indemnified.

We are, sir, your obedient and humble servants, The Woolcombers.

Form of a Petition,

To obtain redress of any grievances, &c.

Sir, or Gentlemen,

Your humble petitioners, confiding in your clemency, hope you will take into your most serious consideration (here state the grievances) which by experience has been found to be so very injurious, (here state the particular bearings they have upon you, and the embarrasments you labour under through them, and endeavour to point out what you conceive would be a remedy) which your humble petitioners having confidence in your wisdom and goodness, hope you will endeavour speedily to adopt (or comply to, as the case may be).

(Here sign all your names, or some in behalf of the whole). . . .

PROTEST OUTLOOK

We know by now that early industrial protest was extremely varied in form and purpose. It ranged from almost inarticulate rage, to coherent attempts to undermine the existing order, to halting efforts to work within that order. Though the general definition of early industrial protest is useful, it does not fit all the actual instances. Economic circumstances varied with time and place. So did the characteristics of different groups of workers and peasants. Evaluation of early industrial protest must therefore be flexible— flexible enough to accommodate protest that reflected an effort to adapt to the new order as well as that which attacked it.

Naturally, the intensity and sweep of the grievance that spurred protest in the first decades of industrialization also varied. Traditions of respect for established institutions and social hierarchy warred with the reaction to rapid change and the sense of growing misery. The following documents do not make it any easier to sum up the meaning of early industrial protest, for motives as well as forms of protest differed from case to case.

The first document came from an embryonic union of weavers, in the Manchester-Bolton area. These were hand weavers, ultimately the group most brutally displaced by new machines but still, in 1799, secure from the worst effects of mechanical competition. The tone of their petition is obvious. Neither a sense of class conflict nor a radical political consciousness is expressed. Yet the remedies suggested are quite radical, for the workers are calling into question the freedom of trade and of untrammeled production on which industrialization in Britain was based. The anti-modern tone of much early industrial protest is clearly suggested.

The second document is a letter from a committee of Manchester weavers to the members of Parliament, in 1818. 1818 was a year of drastic recession that saw many massive strikes in Manchester and elsewhere. Machine competition was also increasing for hand weavers. The letter reflects a mixture of class hostility and deference but stresses material hardship and ultimately points to an essentially Luddite remedy.

The final letter comes from an individual worker, "a journeyman cotton spinner," also in Manchester in 1818. It is certainly more modern in tone than the first two documents, though one may ask if its view of the industrial problem is any less simplistic. The view of class struggle is more sophisticated. It would not have embarrassed an ardent socialist eighty years later. Socialist historians have likewise delighted in finding statements of this type so early in the formation of the working class. I think its importance for understanding workers' protest of this period must be questioned however, though the fact that some individual workers shared similar sentiments cannot be doubted. Few of the actual protests, whether strikes or riots, reveal such a total class warfare position. The question of how representative a viewpoint is frequently arises in social history. Hopefully, in this case, the reader can begin to form some judgment of his own.

The cotton spinner was, of course, a factory worker. Somewhat surprisingly, factory workers were not prominent in early industrial protest. They conducted far less agitation than artisans and usually their protest was strictly tied to situations in which their material conditions were deteriorating; that is, they struck or rioted during economic slumps, when their misery was obvious but unfortunately when they had least chance of winning any gains.[1]

1 See Peter N. Stearns, "Patterns of Strike Activity in France during the July Monarchy," *American Historical Review* 50 (January 1965): 371–94. British factory workers struck more often than French, to be sure, because their conditions deteriorated more frequently in the first half-century of industrialization.

This certainly suggests once again that this cotton spinner's argument, though fascinating, was atypical in the factories. Surrounded by apathetic or even satisfied colleagues, a worker with this acute sensitivity to industrial capitalism must have suffered from more than his work and low wage alone. There is more than a hint of his loneliness in his broadside. But it can be argued that the class-conscious worker, if unusually articulate, was expressing views that his fellows shared even if they were too repressed to give voice to them in direct protest. Or finally, it can be argued that such a worker was a herald of the future, and thus more important if less typical than his factory mates. Once again, when we try to penetrate the mentality of people who did not, like this worker, leave any direct records, we must speculate. I think the indirect evidence—the types of protests that occurred and the absence of sophisticated protest by factory workers—points to the conclusion that class consciousness was yet to develop on a large scale.

The last document certainly helps lead into a discussion of later industrial protest. We can safely assume that class-conscious sentiments of this sort played a much greater role later in the nineteenth century. But note that we have already had other hints of more modern protest and that they do not point in exactly the same directions. Craft unionism changed, but not completely, as we move into a later period. Demands for higher wages and for other gains within the existing system at least hinted at as industrialization got underway, naturally increased in importance. They might lead workers away from full-scale class consciousness. Hence, considerable diversity in modern protest was already being prepared. It would be enhanced by the fact that some of the motives, if not the major forms of early industrial protest, persisted as well.

A Weaver's Statement

The present existing laws that should protect weavers, etc. from imposition, being trampled under foot, for want of a union amongst them, they have come to a determination to support each other in their just and legal rights, and to apply to the Legislature of the country for such further regulations as it may in its wisdom deem fit to make, when the real state of the cotton manufactory shall have been laid before it. The members of this Association have no other object in view but the mutual interest of both employers and employed—well knowing that to combine their interest together is the only method to expect success; being sensible that the fair trader is exposed to difficulties through injurious practices that have crept into the cotton manufactory, and to study his interest is to study their own, for if a fair chance is given to him, theirs of course will follow. These being their sentiments, they flatter themselves with the support of men of this description; earnestly desiring them to give the situations of

From Home Office 42/47. This was a printed statement "to the public."

weavers, etc. their candid consideration, how every necessary of life has increased in price, whilst the price of labour has undergone a continual decrease; this being the case, it becomes a duty incumbent on both parties to search out the cause, and, if possible, remove it, that the effects may cease. And ye who are our enemies, do you not blush to hear these facts repeated—Great Britain holding the reins of universal commerce, is it not shameful that her sons should be thus imposed on? Are you afraid that we should approach the Government, and there tell the truth?—that ye use the mean artifice of stigmatising us with the name of Jacobins, that ye raise your rumours of plots, riots, etc.[1]

We disdain your calumny, and look upon you with that contempt you merit. To the public we address ourselves—rioting, or any illegal behaviour, we detest, and are firmly attached to our King and country, and to promote their prosperity shall ever be the object most dear to our hearts. How unjustly do those calumniate us who assert that our meetings are calculated to sacrifice the independence of our country! It is the reverse, for should the clarion ever sound "To arms! England is in danger!"—we know what is our duty, and what is our interest; and not only ours, but the duty and interest of every individual, to rally round Government, and strike the daring foe prostrate at our feet. These being our genuine sentiments, is there anything to fear by us meeting together? We shall neither interfere with Church nor State, but strictly confine ourselves to a private grievance, which we wish to lay before Government, and it will remain to be determined by it, whether or not our case merits redress; but having that confidence in Government which ought to be universal, we believe that when our real situation is laid before the Legislature, some method will be devised to ameliorate our condition.

There are some as ignorant of the very laws they pretend to administer, that they would willingly confound our meetings with those which are only calculated to undermine Government: it is wonderful that they are not ashamed to expose their ignorance to the public view— but, that their ignorance may not infect you, we will take the liberty to state that it never was the intention of Government to infringe upon the right of meeting together to lay any matter of this kind before them.

On the contrary, the late laws on meetings[2] appear to us to be only

1 This refers to the French revolutionary Jacobins and to the great concern over subversion that developed in Britain during the war against France.

2 The Seditious Meetings Act of 1795 banned public meetings of more than fifty persons unless previous notice had been given in the newspapers and to a Justice of the Peace. It expired in 1799, when an Act was passed "for the more effectual suppression of societies established for seditious and treasonable purposes; and for better preventing treasonable and seditious practices."

intended as a bridle to that wild democratic fury that leads nations into the vortex of anarchy, confusion and bloodshed; if, then, the laws of your country guarantee to you the right of meeting together to consider of a private grievance of this kind, are you so foolish to be deterred in your proceedings by the misrepresentations of ignorant and designing men, who do more hurt to the Government than good? Government does not stand in need of a blind attachment, for the more it is considered the more it is admired; and the friends who are attached to it from understanding are the only real ones to be found:

It is the interest of every occupation to step forward and support us; even the landed property feels the want of regulations in the cotton manufactory; and to convince the landed interest that this is the case, we will point out the situation of those employed in it. They are continually subject to reductions in their wages, which never find their level. Draw the analogy any distant time back, and what we assert will be found true: but to be more particular, we will suppose a man to be married in the year 1792; he at that period received 22s. for 44 yards of cloth. We will follow him year after year; his family keeps increasing, together with the price of every necessary of life, whilst his wages for labour decreases [sic]. Let us look at him in the year 1799, and we shall perhaps find him surrounded with five or six small children, and, lo! instead of 44 yards they have increased the length to 60, and give him only 11s. for it; and, to make ill worse, he must work it with finer weft! No wonder that poor rates increase, when people are situated in this manner. A little reflection will show how matters of this kind affect the landed interest.

It is in vain to talk of bad trade; if goods are actually not wanted, they cannot be sold at any price; if wanted, 2d.[3] or 3d. per yard will not stop the buyer; and whether does it appear more reasonable that 2d. or 3d. per yard should be laid on the consumer or taken from the labourer? A single 2d. per yard would increase the wages from 11s. to 21s., 3d. to 26s. Consider how little it would affect the one, and how important to the other. How impressed with gratitude must that man be with five or six small children, when informed that Government had devised certain measures, that where he now received only 11s., he might receive above 20s. for his work.

Ye whose hardened hearts are dead to humane feelings which should always adorn the human mind, may say it is impracticable, and are we yet to continue suffering on your barely asserting this? No: we are determined that those who are appointed by the Constitution of our country to redress our grievances, shall have our real state laid before them; and it must be their wisdom that must determine this point; and with this determination we shall always think it our duty to com-

3 Two pence. There were twelve pence in the shilling.

ply. A peaceful demeanour shall always guide all our actions, and we trust a candid public will give the subject a mature consideration, and afford us that support we merit.

It was resolved unanimously, that this Address should be printed and distributed in the different towns, in the name of the General Committee, assembled at Bolton, on Monday the 13th of May 1799.

A Weavers' Petition

. . . We Cannot hear, without strong emotions, our Merchants boast their ability to undersell all other Nations, while that ability is acquired by reducing us to the Borders of Starvation, and keeping us but one remove from Slavery.—They boast of underselling foreigners, while foreigners oblige them to pay in the shape of duties what they unnecessarily take from our wages. The average Wages of some hundreds of Weavers, for 4 months, as proved from the Books of their Employers, is now in the Manchester papers: Their wages for that period was 4s. 10d. per week, to each. This may suggest to you the condition that Weavers' families must be in. —The application of many thousands of power-looms to weaving, at the time that many thousands of manual Weavers returned from the Army[1] was altogether unnecessary because, by that Reduction the number of Weavers was more than sufficient to supply the demand. Power-looms by diminishing the demand for manual labour, has put the manual Weaver entirely in the power of his Employer. The Employers can throw their Weavers out of Employ when they please, without injury to themselves, while thousands are glad of Employ at any wages whatever. And Weavers residing in large towns from the number of one to twelve thousands, make it impossible for them either to withhold their labour or to find other Employment. And their long endured poverty has made them incapable of removing to other places. Now, Sir, in this state of things, is it not evident, that Employers have more power over Workmen, than any class of men ought to have over others? I do not mean to insinuate that all our Manufacturers desire that gain, which cannot be had without keeping us at the starving point. —No, Sir, we believe that a greater number of them would rejoice to pay us well. But however good their wishes be, it is impossible for them ever to be realised, while the whole state of our Wages is determined by a few Competitors, who, to effect speedy sales reduce Weavers' wage.

Home Office 40/18. The letter was in response to a speech in parliament which had boasted of England's low rate of wages as the cause of her industrial pre-eminence.

1 After the Napoleonic Wars, which ended in 1815.

—Others discovering the means by which they are under-sold, are, as it were, compelled to reduce Wages in their own Defence. —In our opinion, a Committee, of Masters, or of masters and workmen, chosen by both, fixing the prices periodically, or as often as fluctuations in trade make alterations in the price of labour necessary, would put it in the power of honest Masters to alleviate the Distress of half a million. If, from 1d. to 4d. per yard, were laid on Cotton goods, and that added to the Weaver's Wages, he would not then be half paid as other Branches of the Cotton manufacture are, but still, this trifling advance which the consumer would never know unless by report, would keep the Weaver from pauperism—it would, in a great measure, keep Infancy and age from hunger—it would preserve youth from the demoralisation consequent upon being exposed to all the temptations of want, which has, of late, so crowded our prisons with juvenile Delinquents and too often furnished the platform with victims. —We only wish for such an advance, as the markets without the smallest stagnation can afford; and such as a proper and just regulation would soon produce.

We are sending a petition to parliament; praying for a regulating Committee, such as mentioned above. We also pray for a tax to be laid on power-looms, which are now transferring labour from men to Children and Girls; and from Cottages to Factories. This by depriving parents of sufficient Employ, makes them dependent on their Children for support; which, as experience too tragically proves, deprives them of that authority over youth which is necessary to retard the progress of vice and to promote Virtue. —The evils of a Factory-life are incalculable. —There uninformed, unrestrained youth, of both sexes mingle—absent from parental vigilance; from Reproof and Instruction—confined in artificial heat to the injury of health. —The mind exposed to corruption, and life and limbs exposed to Machinery —spending Youth where the 40th year of the age is the 60th of the constitution, till at last themselves become dependant [sic] on their offspring or the parish. This, Sir, is no overdrawn picture, but, as may be easily proved a very contracted sketch of facts.

In our humble opinion, the evils of multiplying power-looms, by first ruining half a million who depend on manual Weaving for support; and eventually those unhappy young people whom they now employ, are such as no human being can think are counterbalanced by any good expected from them. And if the Capitals now employed in power-looms, were applied the common way, the Manufacturer would have sufficient profit.

The Weavers' Qualifications may be considered as his property and support. It is as real property to him, as Buildings and Lands are to others. Like them his Qualification cost *time, application and Money.*

There is no point of view (except visible and tangible) wherein they differ. And when Buildings are removed, or Land engrossed for Roads, Streets or Canals, the proprietors are paid for them. Then, if two dependencies, of exactly equal value to the proprietors are sacrificed for convenience; does not equity require, that while the one if remunerated, the other ought not to be totally neglected?

Sir, you have now read over the real causes of the tumult so often excited in our Districts; but Weavers too often imputed their misery to other Causes; and manufacturers understood their own interests too well to undeceive them. —Our petition will soon be before you in parliament, we hope the Justice of our Cause will be manifest.

A Spinner's Attack

First, then, as to the employers: with very few exceptions, they are a set of men who have sprung from the cotton-shop without education or address, except so much as they have acquired by their intercourse with the little world of merchants on the exchange at Manchester; but to counterbalance that deficiency, they give you enough of appearances by an ostentatious display of elegant mansions, equipages, liveries, parks, hunters, hounds, &c. which they take care to shew off to the merchant stranger in the most pompous manner. Indeed their houses are gorgeous palaces, far surpassing in bulk and extent the neat charming retreats you see round London . . . but the chaste observer of the beauties of nature and art combined will observe a woeful deficiency of taste. They bring up their families at the most costly schools, determined to give their offspring a double portion of what they were so deficient in themselves. Thus with scarcely a second idea in their heads, they are literally petty monarchs, absolute and despotic, in their own particular districts; and to support all this, their whole time is occupied in contriving how to get the greatest quantity of work turned off with the least expence. . . . In short, I will venture to say, without fear of contradiction, that there is a greater distance observed between the master there and the spinner, than there is between the first merchant in London and his lowest servant or the lowest artisan. Indeed there is no comparison. I know it to be a fact, that the greater part of the master spinners are anxious to keep wages low for the purpose of keeping the spinners indigent and spiritless . . . as for the purpose of taking the surplus to their own pockets.

From Black Dwarf, *September 30, 1818. Reprinted in E. P. Thompson,* The Making of the English Working Class *(New York, 1963) pp. 199–202. Copyright © 1963 by E. P. Thompson. Reprinted by permission of Pantheon Press, a division of Random House, Inc.*

The master spinners are a class of men unlike all other master tradesmen in the kingdom. They are ignorant, proud, and tyrannical. What then must be the men or rather beings who are the instruments of such masters? Why, they have been for a series of years, with their wives and their families, patience itself—bondmen and bondwomen to their cruel taskmasters. It is in vain to insult our common understandings with the observation that such men are free; that the law protects the rich and poor alike, and that a spinner can leave his master if he does not like the wages. True; so he can: but where must he go? why to another, to be sure. Well: he goes; he is asked where did you work last: 'did he discharge you?' No; we could not agree about wages. Well I shall not employ you nor anyone who leaves his master in that manner. Why is this? Because there is an abominable *combination existing amongst the masters,* first established at Stockport in 1802, and it has since become so general, as to embrace all the great masters for a circuit of many miles round Manchester, though not the little masters: they are excluded. They are the most obnoxious beings to the great ones that can be imagined. . . . When the combination first took place, one of thier first articles was, that no master should take on a man until he had first ascertained whether his last master had discharged him. What then is the man to do? If he goes to the parish, that grave of all independence, he is there told—We shall not relieve you; if you dispute with your master, and don't support your family, we will send you to prison; so that the man is bound, by a combination of circumstances, to submit to his master. He cannot travel and get work in any town like a shoe-maker, joiner, or taylor; he is confined to the district.

The workmen in general are an inoffensive, unassuming, set of well-informed men, though how they acquire their information is almost a mystery to me. They are docile and tractable, if not goaded too much; but this is not to be wondered at, when we consider that they are trained to work from six years old, from five in a morning to eight and nine at night. Let one of the advocates for obedience to his master take his stand in an avenue leading to a factory a little before five o'clock in the morning, and observe the squalid appearance of the little infants and their parents taken from their beds at so early an hour in all kinds of weather; let him examine the miserable pittance of food, chiefly composed of water gruel and oatcake broken into it, a little salt, and sometimes coloured with a little milk, together with a few potatoes, and a bit of bacon or fat for dinner; would a London mechanic eat this? There they are, (and if late a few minutes, a quarter of a day is stopped in wages) locked up until night in rooms heated above the hottest days we have had this summer, and allowed no time, except three-quarters of an hour at dinner in the whole day: whatever they eat at any other time must be as they are at work. The negro slave in the West Indies, if he works under a scorching sun, has probably a little breeze of air sometimes to fan him: he has a space of ground, and time allowed to cultivate it. The English spinner slave has no enjoyment of the open atmosphere and breezes of heaven. Locked up in factories eight stories high, he has no relaxation till the ponderous engine stops, and then he goes home to get refreshed for the next day; no time for sweet association with his family; they are all alike fatigued and exhausted. This is no over-drawn picture: it is literally true. I ask again, would the mechanics in the South of England submit to this?

When the spinning of cotton was in its infancy, and before those terrible machines for superseding the necessity of human labour, called steam engines, came into use, there were a great number of what were then called *little masters*; men who with a small capital, could procure a few machines, and employ a few hands, men and boys (say to twenty or thirty), the produce of whose labour was all taken to Manchester central mart, and put into the hands of brokers. . . . The brokers sold it to the merchants, by which means the master spinner was enabled to stay at home and work and attend to his workmen. The cotton was then always given out in its raw state from the bale to the wives of the spinners at home, when they heat and cleansed it ready for the spinners in the factory. By this they could earn eight, ten, or twelve shillings a week, and cook and attend to their families. But none are thus employed now; for all the cotton is broke up by a machine, turned by the steam engine, called a devil: so that the spinners wives have no employment, except they go to work in the factory all day at what can be done by children for a few shillings, four or five per week. If a man then could not agree with his master, he left him, and could get employed elsewhere. A few years, however, changed the face of things. Steam engines came into use, to purchase which, and to erect buildings sufficient to contain them and six or seven hundred hands, required a great capital. The engine power produced a more marketable (though not a better) article than the little master could at the same price. The consequence was their ruin in a short time; and the overgrown capitalists triumphed in their fall; for they were the only obstacle that stood between them and the complete controul of the workmen.

Various disputes then originated between the workmen and masters as to the fineness of the work, the workmen being paid according to the number of hanks or yards of thread he produced from a given quantity of cotton, which was always to be proved by the overlooker, whose interest made it imperative on him to lean to his master, and call the material coarser than it was. If the workman would not submit *he must summon his employer before a magistrate;* the whole of the acting magistrates in that district, with the exception of two worthy

clergymen, being gentlemen who have sprung from the *same* source
with the master cotton spinners. The employer generally contented
himself with sending his overlooker to answer any such summons,
thinking it beneath him to meet his servant. The magistrate's decision
was generally in favour of the master, though on the statement of the
overlooker only. The workman dared not appeal to the sessions on
account of the expense. . . .

These evils to the men have arisen from that dreadful monopoly
which exists in those districts where wealth and power are got into the
hands of the few, who, in the pride of their hearts, think themselves
the lords of the universe.

INDUSTRIAL PROTEST

A mounting wave of protest developed at the end of the nineteenth century in western and central Europe. Anti-semitic agitation spread among segments of the middle classes until 1900, while workers supported hundreds and then thousands of strikes a year in the major industrial countries. Virtually every kind of strike was attempted between 1890 and 1914—many of them for the first time—from nationwide industrial strikes to slowdowns on individual construction sites.[1]

Workers also engaged in other forms of protest. Socialist voting was a vital outlet for aggrieved workers, and elements of other social classes as well. So strikes alone cannot measure the nature of industrial protest. But they did entail an active commitment to agitation. Strikers lost money during their protest; many received no regular strike aid at all, while those who did gained far less than their normal pay. Often, strikers risked their jobs. Dismissals of hundreds of workers were not uncommon after strikes. And, though strikes were now legal in the industrialized countries, they were hemmed in by restrictions, notably those which forbade intimidation of people who wanted to continue their work. Hence, arrests and clashes with the police were frequent. German workers went to jail for shouting "pfui" at strike-breakers, while in the French railroad strike of 1910, some engineers were arrested for merely staring at men on the job. In other words, strikes were becoming a normal part of industrial life, but neither the state nor employers had fully recognized them as such. Strikes therefore

---

1 K. G. J. C. Knowles, *Strikes—A Study in Industrial Conflict* (Oxford, 1952).

constituted the most massive direct-action protest in countries where industrialization was well established.

There is no question that this protest differed from that of the early industrial decades. The very fact that strikes, along with demonstrations and protest voting, had replaced riot and revolution as the key protest forms was significant. Oddly enough, the most interesting historical work on direct-action protest by the lower classes has focused on the early industrial variety, so a definition of industrial or modern protest has not been fully worked out. Nevertheless it has been widely assumed that industrial protest reverses most of the leading characteristics of early industrial protest, and an eminent historical sociologist has developed the definition explicitly, claiming that around the mid-nineteenth century artisans and factory workers in western Europe made the transition to the new protest form.[2] Industrial protest is highly organized, large scale rather than local, organized on class lines, and above all forward-looking in its demands. Protesters now demand new rights rather than looking back to the past for the goals and justifications of protest.

There is no question that protest was tending toward this model at the end of the nineteenth century, but the transition was still incomplete. While large scale strikes did occur, the average strike in Germany embraced only 119 workers, in France about 230 workers, and they were of course purely local in scope. Strikes did involve organization, but often they began spontaneously, invoking organization only after the conflict was underway. Only after 1900, in fact, did even a bare majority of strikes involve union members in countries such as France and Germany. Above all the conversion to progressive demands was incomplete. What is involved here was a major human change. The lower classes had a centuries-old tradition of belief in stability. Early industrial protest had largely been based on this belief. To accept a belief that progress was possible and desirable was no easy matter. Around 1900, the working classes were divided on this point. Some groups of workers could, for example, demand a pay raise without referring to past standards, but others roused themselves only when their pay was cut. Strikes, therefore, deserve careful examination as indicators of working-class outlook and of the level of expectations that had been achieved.

Strikes in the industrial countries were not a revolutionary force. Some labor leaders—notably the revolutionary syndicalists in France— thought they ought to be. And in countries just beginning industrialization they could indeed develop revolutionary implications; the 1905

2 Charles Tilly, "Collective Violence in European Perspective," in Hugh Davis Graham and Ted Robert Gurr, Eds., *Violence in America* (New York, 1969).

revolution in Russia consisted largely of a general strike in the cities. Nothing remotely comparable occurred in the industrialized nations, though it has been argued that labor unrest was contributing to a potentially-revolutionary situation in Britain in 1914, before World War I diverted attention elsewhere.[3] Generally, though, strikers seemed intent on working within the system. Perhaps repression was responsible for their timidity, or undue caution on the part of their professed leaders. More probably the limitations of workers' expectations and their improved political and economic situation combined to infuse a somewhat moderate tone into their protest. In any case, strikers themselves must be studied to determine what protest goals existed and what they implied for the broader society.

In contrast to the early industrial period, the sources for industrial protest are massive. Few, however, come directly from the ordinary striker or voter. If we wish to understand the goals of the protester, the grievances he felt, we are seldom much better off than we were in the pre-industrial period.

In the first place, trade unions and socialist parties were involved in protest even if they did not have full control over it, and they were not reluctant to make pronouncements about its nature. But we cannot take their pronouncements literally, except as expressions of their own intentions. As with leaders like Cobbett, we must try to find independent evidence as to whether actual protesters sought the goals their advisers said they ought to seek. In the 1890s, this often means asking whether workers felt the radical grievances against the existing order that socialist leaders wanted them to. With time, the leader-follower problem changes. Socialist parties and trade unions became more conservative in the industrial countries, particularly after 1900. I would argue that they did so in large part in response to the wishes of their constituents. But there were other factors involved, and it is possible to contend that they were motivated more by their own satisfaction with the positions they had won and by the weight of the bureaucracies they had developed. In this case, protest stemming from workers themselves would have more radical implications. Without any doubt, some strikes in Germany and particularly in England involved discontent against the moderation of the labor movement, particularly after 1909.

We must, then, use the massive documentation which labor leaders produced with great care. When it is possible to cut through it to statement directly from workers, a further problem arises. Workers were not united. The expansion of the scope of protest widened the pos-

---

3 George Dangerfield, *The Strange Death of Liberal England* (New York, 1961); for a more balanced view, E. H. Phelps Brown, *The Growth of British Industrial Relations* (London, 1959).

sible diversity among the participants. When protest was completely illegal, as earlier in the nineteenth century in western Europe, we can usually assume considerable agreement among the small number of highly-aggrieved artisans or peasants who typically risked an outburst. Around 1900, with strikes difficult but basically legal, more cautious, less aggrieved workers might enter the fray. So many strikes produced majority-minority differences, with the majority usually taking the more moderate line. Hence, we must test protest documents for their representativeness, and of course it was the minority that was most likely to issue a formal statement of its beliefs. But there is more than this involved. We must ask if the majorities were genuinely moderate or hemmed in by their sense of tactical difficulties, in which case minority statements might be closer to workers' real goals than the actual progress of most strikes would indicate.

Sources outside the protest increase in volume by the later-nineteenth century, and as before they must be taken into consideration. Reporters of all sorts flocked to major strikes. The police, particularly on the continent, made massive reports of their own. These outside sources often provide details about a protest unavailable from any other material. No only do they discuss the size of a strike or demonstration; they also try to assess causes and real goals. Most of the outside sources, and certainly the police, defended the established order. They typically played down the seriousness of protest and sought prosaic rather than sweeping goals in it. Often they seem more accurate than the wishful thinking of labor leaders. There is something of a vicious circle involved in dealing with accounts of protest in this period, however, because it is impossible to choose among differing accounts without some sense of what the meaning of protest was, yet the choice of accounts is basic to determining the meaning. As in other types of inquiry in history and sociology, a certain amount of intuition is essential, related to the data but not entirely demonstrable from it.

Individual strikes had real drama, particularly when they involved clashes with the police, but overall there is a more prosaic quality to strikes than to the early industrial protests. Protest was becoming partially routinized. It lacked the flashiness of Luddism. But we should not be deterred by surface impressions. Industrial protest directly involved far more people than had ever before regularly participated in agitation and therefore it can tell us more about them. The sources are difficult to handle, but at least they exist. We have a chance to evaluate part of the basic outlook of a large segment of the lower classes, which we could only guess at before. We can study not only the forms and incidence of protest itself but also what they tell us about the nature of industrial life and the ability of workers to adjust to it.

ANTI-SEMITISM AS PROTEST

Anti-Semitic protest at the end of the nineteenth century usefully reminds us that workers were not the only aggrieved group in industrial society. It also suggests the great difficulty of generalizing about the nature of industrial protest. For though anti-Semitic demonstrations only occasionally turned into riots—thus differing in form from the most important early industrial protest—they expressed goals that recall the early industrial type. Anti-Semitism harked back to an idealized past. Most anti-Semites were from social groups that had little experience in protest, so it may have been natural for them to adopt more primitive goals. Furthermore, each new stage of industrialization created new discomforts. If artisans had felt threatened by new machines when they were introduced, so shopkeepers now saw the menace of new, big business activities such as department stores. Anti-Semitism has rarely been included as a form of popular protest at the end of the nineteenth century, partly because it was not based primarily in the working classes and partly because its nature complicates any neat definition of modern protest. It is also true that the sources anti-semitic agitation produced are less direct than those which strikes have left behind. Yet anti-semitic demonstrations commanded hundreds of thousands of participants, particularly in France and, as such, they are worth more than a passing glance.

Anti-Semitism has a long tradition in the Christian world. It is not certain that the recrudescence of anti-Semitism in the late nineteenth century was more than a revival of the tradition, but most historians think it was a new phenomenon—a means of protest against modern political and economic trends that were disturbing to many people. The ideology behind the new anti-Semitism was more racist than religious.[1]

Anti-Semitism appealed mainly to some members of the middle and upper classes, and particularly to shopkeepers and other small property holders who were threatened by the new forms of capitalism. It spread widely in France, even to cities like Nantes, in Brittany, where there were few Jews and scant tradition of anti-Semitism. Its peak occurred in 1898–99, during the Dreyfus affair.[2] Obviously, anti-Semitism was a very indirect form of protest, insofar as it used Jews as the scapegoat for much broader grievances. The methods of protest are also hard to interpret. Anti-Semites relied mainly on propaganda and demonstrations, which occasionally involved some violence but usually did not. The whole point is that anti-Semites wanted desperately to be respectable. They shunned protest methods associated with the lower classes. This makes it difficult to interpret the intensity of their

1 See Robert F. Byrnes, *Anti-Semitism in Modern France* (New Brunswick, N.J., 1950), and P. G. J. Pulzer, *Rise of Political Anti-Semitism in Germany and Austria* (New York, 1964). Insofar as anti-Semitism was a protest of older middle-class elements against further change, it invites comparison with earlier reactions, such as that typified by Vogel and other Germans in 1848; see below.
2 See Gary Chapman, *The Dreyfus Affair* (London, 1955).

grievances. Nor do we have any clear notion of how many people wished to protest in this fashion or believed in anti-Semitism; we certainly cannot assume that whole social classes, some of whose members were anti-Semite, were thus inclined.

The following two documents are typical of the sources available for the history of anti-Semitism. They were associated with several major demonstrations in the streets of Nantes, some of which involved minor skirmishes with the police. The text of the propaganda poster reflects the passions of the Dreyfus affair that were being fanned by national newspapers like Drumont's *Libre Parole* and, in Brittany, by some anti-republican priests. Almost certainly they should not be taken literally. It is inconceivable that many people were worried about a direct Jewish political takeover alone. Even within the text of the poster we can discern other, more understandable grievances. And fortunately a concurrent police report offers greater insight, though it reveals the diversity of composition and motives in the movement. It is, of course, the work of an outsider, interpreting reports by police spies. Note the typical tendency of the French police to find political significance in protest movements and to use them as an opportunity to attack the government's enemies, such as the Church in this case. Before 1914, anti-Semites actually had a great deal of difficulty translating their grievances into politics, though this was partly because they distrusted the parliamentary system; this was the case in Nantes. So we must use the police interpretation with care; but if we do not use it—if we are forced to rely on the rhetoric of anti-semites alone—it is doubtful that we can understand the movement at all. What the police report lacks are the passions and the fears of the people who embraced anti-Semitism. For this we must return to the poster text, combined with the knowledge that in Nantes and elsewhere thousands of usually cautious, conservative people took to the streets.

A Propaganda Statement

Dear Fellow-citizen,

As a Frenchman and a patriot, your heart must throb with indignation as you watch an occult group supported by the whole Semitic race place in doubt the act of justice handed down by a military court which was above all suspicion, hence soiling one of the most sacred Institutions of our country.

To let the opinion of a handful of quasi-French cosmopolitans gain credence would be to profane what we hold most dear in France: Love of Country and Respect for Justice.

A group of patriots at Nantes have felt that the time was ripe to organize, without any spirit of class or partisan politics, a Nantes

Published in the Nouvelliste de l'Ouest, *April 17, 1898. Translated by Peter Meyers.*

patriotic league for the defense of our *Patrie* against the take-over by Jews of more and more public duties and affairs.

Already several French cities, Paris, Lyon, Bordeaux, Poitiers, etc., have preceded us in this course, and we, citizens of Nantes, we should have the courage to remain in the forefront of this wholesome and patriotic movement.

The battle being waged is, alas, only too justified. We have the advantage, as indicated by the adhesion of all decent people to our cause, of not being the *provocateurs*. To convince people of that, without pointing to other proof, we need only read the text of a speech given February 14, 1880 and cited in *Contemporain* of July 1, 1881, which was published by the anti-Semite league of Lyon as well as by several other French journals:

> When we make ourselves the sole possessors of all the gold on earth, true power will pass into our hands, and at last the promises made to Abraham will be fulfilled.

> Gold, the most powerful force in the world; gold, which is the power, the reward, the instrument of all power, all that man fears and all that he desires. . . . There is the only mystery, the most profound science of the spirit which rules the world. . . . Therein lies the future!

> Today, all the emperors, reigning kings, and princes are burdened with debts contracted to support permanent armies, which uphold their tottering thrones. The stock exchange quotes and underwrites these debts, and we are for the most part masters of the Bourse. We must investigate, therefore, how we may grant more and more loans, in order to make ourselves the regulators of all values and, as far as possible, take as security for the capital which we loan to the country, the profits of their railroad lines, their mines, their forests, their big forges and factories, as well as other property, even their taxes.

> Agriculture will always remain the great source of wealth of every country. The possession of large tracts of land will also be worth some honors and exert a great influence on the office holders. Hence it follows that we Jews must make some important territorial acquisitions. We should, as often as possible, use our influence to break up large estates so that we can make our acquisitions more quickly and easily.

> Under the pretext of coming to the aid of the laboring classes, we should see that the large land owners bear the entire tax burden. And after their land has passed into our hands, all the work of the Christian proletariat will become the source of huge profits for us.

> The Christian church is one of our most dangerous enemies and we should work with perseverance to diminish its influence. It is therefore

advisable, whenever possible, to stimulate among those who profess the Christian faith the ideas of free thought, skepticism, and schism and to provoke the religious disputes so naturally fertile in divisions and sects in Christianity.

Logically, it is necessary to start by belittling the ministers of this religion: Let us declare open war on them; let us cast doubt on their private conduct. And by ridicule and gossip we will overcome the consideration attached to the state and to clerical robes.

Each war, each revolution, each political or religious disturbance hastens the day when we will attain our supreme goal.

Commerce and speculation, two branches fertile in profits, must never leave Jewish hands. To begin with we must monopolize the markets for alcohol, butter and wine, for by that we will become absolute masters of all agriculture, and in general of the entire rural economy. We will be the distributors of gains for all, but if it should happen that some discontent is produced by the misery, there will always be time for us to transfer the responsibility to the government.

It is unnecessary, isn't it, to comment on this document, except to point out that in the face of such implacable and inveterate enemies, it is more than time to act: it is the duty of all good Frenchmen.

Toward this end, and in order to defray the various costs of brochures, conferences, circulars, etc., we are enclosing four membership applications which allow you to choose the type of membership you desire.

If, as we hope, you want to adhere to this truly French league, you will fill out one of these forms and return it to the office of the acting treasurer, M. L. Reveillant-Cheval, rue Vauban, # 4 (place Royale), who will collect the fees in his private home.

Some application and subscription forms are available at the same office.

Anonymous contributions will be received with gratitude and will be sent directly to the acting Treasurer.

A general meeting for the election of permanent League committee members will also take place shortly.

At this meeting a speaker will elaborate on the goals of the League, which include the following:

1. Return France to the French.
2. Extract from candidates at the next election a pledge of anti-Semitism.
3. By all legal means battle the take-over of public offices and functions by Jews.

A Police Report
Nantes. Tuesday, 19 April 1898
Report 248

Anti-Semitism

The meeting of members of the Patriotic Anti-Semite League which I reported earlier took place last night in the home of M. Turcand, rue de l'Arche-Sèche. It was presided over by M. de Pontbriand, deputy. Messrs. Garruchaud and the Count de Bellevue, counselor general, were advisors. M. Brincard, attorney, was secretary.

M. de Pontbriand, who is already president of the temporary committee of this association, gave a patriotic speech. The League, he said, is nationalistic; it is against the Jews because they constitute the present danger. It would just as well oppose the English, the Americans, or all other foreigners, if they should become a menace to the *Patrie,* as the Jews are at the present time. He spoke of his proposal to the Chamber of Deputies that French citizenship be granted only to the third generation of foreigners residing in France.

Just as he had done previously, as I reported yesterday, in his new speech last night M. de Pontbriand concentrated on the nature of this association. He specified that it has no political character, since it counts among its members all parties, professing divergent political opinions. He also said that it neither should nor could turn into an association to protect commercial interests; since it includes men of all social conditions, it cannot be considered an instrument of shopkeepers. Finally the League, in its action, espouses no ideological point of view. It is solely against the Semitic race. Unfortunately, the great advantage of the Jews is to bear the name of their religion, so that they can cry religious intolerance when they are attacked. The best defense against them is to label them as foreigners. The Nantes Patriotic Anti-Semite League, concluded M. de Pontbriand, is therefore a nationwide league of defense against the foreigner; it wants to keep France for the Frenchmen.

M. Poulain, Knight of the Legion of Honor, asked the League to appropriate the sum of 700F for the celebration for Joan of Arc. M. de Pontbriand expressed the opinion, for the reasons that he had just given, that no matter how one may admire the solemnity of the occasion, it would be wise to deny the request so that no one could accuse the League of subsidizing political or religious activities. The assembly decided in favor of M. de Pontbriand.

M. Garruchaud then said some words of no importance.

From the M Series of the archives of the Loire-Atlantique department. Translated by Peter Meyers.

The assembly next named a steering committee composed of forty-five members. This committee divided itself into three subcommittees —of commercial affairs, of propaganda, and of press and publicity— at the head of which were placed respectively Messrs.:

Garruchaud, rue de la Poissonnerie
Borgogno, haberdasher, rue d'Orléans
Porcher, rue des Olivettes.

The same committee of forty-five members will meet immediately to name an executive committee of seven members.

It was not the main order of business in the plenary session of last night, as it was in certain meetings of the notables of this League, to choose an anti-Semite candidate and present him to the Nantes electorate. I do not know yet if they have definitely rejected the idea of nominating their own candidate, but it was decided yesterday to demand that candidates for legislative election make some formal anti-Semitic declarations on their campaign posters as well as promise to participate in the anti-Jewish group which will be started in the next Chamber. The candidates who do not subscribe to these conditions will be energetically opposed by the League.

Lastly, at the urging of a number of members, the League decided unanimously to telegraph M. Drumont and General de Boisdeffre in Paris:

To *La Libre Parole*, Paris:

The Nantes Patriotic Anti-Semite League held a general meeting April 18, 1898.
The members send the valiant director of *La Libre Parole* their most sincere thanks for the eminent services that he renders to the *Patrie* in working to deliver it from the influence of the Jewish yoke. The League hopes that, thanks to the patriotism of the Algerians, he will be elected to the Chamber where he will hold his seat with dignity.
The President: de Pontbriand

To General de Boisdeffre, Paris:

The Patriotic Anti-Semites of Nantes, meeting in general assembly the eighteenth of April, affirm their undying confidence in the leaders of our army on the eve of the opening of the trial of the Italian Zola and send their expression of respect.
For the meeting: The President: de Pontbriand

It was announced last night that M. Georges Thiébaud would speak at the next meeting, which would be held in about a week.

As one can see, all the actions of the Nantes Patriotic Anti-Semite League—those of yesterday and those taken in previous meetings—are very clearly contrary to the character credited to it by M. de Pontbriand.

The League, no matter what it says, follows an ideological path of social and political reaction. If this were not so, one could not explain the adhesion of militant reactionaries and ultramontaine clerics, who would not have joined a movement of simple commercial defense. On the other hand, for the shopkeepers who are associated it is a matter of economic defense, no matter what they may claim. I want to do certain men whose names appear on the published lists the honor of believing that they are not there to conspire against the republic but have only wanted to profit from this more or less sincere and spontaneous movement of public opinion against the Jews and hope to attract to their shops the clientele of the Jewish businesses. It would not be necessary to know how things started at Nantes in order to suspect an ulterior motive on the part of those who belong to it. Basically, and it is this which assures the vitality of the association, it will offer to some people certain moral or material advantages which each of the members will use to his profit and which will reduce his scruples to silence.

THE FRENCH EIGHT-HOUR-DAY STRIKE, 1906

In 1904, the Confédération générale du travail—France's central union federation—resolved at its Congress in Bourges to prepare a general strike for an eight-hour day. The C.G.T. was a revolutionary syndicalist organization that wanted to overturn the state as well as the capitalist order, replacing both with local producers' organizations that would give workers true independence. It shunned political means, believing that all politics was corrupt, and instead advocated a general strike that would paralyze the economy and bring the state to its knees. It hoped to use the eight-hour issue to prepare the more sweeping general strike; it was far less interested in concrete gains from the strike than in training and educating the strikers for bigger and more important things. The strike, called for May 1, already a symbolic day for the labor movement, drew over 200,000 participants, mainly in Paris.

First and foremost, then, the strike gives us an opportunity to test the hold of revolutionary syndicalism. The radical intentions of the strike's planners should be tested against the strike itself. The strike was the largest in France before World War I. This should not be forgotten. Something stirred masses of workers, but not necessarily the long range goals of the syndicalists.[1]

1 See Peter N. Stearns, *Revolutionary Syndicalism and French Labor: a Cause without Rebels* (New Brunswick, N. J., 1971).

Even aside from the syndicalist element, the eight-hour day demand was radical, for few French workers worked less than a ten-hour day at this time. Trade union leaders in most industrial countries, whether they were politically radical or not, tried to get workers to strike for reductions of hours, rather than merely for higher wages or other issues. They believed that reductions in work hours would be more permanent than most other gains and would free workers to improve their education and family life, which, in turn, would contribute to a more sophisticated labor movement. Some of these goals are expressed in the C.G.T. proclamations. But workers often sought reductions in hours for different reasons. Sometimes they were not interested in increased leisure time, at least when they weighed this against more pressing concerns. Despite union promptings, less than a fifth of all strikes in any industrial country sought hours' reductions. The course of the 1906 strike suggests some of the reasons for workers' departure from trade union programs in this respect. Obviously, any judgment of workers' intentions depends on distinguishing between what they were willing to settle for, given the realities of a strike situation, and what they really wanted. This is no easy task and cannot really be done definitively. Again, an intuitive element is involved in any conclusion.

The eight-hour demand was unquestionably progressive. Workers who persisted in seeking it were claiming new rights. But some of the workers who quickly turned to other goals were capable of asking for unprecedented gains as well. The strike offers an opportunity to assess the characteristic goals of modern protest. It also suggests some of the divisions among workers in this regard—even among Parisian artisans, who had far more experience in agitation than most workers elsewhere. Construction workers led the way in sophistication. They had long been active in protest. They were also spurred by rapid changes in the construction industry, including the proliferation of large construction crews instead of small operations, and by serious unemployment during the five years previous. Other groups involved in the strike lacked such impetus to develop and maintain progressive demands.

Any interpretation of this strike involves the assessment of various types of sources. Union proclamations give one picture of the strike. Employer statements give another, which must be taken into consideration. Newspaper selections dealing with union meetings give still a third. These selections are excerpted from long accounts in the conservative paper Le Temps. Finally, there is a police report, which included clippings from Le Temps and other newspapers and also referred to reports by police spies in union meetings. All the sources are biassed. In combination, however, they suggest most of the dimensions of the strike. Again, the police report goes furthest in sober analysis of the protest, but its sobriety as well as its more obvious hostility to syndicalism may be serious shortcomings. Again it is the sum of all types of sources, not any single one, that must be stressed.

A Strike Manifesto

POSTER DRAWN UP BY THE C.G.T. COMMITTEE ON EIGHT HOURS

We take advantage of the election period to remind workers that in the midst of the feverish activities of the parties they must not lose sight of the fact that the improvement of their lot should be their constant preoccupation.

To be genuine, this improvement must involve a diminution of capitalist privileges.

This result can be obtained only through the effort of the people concerned, united on the economic plane, in the union of their trade. The union, in its turn, to increase its power, affiliates with its trade federation and the federation adheres to the C.G.T. Thus lines of effective solidarity are established which unite workers in common aspirations and coordinate their diverse demands into general formulas.

Such has been the propaganda campaign to conquer the eight-hour day.

On April 5 and 6, as a consequence of this propaganda, a conference was held in Paris in which delegations of the trade federations participated. It was decided to launch the movement in the following ways:

> To invite workers to participate in a solidarity strike May 1, which will manifest the organized proletariat's power for action.
>
> In addition the conference indicated to the Unions, as a means to realize their lists of demands, the two following forms:
>
> Either cessation of work after the eighth hour or the complete cessation of work from May 1 until satisfaction is gained.

In the first case workers, when they have completed eight hours, will leave the plant, shop, or worksite. In the second case, the strike will continue until complete victory.

The conference leaves the choice between these two tactics to the organizations, which can judge the situation in their trades. It feels obligated to remind them that the diminution of the time of work should not result in a diminution of salary.

Workers!

The need for propaganda is over. Now it is up to the workers, united in their unions, to carry the work to fruition.

It's up to them, inspired by the resolutions of the Congress of

From Le Temps, *April 27, 1906. This and following selections in this section translated by the editor. All dates given are for the year 1906.*

Bourges and the instructions given above, to impose on the employers the demands already formulated.

We urge on the workers the need for economic action, with an eminently social character.

The conquest of the eight-hour day is a step on the road to human emancipation. This step crossed, we'll continue, strengthened by the struggle, our organizational work for new victories, until the complete abolition of wage labor.

Forward for the eight-hour day!

Newspaper Reports

MAY 4

The union of mechanics, which has long led an active campaign to determine its members to demand a reduction of their hours of work, had voted in its last meeting to urge its adherents to seize the occasion of May 1 to present their demands.

Conforming to this decision, a part of the personnel of the following [16] companies have gone on strike demanding a nine-hour day, or 54 hours a week with the same pay as now for 60, as their condition for returning to work. . . .

In certain companies agreement has been reached between the employer and his workers. Thus in the Delaunay-Velleville company, which employs nearly 2,000 workers, a contract has been signed setting the duration of work at 55 hours a week, or 10 hours a day for the first five days and 5 on Saturday morning.

MAY 10

The cabinetmakers, meeting in the great hall of the Labor Exchange, after having heard the readings of the employers' protest against the current strike, realizing that this protest can only be the emanation of capitalists avid for huge profits, reply with scorn to such provocations . . . and declare that they will continue their struggle until complete victory.

MAY 12: A TAILORS' POSTER

Eight days ago the tailors in alterations shops submitted to their respective employers the following just demands: "Ten hours of work, increase of .05 francs per hour."

To this effect and at the wish of the employers themselves, a committee was charged with presenting the demands to the employers' unions, which though finding them very fair said they could not accept the raise and would not accept the application of the 10-hour day unless forced to.

In spite of such a formal refusal, it's been decided to continue the strike until complete satisfaction, as we have legality, in the 10-hour-day law,[1] on our side. These demands are dictated by the greatest spirit of worker solidarity and would have as an immediate effect the diminution of a great amount of unemployment, which the long work days inevitably produce. . . .

MAY 14: A POSTER BY LOCK AND METAL GOODS MANUFACTURERS

As no conflict exists between workers in this industry and the manufacturers;

As in spite of the strike vote by the unions our shops have continued to function normally and the only ones that have had to close are those whose workers have been forced out by violence or by the threats of a tiny minority;

We judge that where demands have been presented they can be ignored and that the shops will remain open or will reopen for the many workers who wish to work as in the past.

MAY 16: BY FUSTER, AN AUTOMOBILE WORKER

Quotes from a speech in a workers' meeting: "I deplore the attitude of those workers who have decreed a strike without engaging in preliminary negotiations with the employers [*hostile shouts*] . . . The leaders of the strike favor foreign competition [*more shouts*].

A subsequent letter: "The great majority of the assembly agreed with my talk. They agree that the reduction of the duration of work in the automobile industry is highly desirable but realizable safely only through an international agreement and by means of successive stages. . . . "

MAY 23

Still more painters have decided to resume work. They adopted this decision yesterday in a general meeting. The increase of ten centimes

1 The law was passed in 1899, came into effect in 1904 with regard to all workers in shops and factories where women were employed. It was unevenly enforced in the small-shop industries.

an hour which the employers' union offered them seemed a concession which was not to be disdained and for which they can renounce their demand for the reduction of the workday.

May 29: Declaration by a Masons' Meeting

As we count only on ourselves, it is therefore by our own energy that we can emerge victorious.

War to the renegades! Let us impose ourselves on those who lack a conscience and take what we have the right to take, even by force.

Police Opinion

Police Report (Unsigned, to the Prefect of Police in Paris, May 20)

Workers on strike yesterday, 55,887.

Workers on strike today, 53,012.

Total number of workers in companies affected by the strike: 281,426.

The strike is virtually over. Many of the remaining strikers are mechanics locked out by their employers. Many are unemployed, particularly in the construction industry, who want the strike to continue so that they can receive some strike aid and so that their misery will have company. It is true that union meetings still shout defiance. The construction workers' union has just warned that their strikers, though "not tired of the fight," are getting excited and that violence could result. This is mostly empty bravado, though it is true that meetings of the strikers are highly charged. In fact the union leaders know that their ranks are thinning by the massive daily defections and that they are powerless to stop this. They seek some way to end the strike without losing face entirely. Almost all the unions are appealing to government ministers for mediation, so that they can win some small concessions. The printers' union has issued a statement recalling that it has "always maintained a conciliatory attitude toward the employers" and announcing its willingness to accept a nine-hour day (which the employers see no need to grant).

The strike has been a great disappointment to all concerned. Many workers thought that victory would be easy, because they were misled by union propaganda. They were quite willing to strike for a few days —most thought that three would be enough—but soon grew tired.

Archives de le Préfecture de la Police de la Seine, B/a 1369.

Many were not so much interested in the eight-hour day as in a raise. Many construction workers have been returning to work for a small raise. Some who won a reduction in hours are already working overtime so that they can earn more money. Many workers did not even try for eight hours, asking for nine hours or Saturday afternoon off instead. Excesses have been committed during the strike. There were some policemen and workers wounded; our most recent count is 43. There were many arrests for threats to policemen and to workers on the job. But there is no death to lament. In effect, everything went along as well as we could hope. The revolutionaries were reduced to impotence and without tragic clashes. Those who were so fearful at first are reassured. Happy to have escaped imaginery dangers they joke about their terror. The revolution which was to come has not come. Never could reasonable and informed men suppose for a moment that the radicals in the labor confederation could overturn the social order. The C.G.T. must try to avoid violence in ending the strike lest it antagonize the public and frighten its own members still further. It will be a long time before it can attempt such a strike again.

A STRIKE SETTLEMENT

Most strikes were settled, and after 1900 a growing number were settled through collective bargaining procedures which resulted in a written collective contract. The following document is typical of such settlements. It followed a strike by cabinetmakers in Rouen, who had demanded a wage raise largely to compensate for rising prices. This was the sort of small strike that proliferated among artisans and factory workers around the turn of the century. Such strikes were calm, unimportant in themselves, but in combination as typical of workers' protest at this point as some of the showier efforts.

Collective bargaining was an important historical development in its own right. It represented something of a revolution in employer-worker relations. Workers were winning new if limited rights of discussion over their conditions, as they forced employers to surrender a bit of their traditional authority. Bargaining also tells us something about the nature of protest. It has implications concerning class relations; clearly the enmity between workers and their employers was not too great to prevent some accommodation. In most strikes, workers' goals were fairly precise and workers were moderate enough to accept compromise. Note that in this case the goals were not simply material. Though wage demands headed the list, workers were also concerned about winning freedom from arbitrary treatment on a whole range of job conditions. Yet, even so, does this prosaic settlement convey the participants' real aspirations? Compromise and recognition of tactical reality were basic to the bargaining system. Some workers were undoubtedly frustrated by these limitations; the most radical workers indeed protested the procedure from

the start, rightly claiming that it would tie their class to the existing system.
Nevertheless, the bargaining system spread steadily and there is every evidence of widespread satisfaction with it. If it left the basic economic and political structure unchanged—among other things, profits continued to rise more rapidly than wages—it did correct some abuses and provide mechanisms for discussing others. This is why such agreements constitute an important measure of industrial protest and the grievances it involved. They force us to realize how important limited gains could seem, just as they point up the kind of expectations that workers had. If documents of this sort can be taken literally—and they are often the only sort of evidence we have on the mass of small strikes—they show that legalized strikes were essentially protests within the system both in goals and methods—unlike agitation in the early decades of industrialization—and that they could be settled within the system.

A Typical Contract

Collective work contract drawn up after the conciliation procedures directly established between the cabinetmakers of Rouen and its environs on strike and the employers in this craft, who have declared that the strike which broke out November 4 has ended amiably on the conditions here listed:

Article I. All cabinetmakers and machinists will receive a 5-centime-per-hour raise. The normal rate and the minimum for hourly wages is set at .60 francs.

Article II. The hours of work will be paid in the following manner: for the first twelve hours, the regular rate; from the twelfth to the fourteenth, time and a half; after the fourteenth, double pay. For Sunday work, when the worker works only until 11 A.M. or noon, an extra hour will be paid; and for afternoon work, he will be paid time and a half. The hour and a half for lunch will be maintained for the summer; to be reduced to an hour in winter, agreement between employers and workers will be necessary.

Article III. During night work, paid at the rate indicated in article II, a meal will be provided by the employer or will be paid for at the rate of 1.50 francs per worker. The time for this meal, which will not exceed an hour, will not be paid for.

Article IV. Wages will be paid in the shops as is customary for each company. And in shops and companies where pay is given every two weeks, an advance of 30 francs will be given the Saturday between paydays, on request. The employers in general pledge morally and in-

From Archives départementales de la Seine-Maritime. Translated by the editor.

sofar as it is possible to use a system of pay, either by their foremen or in some other manner, that will permit payment to be completed by the end of the workday.

Article V. As to the methods of hiring and firing, no change will be made in the usages and customs of the craft. However, any employer who fires a worker for insufficient work should warn him an hour before the end of the day. Any worker who quits voluntarily or is dismissed by the employer will be paid immediately and should take his tools away, and the employer is not responsible and cannot be sued for disappearance, loss, or theft of tools or wood.

Article VI. A bonus of .50 francs per fortnight will be paid to each worker for supplying and maintaining his tools.

Article VII. For every job between one and five kilometers outside town, the travel expenses will be paid, plus an hour's extra wages.

Article VIII. For every job requiring the worker to stay overnight, 2.50 francs per day extra will be paid, Sundays and holidays and losses of time included; however, when the worker cannot work at least a half day on Sundays and holidays, the displacement fee will be three francs. Each worker will be given a paid trip every four weeks, up to a distance of 30 kilometers; beyond this, an agreement will be made between employer and worker.

Article IX. No worker will be dismissed for wishing to limit his work day to 11 hour, or for the strike. The employers pledge not to put any worker on the index.

Article X. The present collective agreement is valid for three years, beginning Jan. 1, 1911, with retroactive effect from Nov. 8, 1910, the day when work was resumed. The contract will be renewed for new periods of three years. It can be denounced by either party three months before its expiration. The present contract has been drawn up before the Justice of the Peace of the 3rd canton.

OTTO HUÉ

The Ruhr miners' strike of 1905 resulted from a variety of causes. It followed an economic slump and falling wages. It also followed two years during which a worm disease had spread among the miners; the treatment, which was compulsory when the disease was discovered, was exceedingly painful and cost the victims much of their wages for two or three weeks. The strike was probably deliberately provoked by the owners, who were hostile to the growing trade unions and saw a premature strike as a good way to deflate the workers. The strike broke out suddenly in one pit, the Bruchstrasse, owned by the giant industrialist Hugo Stinnes, in protest over a lengthening of the workday. In other words, the strike was really a reaction to deteriorating conditions, both in its general and in its immediate causes. The strikers ultimately asked for a raise and other gains, but they were trying to compensate for their losses, not to win new rights. Hence, this was a less sophisticated strike than those thus far considered. Relatedly it was not planned in advance. In many ways it resembles some of the early industrial efforts, but it drew massive support, from close to 200,000 workers. This kind of strike, in other words, was still important. There is little evidence that the Ruhr miners were ready for a more progressive effort.

The following passage relates many of the difficulties encountered in conducting the strike. Among them was the fact that the organized miners were divided among the socialist union (which was larger than all the other groups combined), a powerful Catholic union, a union of Polish workers, and some other groups. Divisions of this sort were not uncommon. Even when they were not institutionalized, as in this case, religious and ethnic differences hampered labor protest. Most important, and again this was typical for the period, the majority of workers were not unionized at all. Many of them refused to strike and fought with strikers who tried to intimidate them. Others quickly defected.

The unions, drawn into a strike they had not called, faced a body of strikers unaccustomed to organized protest and incapable of articulating extensive demands. They undoubtedly had massive grievances, but there was a gap between having them and making them effective. To keep what unity they had and to prevent complete defeat, the unions agreed on a compromise with the owners (who had refused to negotiate directly), which improved wages somewhat but brought few other gains to the workers. Although this was not genuine collective bargaining, it reveals another reason that compromise settlements spread: unions had to salvage what they could when workers grew confused about their own purpose. The strike thus embodied three major elements: extensive discontent, limited experience in expressing and organizing it, and formal labor organizations concerned about protecting their own future. Protest of this sort was transitional between traditional and modern. As unions spread but won only a limited hold over most workers, they frequently became involved in such protest.

Much of our information about industrial protests comes from union leaders. Otto Hué, the head of the socialist union, here speaks to a union congress explaining his conduct of the strike. It is obviously a defensive speech, casting as much blame as possible on the owners. It also says a great deal about the majority of the Ruhr miners. It reflects their limited ability to form positive expectations and their dependence on a deterioration of conditions to rise in protest. Though historically miners are in the forefront of solid labor agitation, many German miners had only recently come in from the countryside, often from eastern Germany. They were not prepared for the type of protest more experienced miners in France and Britain undertook in these same years. But their outlook was typical of many workers in Germany and elsewhere, including some with considerable experience in industry.

Yet there are questions, of course. Hué clearly implies that his caution was compelled by the attitude of most workers. But it is not fully clear whether they too were cautious or rather suffered from a lack of ability to express their discontent which could have been remedied by more daring leadership during the strike itself. We're back to the issue, basic to this period of working-class history, of whether most workers were really moderate or simply too frustrated to convey fully their deep unhappiness in protest. Clearly there was division in their ranks. Hué refers to a radical minority which continued to criticize his caution. His statement that no union could afford to follow the dictates of such a minority is characteristic of union leaders in actual strikes. Even the most radical in theory insisted on pleasing the majority, which almost always meant behaving moderately. Perhaps they were wrong, and should have followed the articulate minority. Certainly the minority itself is interesting. We must ask what made it more demanding and whether it differed from the majority in the depth of its discontent or more in its ability to express it. We must also ask what its reaction was, aside from grumbling, when it was put down by organized labor.

Hué thus suggests many of the problems in the relationship between formal organizations and protest. He represents a classic trade union position—protect the organization at all costs. In his case, since he was also a socialist deputy in parliament, he even refers to the need to save the country from a rightist coup d'état. The burden of responsibility oozes from every word. His remedies are better organization, fuller planning, more information—in other words, more trade unionism. Many workers were repelled by this bureaucratic approach, this effort to stamp out spontaneity; this was one of the reasons they were divided and unprepared. Only grudgingly did they admit the need for organization. The tension between bureaucratized protest and the workers' desire for freedom from constraint has continued in the development of the industrial working class. Before 1914 many workers, even some with extensive expectations, preferred to indulge their distaste for regimentation. For them, clearly, the record of actual protest does not describe their aspirations.

Hué gives us a picture of the agonizing dilemma which the conscientious union leader experienced in most strikes of any consequence. To go beyond this, to judge how this dilemma reflected the outlook of most protesting workers, no source yet discovered is entirely adequate.

Strike Report to Union Delegates

Worthy comrades! I understand very well that all of you expect this report with some degree of suspense. But should you assume that I could or would tell you which strategy to apply in all future strikes I have to explain to you in advance that you must not nurse this expectation. Should we agree today on the tactics I would like to propose that we take up these discussions in a session excluding the public. (*Quite correct!*) The Porcelain Workers' Association which is presently

From Otto Hué, Unsere Taktik beim Generalstreik (*Bochum, 1905*), pp. 1–11. Translated by Gabriela Wettberg.

also in session in this building as well as the Bricklayers' in their general assembly have debated this point of the "tactics in wage disputes" in closed sessions. We, too, would say many a thing that does not necessarily have to reach the ears of the factory owners or their agents.

I will not tell or be able to tell you how to conduct future strikes but I will only speak of what lies behind us. I will do so because the last general strike which just occurred has produced extraordinarily extensive critiques. It has resulted in after-effects which could be clearly sensed in the previous debates, as you saw. Now, it is true that no certain tactic can be determined for all times and all strikes. We are however dealing with a gap in our union and socio-political literature concerning the theory of strike. A sort of "general staff work" could be indeed created about the experiences in strikes at home and abroad. From it we could deduce which strikes hold greater promise under certain circumstances and whether defensive or aggressive strikes are preferable. One could discuss whether partial strikes or general strikes are better under given conditions. Furthermore, the question could be discussed as to whether it is better to limit an impending mining strike to one single precinct or to expand it immediately to the entire country and maybe even carry it out internationally. I recall a highly interesting episode from the big strike of the American miners. When the anthracite miners of Pennsylvania were on strike for several months the question arose whether the soft coal miners should join the strike to increase economic pressure. At the time, John Mitchell, director of the American strike, argued fervently in favor of the miners continuing their work. And experience has shown that the conference was correct in following Mitchell's advice to let the soft coal miners continue to work. It is consequently not always correct to assume that expanding a general strike to all areas is more advantageous. Circumstances might exist which could render a partial strike much more effective. Sometimes circumstances predestine offensive strikes to failure while they offer best prospects for a defensive strike. The desired "general staff work" would have to examine all this and more. Our literature indeed lacks a theoretical discourse on strikes, a scientific presentation of strike experiences on an international basis. I do not know whether this work will be written soon nor who will write it. But even if it already existed it could only provide us with conclusions on past strikes and show us what happened under these other circumstances. But it would not be possible to avail oneself of this book as a kind of "handbook for strike leaders" at a given moment nor to say how one would have to act on such and such a page.

The actual conditions are decisive factors for strike tactics. It is the very skill of the strike leadership to consider these decisive forces. But one has to know them thoroughly—and in advance. He who does not know them can easily make the mistake of judging from his own environment which appears quite favorable for a strike. But if this judgment were applied to the general situation it would prove quite faulty. It is clear to everyone who has come to know the critics as well as the type of critique, that these sweeping judgments were made from a limited knowledge of certain areas, certain locations or even a certain group of people. And it was these judgments which primarily provoked the negative critique after our last general strike. But I believe that I act according to your wishes if I do not in my speech attempt to cause friction between persons who have been mentioned here and there and myself. I will limit myself to the purely factual in considering that necessary enlightenment can hardly be furthered by personal polemics. But sometimes it will be difficult for me to speak in a purely factual manner because as of late press polemic has arisen after the Union Congress at Cologne. There were attempts at creating acute opposition between "practitioners" and "theoreticians." While in earlier times praxis was preferred and it was said "Workers must educate the academics," "workers have to liberate themselves," one has unfortunately arrived at a different standpoint today. In some circles one speaks of "practitioners" only in quotation marks ("") and considers them minor human beings. According to my knowledge of marxist teachings this low appreciation of the practitioner, which also entails a low appreciation of the economic structure, does not appear to coincide with the teachings of Marx which some of our critics in particular profess to represent. . . .

Let us first ask whether the strike was insufficiently prepared. We concede candidly that this general strike was practically not prepared at all. This simply and convincingly proves the fact that this strike was neither intended nor instigated by us but rather suited the entrepreneurs well. The critics' reproach is in fact irrefutable evidence that we are dealing with a spontaneous rebellion of an oppressed working class in this general strike and not with a "mass stirred up by social democracy." I am speaking of the fact that no care was taken for things to be in order when the strike began. If the general strike had not been such a spontaneous event, if it had been instigated, desired by us, we certainly believe that we would have made preparations. We would have had all strike lists, all offices etc. in order at the strike proclamation. But because this was not the case, because we were faced with a *fait accompli* all insults which have been cast against our association and the social democratic party by the House of Lords and the House of Representatives are groundless. Namely we are supposed to have created the movement, incited and unchained it.

Why had we then not prepared the general strike? Is it not known to you that we have been covering the country for 15 years with redoubled energy since our association nearly collapsed completely in the years of 1894 and 1895 in order to bring the ideas to the masses with hundreds of thousands of pamphlets? Is it not known that we have not neglected to strengthen our association by agitating as well as our financial resources permitted? Why did the masses not come, why did they not place the association in the position that would have been necessary for the leadership of such a powerful fight? Is it the fault of the strike leadership, is it the fault of the board of the mining association? Or is the weak organization not rooted in the miserable conditions of indifference and the economic situation of the people existing in the mining districts? It is not our fault that the organization was not sufficiently strong at the eruption of the general strike. There were too many people who refused to join the association in spite of many decades of admonition.

How many times during the economic boom of 1895–1900 and in how many meetings in the Ruhr area did I not say that we could not always have prosperity? That times would come not to our liking and that then the entrepreneurs would take advantage of their power in order to torture and gag the workers? Then a rebellion would break loose but we would not be armed for such powerful struggles. Thus all workers should speedily join the association and arm themselves. We could talk our lungs out to no avail. All of our agitators and those comrades particularly active in that area have suffered in health to a greater or lesser degree because of their intensive activities. Our lung diseases, our chest illnesses did not come from not accomplishing sufficient agitation. One can therefore not reproach us for not having prepared the general strike in terms of not taking care to have a strong organization. When the storm broke loose it was not there. Of the 270,000 Ruhr miners only 60,000 belonged to our association. And of these, tens of thousands were not as permeated by the ideas of the association as would be necessary to call them adamant fighters. (*Agreement.*) We knew that. But we knew still more. We knew that this spring no one but the entrepreneurs could have an interest in the outbreak of a strike. We knew that when we delivered our demands in the year of 1900, this was a time where we could fight with the greatest certainty for victory, where it would be unavoidable. There was a general strike in Belgium and Austria, there was also a strike in Saxony, and if the employers had wanted a strike then they would not have emerged as total victors because we had prosperity then. It is significant that just a few days ago mining master Engel corroborated our opinion in a delightful way. Namely he said in court that then— in 1900—our request was answered "politely and thoroughly" because there was a boom then and the entrepreneurs feared a strike. (*Hear, hear!*) But how was it in 1905? Then, too, we made a request. But the way in which the answer was delayed, the format of the answer, the fact that it was transmitted to the press before handing it to the representatives of the Commission of the Seven convinced me beyond any doubt that the mine owners were aiming to heighten the tension among the laborers. My opinion was reinforced by the remark repeated by master Engel in court: The mining association had not actually convened in order to debate the answer to the Commission of the Seven but it had merely handled the matter incidentally. I am completely convinced that we had good reasons to put on the brakes energetically before the strike. Especially since the testimony of master Engel I cannot rid myself of the impression that this year the strike has come quite unwantedly considering the unfavorable situation of the coal market.

The entrepreneurs wished for the strike for yet another reason: because of the delightful rise of our association. The capitalists watched with horror how during the last years miners turned to the association by the ten thousands. They probably reasoned along the familiar lines: before we get another boom we have to gain a respite from the mining association. Whenever prosperity returns we must not have to reckon with a strong miners' organization. (*Quite correct!*) The exciting subsequent attempts to prolong the shifts in the Oberhausen mine in February, then in the Baaker Mulde mine in the summer, finally in the Bruchstrasse mine in December of the previous year made their intention clearly recognizable. The masses became increasingly irritable. By those actions they were systematically incited to feel that a longer shift would be imposed on them if they did not defend themselves. Through systematic, inconsiderate measures which cannot at all be explained as "technical maneuvers", the miners had to be persuaded that they had to strike now even though the coal storages were filled and their organization was not sufficiently strong. Anyone who reads the speeches from the provincial diet and House of Lords will corroborate my view. They wanted to pound us into the ground with this strike. They wanted to destroy the miners' association! (*Vivid agreement.*) That is my conviction. From the history of the workers' movement sufficient examples could be cited thoroughly illustrating what I have just told you.

We were certainly ill prepared. I have already told you why. But more yet. We have many comrades in our organization who are very critically inclined and extremely keen on preventing the slightest upsurge of a "dictatorship" or "pontificate." (*Laughter.*) It would be excellent if the comrades could also claim to have grasped the needs of our organization. In the months and weeks preceding the strike I often pointed out the necessity of knowing how large the supply of coal was. The board has indicated in I do not know how many intimate conferences that the stocks were bursting and that the syndicate did not know what to do with the supply piled up near Bottrop. But the comrades paid no attention to our arguments. We have asked them to notify us how much of a supply there was in their mines, whether they put in holiday shifts and how much coal and coke were amassed in storage. If the comrades, the confidants, had understood then how extraordinarily important it is for us in leading this fight to know the supply of arms of our enemy they would have answered accordingly when we inquired. But there was hardly an answer to all of these questions and appeals in the papers. We were only able to estimate approximately the coal and coke supplies through the business reports of the single plants and the coal syndicate. We would have a general view if in the future things were to be different, if the comrades could become accustomed to keep their eyes open in the mines and observe how many wagons were being mined and how many stored, and were to tell us this regularly every month. We could then demonstrate the following calculation to them: there are these specific supplies, we have to hold out with our strike until the time just before real coal need sets in. But today our friends and comrades still frequently hold the opinion that they can throw the coal syndicate over in one forceful offensive. If they were indeed ill prepared it was not the fault of the strike leadership but also the responsibility of the local administrations. And in the final analysis the cause is our lack of organization.

Comrades, that is why we have put on our brakes. In the meetings they called to me "Throw away the brake blocks at last!" And as they had already called to Sachse and Husemann on several occasions "Do not always bring along brake blocks!" They thought they could win a gigantic strike in 8 or 14 days. A year ago I already declared explicitly in Stadthagen that we should not delude ourselves about the decisive fight which we have to sustain when some comrades spoke of a short, forceful strike, certain of their victory. It would rather have to be fought to the last extremity. I have also repeated this before the general strike, but no one listened to me. In 1889 there was a much greater need for coal after a strike duration of 8 days than after 4 weeks of general strike. Today the entrepreneurs take care to collect reserves so that they can endure the strike for weeks, even months without their buyers experiencing any hardship. I have said this in the meetings in which the comrades were animated by a child-like joy of hope. . . . But when I told this to the comrades of Essen they said to me: "You want to bring us back to work at any cost." The empirical evidence was disregarded.

One can easily see why it had to be this way. The great masses of miners, still unorganized for the most part, possess an insufficient

theoretical knowledge of the economy and practically no union discipline. Again it was a wild strike, as in 1889. It was one of the kind
Upper Silesia has repeatedly experienced during the past years. It was
no actual union strike which we could have induced and conducted
with the help of a strong organization. The peculiarities of the strike
and the critiques which succeeded it can be explained by this fact . . .
Because of this knowledge we stopped the strike. I am convinced, and
no one can change my mind, that the workers have been driven into
this strike at a time that was unfavorable to them. The employers intended to destroy the organization. Besides it also permitted the syndicate to raise the price of coal accordingly! . . . I have already stated
explicitly in the "Miners' Newspaper" and in the Imperial Diet who
incited the strike, namely those to whom it promised to be profit-
able. . . .

We were completely prepared for the strike in the Bruchstrasse
mine. The strike was begun with the approval of the board of the association. Everything was ready or could be readied within a few days.
At this point I would like to interject: there were differences, factual
differences within the board and among the directors, and they will
exist today. They deal with the question of whether a partial or general strike would be more beneficial at a given time. Comrades with
wide union experience dceided upon partial strike. We were to "im-
mobilize" that high and mighty Stinnes just once . . . Be this as it
may. In any event, on Dec. 26, 1904, a conference of confidants had
explicitly decided not to start a general strike. The fact is that even
those comrades knew of the decision who later loudly and forcefully
advocated an expansion of the general strike in word and writing. But
the fact that the strike spread from Bruchstrasse to the district of
Dortmund, from there to Oberhausen and then to Essen, that it gradually spread is only further evidence of our defective organization.
Partial strikes, especially here in the Ruhr area or in mining areas in
general can only be carried out if the organization functions flaw-
lessly. (*Quite correct.*) The fact that the strike spread to other mines
proves that the organization was faulty. (*Quite correct.*)

I have already previously stated what needs to be said against the
reproach that we had not prepared the general strike. But something
else must be considered. We had to reckon with unknown factors which
we could not ignore. Who would have vouched before the general strike
that the Christian Mining Union or the Association of Poles, that
those of Hirsch-Duncker would go along with us? . . . Did we not risk
the whole organization of miners when the fratricidal struggle flared
up again in high flames? . . . But he who always agitates and protests against our amiable relations to the other organizations is also
partly responsible for the fact that we did not know whether the others

would participate whenever the strike in the Bruchstrasse mine began. Comrades! They told us that we could carry out the strike on our own. I would not wish it upon any of you to experience the days through which we have lived before the outbreak of the general strike when we did not know what decision the other side would finally make. I do not wish the tensions on any of you nor the deeply stirring turmoil which these days have brought us. There was more at stake than the miners' movement in the Ruhr area. There was more at stake than merely the miners' association—the entire workers' movement was at stake. The question was whether the firebrands would win, whether they would destroy us and then exploit their power for a *coup d'état* from above in order to abolish the rights of the people. At the time we all felt what immense significance the mining association possessed among the economic organizations. Our association will speak a powerful word in the history of Germany if it is strong and mighty. We could not proceed alone with 60,000 men against 200,000 even with more than 100,000 unorganized men on our side . . .

I therefore propagate the following: tactics of strikes must not be directed by our own will or wishes but by the demands of the given moment. (*Quite true.*) The strike leader who does not know how to take advantage of a given moment may be highly educated theoretically, he may be a doctor of all four disciplines, but he is of no use as strike leader. Practice, as you know, is mother to success here, and practice must decide. Had we let that which others wanted become decisive we would have experienced a miserable fiasco. Of course we would much rather have dealt with one single organization of miners. How much simpler our task would have been then and how much easier it would have been to conduct the strike uniformly. The comrades of other organizations, of the union association, would also much prefer to exist and decide for themselves. It is self-evident and beyond any doubt that we might have employed different tactics had we been the sole organization in existence. This applies to the other organizations as well. But not our will and wishes but cold, indisputable facts determine our actions.

A RADICAL CALL TO ARMS

This is one of the most radical documents spawned by workers' direct action before World War I. More remote from the fray, socialists and even trade union congresses could develop more sweeping condemnations of the existing order, but this was a program for immediate agitation. In some respects it recalls the most intense pre-industrial attacks on the industrial system. But this is no mere throwback. Its radicalism can also be measured by comparing its demands for higher wages and lower hours against labor protest elsewhere in these same years. Above all, it challenged the collective bargaining system that had developed more elaborately in Britain than anywhere else in Europe and, along with this, it attacked the established trade union leadership. Here, the pamphlet can be directly compared with Otto Hué's approach, for when it talks of union leaders ensconced in the political establishment it was talking of a phenomenon that developed wherever unions created powerful bureaucracies. The pamphlet clearly expresses the tension between workers' grievance and the compulsions and temptations of a union organization.

Sparked by the South Wales miners, British workers of many types rose in unprecedented protest between 1910 and 1912.[1] Inflation was cutting into their wages. In the mines, British unions had long maintained a policy of tying wages to the selling price of coal. This assured that when the coal price went up, wages would rise; but it did not guarantee that wages would rise as fast as general prices or as fast as either profits or the intensity of work increased. This policy had kept the peace between miners and their employers for over a decade but the workers grew increasingly resentful of it; with inflation and changes of work organization, South Wales miners could no longer contain their resentment. Like so many protest documents, *The Miners' Next Step* demands an assessment of the degree to which particular material grievances predominated, even in a more general statement of demands.

South Wales miners conducted a long, painful strike in 1909–10. Their agitation was unusually intense, partly because their union was badly organized, with a remote, autocratic leadership and with no middle-level bureaucracy to retain contact with and control over ordinary members. The miners also encountered growing difficulties at the pit face which reduced their production and, therefore, their wages. For several years prior to the strike, intelligent young miners had been sent for a year to Ruskin College in Oxford, where they were exposed to new ideas—though not primarily from the College, against which the most radical workers rebelled in 1910. Revolutionary syndicalist ideas were in the air, and some of the educated, young Welsh miners encountered them as well as Marxist theory. Then the 1910 strike collapsed, the miners returning to work with very few gains. *The Miners' Next Step* was the product of the sharp disappointment that resulted, after the effervescence of the previous months and years. A group of the young radicals drew it up.

The pamphlet is fine reading for those who believe that workers before World War I were, or should have been, revolutionaries. It reveals grievances that most labor organizations ignored. It shows the thinking of the radical minorities that most unions tried to bypass. Yet it was an unrepresentative approach for most workers in protest. Most workers were not actively revolu-

---

1 George Dangerfield, *The Strange Death of Liberal England 1910–1914* (New York, 1961), stresses the revolutionary implications of this labor agitation; but a far more cautious account is E. H. Phelps Brown, *The Growth of British Industrial Relations* (London, 1959). On the miners, see R. Page Arnot, *The South Wales Miners* (London, 1966).

tionary—hence no serious revolutionary effort occurred in the industrial countries. British miners outside Wales refused to back the 1910 Welsh strike, but they conducted their own agitation soon afterwards and did demand and win a legislated minimum wage as the basis for further collective bargaining. So some of the specific ideas of the South Wales radicals were shared by a larger group, even if the revolutionary tone was not. But miners had always been in the vanguard of the working class; few other groups of workers could raise such sophisticated demands. *The Miners' Next Step* was the work of a minority. It reveals at most the excitement that could seize a larger number of workers when conditions deteriorated, as they did with rapid inflation after 1910. The grievances against the union leaders cannot be lightly dismissed. Many workers shared them. It can of course be argued that without the cautious direction of the union leadership more workers would have pursued a radical course. I think the general tenor of protest in these years suggests the contrary. Union leaders were not only well entrenched, but also far more representative of the wishes of most workers than the radical minority would admit.

Even if these points are granted, the debate over the significance of this sort of document cannot be ended. Minority sentiment may be truer and more important than majority outlook when the majority is disadvantaged and repressed. No single protest document allows us to deal with this approach. Larger numbers of documents help the historian form an opinion, for the final judgment involves a grasp of the nature of working-class life and protest. Without this grasp, minority sentiment can easily be given too much importance, for it often expresses what historians want workers to have wanted. Perhaps a more promising, and certainly a more testable approach, would be the claim that the new, sweeping protest suggested by *The Miners' Next Step* was the wave of the future; a foretaste of a period in which far more workers would be capable of raising positive demands. This, in turn, requires an assessment of protest after World War I.[2] The ambiguities of the first wave of industrial protest, the division among workers, and the moderation of most demands, raise genuine questions about when, to what degree, and why workers united in more thoroughly progressive agitation.

The pamphlet suggests one final set of complications, basic to an assessment of the nature of industrial protest. The authors were hostile to existing unions, profoundly anti-capitalist, and they make telling points. But the alternatives they propose are less clear. What kind of organization could be developed to avoid the trammels of bureaucracy? Modern protest involves masses of people. This, as well as the power of the industrial state and capitalism, requires that it be carefully organized. But careful organization, though it may be launched by genuine radicals, tends to become committed to defense of the organization and, so, more cautious. Even before World War I, the existence of this vicious circle was visible. The perceptive authors of *The Miners' Next Step* were aware of it. It is not clear that they knew what to do about it, even if they could rally masses of workers behind them, nor is it clear that the tension

2 For Britain, this can be started by a careful reading of Charles Mowat, *Britain Between the Wars 1918–1940* (Chicago, 1963), as well as K. G. J. C. Knowles, *Strikes —A Study in Industrial Conflict* (Oxford, 1952).

between organization and protest has been resolved anywhere in industrial society during the twentieth century, except where the dictates of organization triumph completely and real protest withers.

The Miners' Next Step

FOREWORD

A few words are necessary to explain how this pamphlet came to be written. All the suggestions in the preamble, programme, constitution, and policy have been sent from one lodge or another, through their districts to the Executive of the South Wales Miners' Federation. The Executive appointed a sub-committee to sit on them and draft out a programme. This programme was submitted to the Federation "Reform" Conference in March, 1911. It consisted of a recommendation to increase the contribution to 2/- per month, and a very worthless and highly bureaucratic scheme of centralization. The people responsible for the resolutions from the lodges realized that it was hopeless to expect any reform from that quarter, and in the course of time, they got together and held meetings in every part of the coalfield.

OLD POLICY OUTWORN

The present policy of the Federation since 1900 may be called the Conciliation policy. We have to briefly examine its usefulness as a wage getting policy, for that is the best and the only real test of any policy.

HAS CONCILIATION SECURED WAGES?

From the year 1900 there has been an enormous increase in the price of coal, averaging nearly 6/- per ton. This would have in itself automatically secured for us 60% on the standard, whereas we are only paid 50% . . . Dismissing then the illusion that our policy has kept up prices, how are we to account for the 10% reduction we have suffered? By the facts, and here they are. When Sir David Dale gave his award in 1902, he increased the price which was the equivalent of 30% (under the Sliding Scale) from 11/3 to 11/10. A direct reduction of over 5% in all our standard rates. There goes one Chunk. When the last agreement (1910) was arrived at we allowed 9d. per ton over 14/- to be free from percentages. There goes another 6% (?) reduction. These are facts. It is a fact (from reasons we have already

Published anonymously in Tonypandy in 1912.

explained) that the price of coal has never gone down to 11s. 10d. since the great (?) principle of minimum percentage was established. Thus, while we were clapping our hands in enthusiastic joy over the securing of a *great principle* the employers were quietly pocketing the 5% proceeds. This is a distinct feature of our recent reductions. The other serious reduction was granted on grounds, that if logically carried out, would mean the final end of progress, and the commencement of a battledore and shuttlecock game, of changing the persons to whom we were paying our reductions. The owners said said that cost of legislative reforms[1] had increased the cost of production. So we relieved them to the extent of 9d. on the ton after 14/-, *i.e.* 6%. This means that if we get any improvements, we must pay for them. We can go on like this for centuries securing great principles and legislative reforms, while all the time our pockets grow emptier. This is a fiendish principle that no sane man can countenance. *Yet these are facts.* That is one part of our indictment against the policy of conciliation.

Space prevents us from going into exhaustive detail as to the "tying up" and "delay" character of conciliation. But they are so well known, that it is superfluous really to detail them. We shall briefly summarize our objections. First the process.

DELAY

A dispute occurs in a colliery. The ordinary lodge negotiations are carried on, resulting in failure. The Agent is called in. Still failure. The matter is sent to the Executive and finally the Board. Here it takes its place with other matters on the agenda. In the course of time, after some months of waiting, it is reached and brought up for discussion. It is then referred to a sub-committee. These take time to see the management, and the colliery. Then they negotiate. Sometimes, as in the case of Rhymney,[2] they negotiate for two years Even then the owner's side refuse to report failure to agree. Eventually this may be done. Then, and then only, the colliery may give a month's notice. Need we say anything more in condemnation of this? We think not.

BASIS OF CONSIDERATION

On the Board all things have to be considered from the employers' standpoint. They alone have the inside information. We don't audit their books, and we have no means of judging the truth of their asser-

1 Notably the 8-hour day law.
2 Where the South Wales strike first broke out, in 1909.

tions. They say the colliery won't pay. We must accept their word. When we are considering principles, they have only to show that some wretched little colliery employing 10 men will have to close if we insist on our demands. That silences us. The little colliery belongs to a method of production that is almost a century old. Yet we must allow *their* conditions to govern us. *Reason* in such a case means, in plain English: *the Employers interest and outlook.* After 10 years of such a game, we find our customs broken down, and our price lists a farce, *and in the face of a very serious rise in the cost of living* (which many of us have nick-named prosperity) we have been *reduced* 10% in the standard rates. Is this enough?

CONCILIATION AND LEADERS

Here is perhaps after all our strongest indictment. The policy of "collective bargaining" will be dealt with later on. But we have here to point out why there is discontent with "leaders." The policy of conciliation gives the real power of the men into the hands of a few leaders. Somebody says "What about conferences and ballots"? Conferences are *only called,* and ballots *only taken* when there is a difference of opinion between leaders. The conference or ballot is only a referee. Can this be denied? In the main, and on things that matter, the Executive have the supreme power. The workmen for a time look up to these men and *when things are going well* they idolise them. The employers respect them. Why? Because they have the men—the real power—in the hollow of their hands. They, the leaders, become "gentlemen," they become M.P.'s, and have considerable social prestige because of this power. Now when any man or men assume power of this description, we have a right to ask them to be infallible. That is the penalty, a just one too, of autocracy. *When things go wrong,* and we have shown that they have gone wrong, they deserve to be, and are blamed. What really is blameworthy, is the conciliation policy which demands leaders of this description. For a moment let us look at this question from the leaders' standpoint. First, they are "trade unionists by trade" and their profession demands certain privileges. The greatest of all these are plenary powers. Now, every inroad the rank and file make on this privilege lessens the power and prestige of the leader. Can we wonder then that leaders are averse to change? Can we wonder that they try and prevent progress? Progress may arrive at such a point that they would not be able to retain their "jobs," or their "jobs" would become so unimportant that from their point of view, they would not be worth retaining. *The leader then has an interest—a vested interest—in stopping progress.* They have therefore in some things an antagonism of interests with the rank and file. The conditions of things in South Wales has reached the point when this difference of interest, this antagonism, has become manifest. Hence the men criticise and are discontented with their leaders. But the remedy is not new leaders. But—well, we shall see. . . .

It becomes necessary then to devise means which will enable this new spirit of real democratic control to manifest itself. Which will not only *enable* the men, but which will encourage, nay *compel* them, to take the supreme control of their own organisation. . . .

WORKMEN THE "BOSSES," "LEADERS" THE SERVANTS

Is it possible to devise such an organization as will bring the above from the realm of the ideal to the realm of practicability? Those responsible for this pamplet, men who, residing in all parts of South Wales, have given their time and thought to this problem, answer confidently in the affirmative. In these chapters they present their scheme, believing it to be not only possible, but the only practicable form of organization for us to achieve. . . .

I.—A united industrial organisation, which, recognising the war of interest between workers and employers, is constructed on fighting lines, allowing for a rapid and simultaneous stoppage of wheels throughout the mining industry.

II.—A constitution giving free and rapid control by the rank and file acting in such a way that conditions will be unified throughout the coalfield; so that pressure at one point would automatically affect all others and thus readily command united action and resistence.

III.—A programme of a wide and evolutionary working class character, admitting and encouraging sympathetic action with other sections of the workers.

IV.—A policy which will compel the prompt and persistent use of the utmost ounce of strength, to ensure that the conditions of the workmen shall always be as good as it is possible for them to be under the then existing circumstances. . . .

IMMEDIATE STEPS—INDUSTRIAL

I.—That a minimum wage of 8/- per day, for all workmen employed in or about the mines, constitute a demand to be striven for nationally at once.

II.—That subject to the foregoing having been obtained, we demand and use our power to obtain a 7 hour day.

PROGRAMME—POLITICAL

That the organisation shall engage in political action, both local and national, on the basis of complete independence of, and hostility to all capitalist parties, with an avowed policy of wresting whatever advantage it can for the working class.

In the event of any representative of the organisation losing his seat, he shall be entitled to, and receive, the full protection of the organisation against victimization.

GENERAL

Alliances to be formed, and trades organisations fostered, with a view to steps being taken, to amalgamate all workers into one National and International union, to work for the taking over of all industries, by the workmen themselves.

The Programme is very comprehensive, because it deals with immediate objects, as well as ultimate aims. We must have our desired end in view all the time, in order to test new proposals and policies, to see whether they tend in that direction or not. For example, the working class, if it is to fight effectually, must be an army, not a mob. It must be classified, regimented and brigaded, along the lines indicated by the product. Thus, all miners, &c., have this in common, they delve in the earth to produce the minerals, ores, gems, salt, stone, &c., which form the basis of raw material for all other industries. Similarly the Railwaymen, Dockers, Seamen, Carters, etc., form the transport industry. Therefore, before an organised and self-disciplined working class can achieve its emancipation, it must coalesce on these lines.

It will be noticed that nothing is said about Conciliation Boards or Wages Agreements. The first two chapters will, however, have shown you that Conciliation Boards and Wages Agreements only lead us into a morass. As will be seen when perusing the policy and constitution, the suggested organisation is constructed to fight rather than to negotiate. It is based on the principle that we can only get what we are strong enough to win and retain.

The great merit of the minimum wage, is that it makes conciliation unnecessary. A man either receives the minimum or he does not. There is nothing to conciliate or negotiate upon. There is further in the minimum wage two diverse tendencies. On the men's side it will tend, as the organization develops its power, for the minimum to be so increased as to become the maximum possible to be earned on the price lists. On the employers' side, the tendency will perforce always be to offer some inducement to the men, to earn something above the minimum, in order to expedite production and thus maintain profits.

There is little need to dilate upon the proposal for a seven-hour day, conditional as it is upon the minimum wage being obtained. To those, however, who would still be earning (on the price list) wages above the minimum, it may be pointed out that this would supply the necessary stimulus for further increases in the minimum. Reductions of hours have always ante-dated increases in wages. The operation of the Eight Hours Act will supply an instance. This present struggle for a minimum wage is a direct outcome of that Act.

Political action must go on side by side with industrial action. Such measures as the Mines Bill, Workmen's Compensation Acts, proposals for nationalising the Mines, etc., demand the presence in Parliament of men who directly represent, and are amenable to, the wishes and instructions of the workmen. While, the eagerness of Governments, to become a bludgeoning bully on behalf of the employers, could be somewhat restrained by the presence of men who were prepared to act in a courageous fashion. . . .

POLICY

I.—The old policy of identity of interest between employers and ourselves be abolished, and a policy of open hostility installed.

II.—No dispute to be considered by the Executive Council until after failure is reported by the Lodge affected.

III.—Lodges failing to settle disputes arising in their respective collieries, must immediately report the same to the Secretary, together with all information relative to the cause, and subsequent conduct of the fight.

IV.—The Secretary on receipt of such information, must immediately call on the services of an Agent, the three parties to consult together, with a view of arriving at a policy mutually agreeable.

V.—Failing mutual agreement on a policy, the Lodge must be allowed to carry out their own, or the one favoured by them, until rescinded or altered by a Conference, whose decision must be final.

VI.—Any dispute not settled within 14 days after its report to the Executive Council, the Council to have power to call a special conference to deal with the same.

VII.—Any Lodge desiring to bring any grievance before a Conference, which has not been reported in the usual way, must first receive the sanction of the Business Committee, who must have due regard to its importance.

VIII.—For the purpose of giving greater strength to Lodges, they be encouraged to join together to form Joint Committees, and to hold joint meetings.

IX.—These Committees to have power to initiate, and carry out any policy within their own area, unhampered by Agent or Executive Council, so long as they act within their own financial resources. . . .

Decentralization for Negotiating

The Lodges, it will be seen, take all effective control of affairs, as long as there is any utility in local negotiation. With such a policy, Lodges become responsible and self-reliant units, with every stimulus to work out their own local salvation in their own way.

Centralization for Fighting

It will be noticed that all questions are ensured a rapid settlement. So soon as the Lodge finds itself at the end of its resources, the whole fighting strength of the organisation is turned on. We thus reverse the present order of things, where in the main, we centralize our negotiations and sectionalize our fighting.

Industrial Democracy the Objective

. . . Every fight for, and victory won by the men, will inevitably assist them in arriving at a clearer conception of the responsibilities and duties before them. It will also assist them to see, that so long as shareholders are permitted to continue their ownership, or the State administers on behalf of the Shareholders, slavery and oppression are bound to be the rule in industry. And with this realization, the age-long oppression of Labour will draw to its end. The weary sigh of the over driven slave, pitilessly exploited and regarded as an animated tool or beast of burden: the mediæval serf fast bound to the soil, and life-long prisoner on his lord's domain, subject to all the caprices of his lord's lust or anger: the modern wageslave, with nothing but his labour to sell, selling that, with his manhood as a wrapper, in the world's market place for a mess of pottage: these three phases of slavery, each in their turn inevitable and unavoidable, will have exhausted the possibilities of slavery, and mankind shall at last have leisure and inclination to really live as men, and not as the beasts which perish.

MAJOR SOCIAL
CLASSES

If we had only the records of protest to guide us, we would have an incomplete picture of the impact of industrialization on society. Too many people did not protest at all. Some, although hostile to industrial society, found it beneath their dignity to take to the streets. Others were so completely disoriented by industrialization that they could not even coherently formulate their grievances. Still others, and not only among the upper classes, adapted successfully to industrialization. So protest leaves out a lot of people. Furthermore, it does not always convey the deepest concerns of those who did protest. In the late 1890s, a survey of German workers in three industries revealed that sixty to eighty percent of the workers found no satisfaction in their work. Yet German strike rates were still rather low and the goals of strikes did not usually deal with the work situation. Seventy percent of the strikes—an unusually high figure for an industrial country—concerned wages.[1] In other words, there is evidence that workers were not able to articulate some of the problems that most concerned them and/or that prosaic strike demands, particularly over wages, stemmed from intense dissatisfaction over issues at work.

Protest through direct action, then, advances us only part of the way. It may be a less accurate measure of conditions and outlook as industrialization progresses then when the first shock of change was felt.

[1] Peter N. Stearns, "Adaptation to Industry: German Workers as a Test Case," *Central European History* (1971); E. J. Hobsbawm, *Labouring Men* (New York, 1967), pp. 405–36.

Fortunately, we have other sources, written about the industrial classes and by individuals within them. What follow are mostly individual reactions to industrial society or accounts by observers of larger groups. Obviously, many other types of sources can be used, including novels of the time. But it is best to start with statements by and about ordinary people. They may not always have been as perceptive about their situation as more articulate and farther removed observers, but their own reactions are the most certain indicators of what industrial society was like.

Not surprisingly, the outlook toward this new society differed not only from one class to the next, but also within what we normally consider each major social group. The study of protest has already revealed considerable variations in goals among different types of workers; direct statements by and about workers will confirm this diversity. The middle class was, if anything, even more divided. While direct statements indicate the nature of various views, they do not give much evidence about the extent to which they were shared. In this sense, the following documents are less satisfactory than the protest records. While protest statements must be tested against actual behavior to determine how representative they are, particularly when they emanate from self-professed protest leaders, at least we know how many people participated in the major types of protest and can assume some relationship between the protest records and widely-shared grievances. Statements made outside a direct protest situation have no such clear relationship to groups of people. Hence, the question of how typical they are is rarely easy to answer. The insight these statements give into life in societies undergoing industrialization is too great to ignore because of problems of representativeness, but it is true that the social historian must seek other sources, including protest records and other evidence of actual behavior, to test the significance of each type of reaction.

THE MIDDLE CLASSES

During the decades when countries in western and central Europe launched their industrialization, a large segment of the urban population—twenty to thirty percent—can be counted as middle class. Certainly they were in the middle in terms of wealth. Propertied, with at least twenty times as much capital as the better-paid wage earner possessed, the middle class could not yet rival the wealthy aristocrats in income or style of life. There is, of course, some overlapping at each end of the spectrum, where shopkeepers blend with artisans and rich businessmen with aristocrats, but these are minor problems of definition.

Until recently we thought we knew the characteristics of the middle class, and most textbooks still repeat the standard definitions. The middle class was liberal, confident if not brash, the motive force behind the twin political and industrial revolutions of the late eighteenth and early nineteenth centuries. It fought the old aristocratic order based on privilege of birth. It welcomed change and vaunted its belief in progress. At the same time, it valued order, as befit a propertied group, and so rarely participated in protest in the streets. It might use lower class unrest to support its own political ambitions and thus take the leadership role in revolutions, but it shunned direct contact with violence and most other illegal agitation.

The middle class shared a personal ethic on which it based its own behavior and by which it judged, and usually condemned, all other social groups. Hard work, thrift, individual initiative, personal sobriety and restraint—these were the hallmarks of the class. Toward the poor, the middle class applied its individualism most harshly. The poor were poor because they lacked personal merit. They deserved no charity or other assistance. At most they might be encouraged to develop the virtues they lacked on their own, so the middle class sponsored a variety of moralization projects, including education and savings banks.

We are now learning, however, that the middle class was not as united as many historians had formerly assumed. There were certainly important political divisions within it. Many liberals came from other classes and many members of the middle class opposed liberalism. Attitudes toward the poor varied. Some groups urged charity and even state aid to the poor; they did not believe that poverty was the fault of the poor alone. The middle class did not even share a common economic ethic. Some believed in economic change and personal advancement and others bitterly resisted both. There is abundant documentation for contradictory positions on all these matters. Perhaps the middle class did agree on certain personal virtues, such as cleanliness and hard work, but their range of shared values was quite limited.[1]

There was, then no single middle class. Definition by income is almost meaningless. The key division in the middle element was between those who sponsored and favored industrialization and related political changes and those who opposed both.

The innovating middle class included industrialists who introduced new machines and who extended the factory system. It also included political reformers—few of whom were businessmen themselves— and many professional people who thought of their professions not as almost inherited stations but as careers open to talent, competitive, and requiring rigorous training. This middle class did possess many of the classic characteristics attributed to it. It valued money and striving and it was not disturbed by social change.

The old middle class, which long outnumbered the new elements, saw society in a different way. It believed in a stable hierarchy. It was quite content that some groups were superior to it; it was sufficiently secure in its position that it could extend a charitable hand to the poor. It did not really believe in classes in the modern sense, for its view of the social order was based on birth, not on money. Therefore social mobility and changes that threatened the old ways were anathema. This group, which included large numbers of businessmen, shunned economic innovations. Often it was ignorant of new techniques and lacked the capital to introduce them, but this was not the

---

1 The current debate on the middle class is well presented in two articles: Lenore O'Boyle, "The Middle Class is Western Europe," *American Historical Review* (April, 1966), and Alfred Cobban "The 'Middle Class' in France, 1816–1848," *French Historical Studies* (1967).

main barrier. The old middle class simply lacked the incentive to innovate. Since it did not expect to improve its status and did not believe in rapidly advancing wealth, it simply hoped to behave as it always had. With industrialization on the horizon, however, it could not. It either had to change or lose its status. The process was often agonizing. The old middle class rarely suffered the physical misery that industrialization forced on some elements of the lower classes, although certain families came close to starvation as they tried to maintain a traditional front while their business or professional income declined. The psychic damage, however, was immense. And it was from the old middle class that the most consistent opposition to industrialization came. There was nothing so dramatic as Luddism, though we have seen that important middle class elements sympathized with the Luddites. But petitions, pamphlets, even demonstrations occurred frequently, and they recurred through the nineteenth century and beyond. Anti-Semitic protests was one outgrowth of this tradition.

The old middle class was more often found in smaller towns than in big cities. It included more professional people and civil servants than businessmen. But all major middle-class occupations were divided between old and new.

Historians have long known that middle classes differed from one country to the next. The German middle class was relatively illiberal; the French, comparatively undynamic in business. Differences of this sort might explain at least some of the ambiguities in the documentation on the middle class. But this argument cannot be pushed too far. Indeed, there may have been a slightly different balance of viewpoints from one nation's middle class to the next, but all the elements were represented everywhere. There were dynamic French industrialists. There were Britishers shocked by change; indeed, it is now recognized that the majority of the British middle class was opposed to industrialization early in the nineteenth century. So we need not assess each nation's middle class separately.

Rather, we must try to understand the basic divisions within the middle element of society. We should not expect complete contrasts. Much of the new middle class came from its older counterpart. It would long retain some traditional thinking. It was slow, for example, to replace the charitable approach to the poor with a more individualistic approach.[2] Even the most dynamic industrialists sometimes longed for a simpler past amid all the risks they were taking. But crucial differences did exist. Besides identifying them we must ask

2 Reinhard Bendix, *Work and Authority in Industry; Ideologies of Management in the Course of Industrialization* (New York, 1956) documents this process for Britain.

why they arose. Differences in family upbringing, in education, and in personal psychology were clearly involved. We do not yet have final answers on the reasons a new middle class developed or, relatedly, on the reasons members of the old middle class could not make a comparable transition. Yet the documents each group has left us may provide some clues.

Whatever the causes of their differences, the two middle classes were in a state of undeclared war with each other. The new middle class eventually eroded or converted the older group, but only gradually. The old middle class had weapons of its own and it won some important, if usually fleeting, victories.

SAMUEL SMILES

We can begin with the obvious, for the obvious is usually important. Samuel Smiles—his very name seems appropriate—was the leading propagandist of "middle-class values" in mid-nineteenth century Britain. Himself a doctor from a small town, Smiles early turned to writing and made his living from it. His books sold widely; *Self-Help* went through many editions. He preached what we would expect from the middle class: hard work, self-denial, and advancement in position. There are, however, some interesting ambiguities in his values. The tension in his view of the proper role of the working class is most obvious: workers are supposed to convert to middle-class values *except* the value of advancement, for, after all, God and the necessities of life dictate that contented workers are essential. There was also, for the middle class itself, a possible contradiction between the idea of advancement and the preaching of restraint and self-denial. Self-denial could of course aid mobility—clearly, here was one of the motive forces of the new middle class —but the old middle class could value self-denial alone and resist changes in station on that basis. Note also Smiles' implicit anti-intellectualism. Here was another middle-class ambiguity, and a durable one. The middle class was defined in part by superior education; Smiles himself was of course educated for the medical profession. And many outright intellectuals had middle-class origins. But very early in the rise of the new middle class hostilities developed, with business people professing distrust of impractical theorists and the theorists often replying in kind. In sum, Smiles suggests inconsistencies that characterized even the new middle class alone, reminding us that we cannot expect fully consistent values from any social group.

As a type of document, Smiles' piece presents an obvious problem. We cannot know exactly who read his work and we cannot know if those who read it believed it. There is some evidence that most of Smiles' readers came from the lower reaches of the middle classes and from the artisans, which is a sign that middle-class values were spreading, and which also suggests one of the major sources of the growth of the new middle class. But to be positive that Smiles' values were important for any segment of the middle class we need additional evidence. Letters and other documents exist which show that many members of the middle class taught their children the virtues Smiles urged. Certainly belief in the virtues of the self-made man was widespread. Smiles himself illustrates the power of this belief in the reaction of the House of Commons to Joseph Brotherton, a manufacturer of working-class origin. Nor, of course, was Smiles alone in his preachings. Many similar if less famous tracts were produced throughout western and central Europe. They flourished through mid-century and then declined. Sales of Smiles' own work trailed off dramatically in the 1870s. The middle-class spirit, part of which Smiles had represented, was beginning to change.

During his period of popularity, Smiles' role in the rise of the new middle class was not fully clear. This is a problem in the interpretation of anyone who consciously wrote for a reading public. We know Smiles was read, and we have good evidence that he was believed. Yet it is difficult to decide if his writings confirmed values already present or caused them. We can see his books eagerly read by aspiring artisans, who learned from them what values they needed to become middle class. But this leaves unanswered the question of why artisans read the books in the first place. Certainly most artisans were not sufficiently interested in changing their status to buy such blatantly middle-class propaganda. So the causation of mobility strivings remains unclear. What is certain is that the new middle class was a missionary group, proud of its virtues and eager to advertise them. Anyone open to the desire to rise in society would find ample advice available. The following passages suggest the variety of middle-class propagandists ready and willing to tell other people how they should behave. Publicists like Smiles and the politician-lecturers he cites played a vital role in the spread of the middle-class ethic, and they could make a tidy profit for themselves in the process.

Self-Help with Illustrations of Conduct and Perseverance

All nations have been made what they are by the thinking and the working of many generations of men. Patient and persevering labourers in all ranks and conditions of life, cultivators of the soil and explorers of the mine, inventors and discoverers, manufacturers, mechanics and artisans, poets, philosophers, and politicians, all have contributed towards the grand result, one generation building upon another's labours, and carrying them forward to still higher stages. This constant succession of noble workers—the artisans of civilization —has served to create order out of chaos in industry, science, and art; and the living race has thus, in the course of nature, become the inheritor of the rich estate provided by the skill and industry of our forefathers, which is placed in our hands to cultivate, and to hand down, not only unimpaired but improved, to our successors.

Self-Help *was first published in 1859. In the Centenary Edition (London, 1958), the following passages can be found on pp. 38–39, 47–48, 115–19, 281–84.*

The spirit of self-help, as exhibited in the energetic action of individuals, has in all times been a marked feature in the English character, and furnishes the true measure of our power as a nation. Rising above the heads of the mass there were always to be found a series of individuals distinguished beyond others, who commanded the public homage. But our progress has also been owing to multitudes of smaller and less known men. Though only the generals' names may be remembered in the history of any great campaign, it has been in a great measure through the individual valour and heroism of the privates that victories have been won. And life, too, is 'a soldiers' battle,'—men in the ranks having in all times been amongst the greatest of workers. Many are the lives of men unwritten, which have nevertheless as powerfully influenced civilization and progress as the more fortunate Great whose names are recorded in biography. Even the humblest person, who sets before his fellows an example of industry, sobriety, and upright honesty of purpose in life, has a present as well as a future influence upon the well-being of his country; for his life and character pass unconsciously into the lives of others, and propagate good example for all time to come.

Daily experience shows that it is energetic individualism which produces the most powerful effects upon the life and action of others, and really constitutes the best practical education. Schools, academies, and colleges, give but the merest beginnings of culture in comparison with it. Far more influential is the life-education daily given in our homes, in the streets, behind counters, in workshops, at the loom and the plough, in counting-houses and manufactories, and in the busy haunts of men. This is that finishing instruction as members of society, which Schiller designated 'the education of the human race,' consisting in action, conduct, self-culture, self-control,—all that tends to discipline a man truly, and fit him for the proper performance of the duties and business of life,—a kind of education not to be learnt from books, or acquired by any amount of mere literary training. With his usual weight of words Bacon observes, that 'Studies teach not their own use; but there is a wisdom without them, and above them, won by observation'; a remark that holds true of actual life, as well as of the cultivation of the intellect itself. For all experience serves to illustrate and enforce the lesson, that a man perfects himself by work more than by reading,—that it is life rather than literature, action rather than study, and character rather than biography, which tend perpetually to renovate mankind.

The instances of men, in this and other countries, who, by dint of persevering application and energy, have raised themselves from the humblest ranks of industry to eminent positions of usefulness and influence in society, are indeed so numerous that they have long ceased to be regarded as exceptional. Looking at some of the more remarkable, it might almost be said that early encounter with difficulty and adverse circumstances was the necessary and indispensable condition of success. The British House of Commons has always contained a number of such self-raised men—fitting representatives of the industrial character of the people; and it is to the credit of our Legislature that they have been welcomed and honoured there. When Joseph Brotherton, member for Salford, in the course of the discussion on the Ten Hours Bill, detailed with true pathos the hardships and fatigues to which he had been subjected when working as a factory boy in a cotton mill, and described the resolution which he had then formed, that if ever it was in his power he would endeavour to ameliorate the condition of that class, Sir James Graham rose immediately after him, and declared, amidst the cheers of the House, that he did not before know that Mr. Brotherton's origin had been so humble, but that it rendered him more proud than he had ever before been of the House of Commons, to think that a person risen from that condition should be able to sit side by side, on equal terms, with the hereditary gentry of the land. . . .

Fortune has often been blamed for her blindness; but fortune is not so blind as men are. Those who look into practical life will find that fortune is usually on the side of the industrious, as the winds and waves are on the side of the best navigators. In the pursuit of even the highest branches of human inquiry the commoner qualities are found the most useful—such as common sense, attention, application, and perseverance. Genius may not be necessary, though even genius of the highest sort does not disdain the use of these ordinary qualities. The very greatest men have been among the least believers in the power of genius, and as worldly wise and persevering as successful men of the commoner sort. Some have even defined genius to be only common sense intensified . . . owing their success in a great measure, to their indefatigable industry and application. They were men who turned all things to gold—even time itself. Disraeli the elder held that the secret of success consisted in being master of your subject, such mastery being attainable only through continuous application and study. Hence it happens that the men who have most moved the world, have not been so much men of genius, strictly so called, as men of intense mediocre abilities, and untiring perseverance; not so often the gifted, of naturally bright and shining qualities, as those who have applied themselves diligently to their work, in whatsoever line that might lie. 'Alas!' said a widow, speaking of her brilliant but careless son, 'he has not the gift of continuance.' Wanting in perseverance, such volatile natures are outstripped in the race of life by the diligent and even the dull.

'Che va piano, va longano, e va lontano,' says the Italian proverb: 'Who goes slowly, goes long, and goes far.'

Hence, a great point to be aimed at is to get the working quality well trained. When that is done, the race will be found comparatively easy. We must repeat and again repeat; facility will come with labour. Not even the simplest art can be accomplished without it; and what difficulties it is found capable of achieving: It was by early discipline and repetition that the late Sir Robert Peel [1] cultivated those remarkable, though still mediocre powers, which rendered him so illustrious an ornament of the British Senate. When a boy at Drayton Manor, his father was accustomed to set him up at table to practise speaking ex tempore; and he early accustomed him to repeat as much of the Sunday's sermon as he could remember. Little progress was made at first, but by steady perseverance the habit of attention became powerful, and the sermon was at length repeated almost verbatim. When afterwards replying in succession to the arguments of his parliamentary opponents—an art in which he was perhaps unrivalled—it was little surmised that the extraordinary power of accurate remembrance which he displayed on such occasions had been originally trained under the discipline of his father in the parish church of Drayton.

It is indeed marvellous what continuous application will effect in the commonest of things. . . .

Progress, however, of the best kind, is comparatively slow. Great results cannot be achieved at once; and we must be satisfied to advance in life as we walk, step by step. De Maistre says that 'to know *how to wait* is the great secret of success.' We must sow before we can reap, and often have to wait long, content meanwhile to look patiently forward in hope; the fruit best worth waiting for often ripening the slowest. But 'time and patience,' says the Eastern proverb, 'change the mulberry leaf to satin.'

To wait patiently, however, men must work cheerfully. Cheerfulness is an excellent working quality, imparting great elasticity to the character. As a bishop has said, 'Temper is nine-tenths of Christianity'; so are cheerfulness and diligence nine-tenths of practical wisdom. They are the life and soul of success, as well as of happiness: perhaps the very highest pleasure in life consisting in clear, brisk, conscious working; energy, confidence, and every other good quality mainly depending upon it. Sydney Smith, when labouring as a parish priest at Foston-le-Clay, in Yorkshire,—though he did not feel himself to be in his proper element,—went cheerfully to work in the firm determination to do his best. 'I am resolved,' he said, 'to like it, and reconcile

---

1 British statesman and moderate reformer (1788–1850), son of a successful cotton manufacturer.

myself to it, which is more manly than to feign myself above it, and to send up complaints by the post of being thrown away, and being desolate, and such like trash.' So Dr. Hook, when leaving Leeds for a new sphere of labour, said, 'Wherever I may be, I shall, by God's blessing, do with my might what my hand findeth to do; and if I do not find work, I shall make it.' . . .

How a man uses money—makes it, saves it, and spends it—is perhaps one of the best tests of practical wisdom. Although money ought by no means to be regarded as a chief end of man's life, neither is it a trifling matter, to be held in philosophic contempt, representing as it does to so large an extent the means of physical comfort and social well-being. Indeed, some of the finest qualities of human nature are intimately related to the right use of money; such as generosity, honesty, justice, and self-sacrifice; as well as the practical virtues of economy and providence. On the other hand, there are their counterparts of avarice, fraud, injustice, and selfishness, as displayed by the inordinate lovers of gain; and the vices of thriftlessness, extravagance, and improvidence, on the part of those who misuse and abuse the means entrusted to them. 'So that,' as is wisely observed by Henry Taylor in his thoughtful *Notes from Life,* 'a right measure and manner in getting, saving, spending, giving, taking, lending, borrowing, and bequeathing would almost argue a perfect man.'

Comfort in worldly circumstances is a condition which every man is justified in striving to attain by all worthy means. It secures that physical satisfaction which is necessary for the culture of the better part of his nature; and enables him to provide for those of his own household, without which, says the Apostle, a man is 'worse than an infidel.' Nor ought the duty to be any the less indifferent to us, that the respect which our fellow-men entertain for us in no slight degree depends upon the manner in which we exercise the opportunities which present themselves for our honourable advancement in life. The very effort required to be made to succeed in life with this object is of itself an education; stimulating a man's sense of self-respect, bringing out his practical qualities, and disciplining him in the exercise of patience, perseverance, and such like virtues. The provident and careful man must necessarily be a thoughtful man, for he lives not merely in the present, but with provident forecast makes arrangements for the future. He must also be a temperate man, and exercise the virtue of self-denial, than which nothing is so much calculated to give strength to the character. John Sterling says truly that 'the worst education which teaches self-denial is better than the best which teaches everything else, and not that.' The Romans rightly employed the same word (*virtus*) to designate courage, which is in a physical sense what the other is in a moral; the highest virtue of all being victory over ourselves.

Hence the lesson of self-denial—the sacrificing of a present gratification for a future good—is one of the last that is learnt. Those classes which work the hardest might naturally be expected to value the most the money which they earn. Yet the readiness with which so many are accustomed to eat up and drink up their earnings as they go renders them to a great extent helpless and dependent upon the frugal. There are large numbers of persons among us who, though enjoying sufficient means of comfort and independence, are often found to be barely a day's march ahead of actual want when a time of pressure occurs; and hence a great cause of social helplessness and suffering. On one occasion a deputation waited on Lord John Russell,[2] respecting the taxation levied on the working classes of the country, when the noble lord took the opportunity of remarking, 'You may rely upon it that the Government of this country durst not tax the working classes to anything like the extent to which they tax themselves in their expenditure upon intoxicating drinks alone!' Of all great public questions, there is perhaps none more important than this,—no great work of reform calling more loudly for labourers. But it must be admitted that 'self-denial and self-help' would make a poor rallying cry for the hustings; and it is to be feared that the patriotism of this day has but little regard for such common things as individual economy and providence, although it is by the practise of such virtues only that the genuine independence of the industrial classes is to be secured. 'Prudence, frugality, and good management,' said Samuel Drew, the philosophical shoemaker, 'are excellent artists for mending bad times: they occupy but little room in any dwelling, but would furnish a more effectual remedy for the evils of life than any Reform Bill that ever passed the Houses of Parliament.' Socrates said, 'Let him that would move the world move first himself.' Or, as the old rhyme runs:

> If every one would see
>   To his own reformation,
> How very easily
>   You might reform a nation.

It is, however, generally felt to be a far easier thing to reform the Church and the State than to reform the least of our own bad habits: and in such matters it is usually found more agreeable to our tastes, as it certainly is the common practice, to begin with our neighbours rather than with ourselves.

Any class of men that lives from hand to mouth will ever be an in-

2 Whig politician (1792–1878).

ferior class. They will necessarily remain impotent and helpless, hanging on to the skirts of society, the sport of times and seasons. Having no respect for themselves, they will fail in securing the respect of others. In commercial crises such men must inevitably go to the wall. Wanting that husbanded power which a store of savings, no matter how small, invariably gives them, they will be at every man's mercy, and, if possessed of right feelings, they cannot but regard with fear and trembling the future possible fate of their wives and children. 'The world,' once said Mr. Cobden[3] to the working men of Huddersfield, has always been divided into two classes,—those who have saved, and those who have spent—the thrifty and the extravagant. The building of all the houses, the mills, the bridges, and the ships, and the accomplishment of all other great works which have rendered man civilized and happy, has been done by the savers, the thrifty; and those who have wasted their resources have always been their slaves. It has been the law of nature and of Providence that this should be so; and I were an impostor if I promised any class that they would advance themselves if they were improvident, thoughtless, and idle.'

Equally sound was the advice given by Mr. Bright[4] to an assembly of working men at Rochdale, in 1847, when, after expressing his belief that, 'so far as honesty was concerned, it was to be found in pretty equal amount among all classes,' he used the following words: 'There is only one way that is safe for any man, or any number of men, by which they can maintain their present position if it be a good one, or raise themselves above it if it be a bad one—that is, by the practice of the virtues of industry, frugality, temperance, and honesty. There is no royal road by which men can raise themselves from a position which they feel to be uncomfortable and unsatisfactory, as regards their mental or physical condition, except by the practice of those virtues by which they find numbers amongst them are continually advancing and bettering themselves.'

There is no reason why the condition of the average workman should not be a useful, honourable, respectable, and happy one. The whole body of the working classes might (with few exceptions) be as frugal, virtuous, well-informed, and well-conditioned as many individuals of the same class have already made themselves. What some men are, all without difficulty might be. Employ the same means, and the same results will follow. That there should be a class of men who live by their daily labour in every state is the ordinance of God, and doubtless is a wise and righteous one; but that this class should be otherwise than frugal, contented, intelligent, and happy is not the design of

3 Liberal economist and politician (1804–65).
4 Liberal politician and propagandist (1811–89).

Providence, but springs solely from the weakness, self-indulgence, and perverseness of man himself. The healthy spirit of self-help created amongst working people would more than any other measure serve to raise them as a class, and this, not by pulling down others, but by levelling them up to a higher and still advancing standard of religion, intelligence, and virtue.

NARCISSE FAUCHEUR

Narcisse Faucheur was one of thousands of industrialists who set up factories with power equipment in France in the 1820s and 1830s. Note that he was not an industrial pioneer; his enterprise remained modest. This makes his outlook all the more interesting, in that industrialization really caught on only because of efforts by such men to imitate innovations conceived by others. But one must also ask whether top success in industry would require a still more ambitious, less cautious approach. And is there something distinctively French in the approach? Certainly Faucheur suggests French dependence on British example in industrialization; he may indicate also a reluctance to follow this example too closely, as he only slowly was convinced of the usefulness of new techniques.[1] Faucheur describes his behavior rather than his system of values, but the values can be derived from his account and they invite comparison with Smiles. Beyond this, Faucheur gives us an insight into the day-to-day business world in early industrialization and into family life and the role of women in the middle class.

Very few industrialists wrote anything at all about their activities and outlook. An autobiography is most unusual. As a source it is less than completely reliable, for it depends on a human memory that is faulty anyway and open to doctoring to make the author look good. Faucheur may be projecting more confidence than he actually felt while undertaking risky technical innovations. The values he suggests may be those he knows to be appropriate for public display or for training his grandchildren (for whom the book was published in a very limited edition), rather than those he actually held during his business career.

These cautions aside, the important fact is that we have a statement from one of the thousands of manufacturers who brought the industrial revolution into being. Faucheur never reached great heights; his business remained medium in size. During the period he discusses here he never employed more than fifty people in his mechanized shops. Correspondingly he amassed a solid by not unusual fortune. There were many industrialists in Lille who did as well or better as they introduced new techniques; Lille became one of the centers of factory production of cotton thread and cloth in France. So Faucheur gives us an indication of the outlook of the ordinary industrialists,

1 See David Landes, "French Entrepreneurship in the Nineteenth Century", *Journal of Economic History* (1949); Arthur L. Dunham, *The Industrial Revolution in France, 1815–1848* (New York, 1955).

who in combination were doing extraordinary things. His statements should be examined not only for what they say but also for what they do not say. Note the absence of significant reference to religion or cultural activity or to workers (except a few skilled workers on whom Faucheur had particularly relied and whose competence and ambition he could appreciate). The industrialists' horizon was a narrow one. Faucheur reveals some of the advantages and disadvantages of this narrowness for people who were building a new economic world. He also shows why he could be satisfied with this narrow focus.

What motivated men like Faucheur? In France thousands of them swarmed into new industries during the 1820s. Faucheur's autobiography gives at least some hints of his motives. He came from a family of petty merchants. Like most industrialists he was not entirely new to the middle-class world. Like many of the 1820s breed in France he had served in the army, which may have helped develop new ideas and expectations. Military service often shakes old values, and service in Napoleon's armies helped spread a belief in careers open to talents—if only because so many officers had risen from humble ranks—that could be applied to industry when the wars were over. Petty motives could play a role in impelling an individual to seek improvement in his wealth and status; Faucheur, for example, mentions his desire for good clothing. Faucheur cannot give us the whole answer about motivation; he undoubtedly never really asked himself why he did what he did. He assumes that the desire to make more money is normal, whereas the real question is why this desire spread so rapidly.

An Autobiography

I left Paris during the early part of June, 1815. As soon as I arrived at Clermont I went to see M. Paty, who promised me the post of regimental warrant officer. I re-enlisted into the army, therefore, at a very nice rank. I was delighted, for during my entire stay at Paris my poverty had imposed some very painful sacrifices, which were difficult to endure at my age. It was especially difficult for me because I could not foresee how long my sad situation would last. I was equally delighted to serve under M. Paty, whom I knew from frequent meetings at Clermont following my first return from the army. He was a veteran battalion leader, capable, educated, a good soldier with whom I had often chatted about my army experiences, and who, since our first encounter, had always been very friendly.

I had been at Clermont for barely eight days when I learned of the disaster at Waterloo, the new abdication of the Emperor, his departure for Rochefort, the return of the Bourbons, etc. All these events naturally meant that the battalion in which I was to serve was not com-

From *Narcisse Faucheur-Deledicque*, Mon Histoire: à mes chers enfants et petits enfants *(Lille, 1886), pp. 339–42; 347–48; 356–57; 358–61; 362; 367–70; 377–82. Translated by Peter Meyers.*

missioned. I was, therefore, once again "Gros-Jean as before," reduced to lamenting my own position and that of my country in her humiliation by the foreigners.

The French army, which at first had withdrawn behind the Loire, was then disbanded. Every day officers arrived who didn't know what to do. Some even left France and went to seek their fortunes in foreign lands. The idea of leaving for America again struck my fancy, but my parents were absolutely opposed to it. I yielded to their wishes rather than cause them the least unhappiness. The question of returning to Paris was soon raised, but the conditions for finding a job were hardly favorable, and moreover my parents were not anxious for me to leave, fearing that in Paris I would more easily find an opportunity to emigrate. They begged me, therefore, to stay with them until calmer times when I could more easily make long-range plans. One of our friends promised to do all he could to find me any sort of job while I was waiting better opportunities. Finally, after a long and very arduous search, our friend announced that he had found a position for me with the most important wholesalers in Clermont. I will tell you more about it. . . .

The friend whom I mentioned in the last chapter had found an opening for me in the firm of M. Cassan-Guyot, who was a wholesale dealer in the products of Roubaix, Lille, Amiens, Rouen, and the cloth trade of the Midi. This firm was, without doubt, the most important in Clermont. Unfortunately, I received a very meager salary, and because I was living with my parents I gave my mother all my earnings to help with the household expenses, which had risen sharply upon my arrival. I had rather quickly observed how poor my unfortunate parents were, so it was with real joy that at the end of each month I placed into my mother's hands the paltry sum I had earned.

The commercial apprenticeship that I had served in Paris helped me quickly to put the affairs of my new employer in good order. I displayed for his interests all the zeal, all the ardor and all the activity of which I was capable. I saw with satisfaction that my efforts were appreciated and that my employer held me in high regard. I was deeply touched by this attitude, which increased greatly my self-esteem; nevertheless I was quick to realize that my salary remained rather low. Yet he had made an unheard of gesture in giving me a salary right from the beginning, when he could have had as many clreks as he wanted without paying them at all. The firm enjoyed such a good reputation that for miles around all the young men who wanted to enter into business sought the honor of serving *gratis* such a renowned company. Besides, this company practiced the strictest economy, and it was precisely such thrift which had made the fortune of my employer and his two predecessors, this being the third generation that had carried on the same kind of business in this place.

I soon saw, therefore, that it would be necessary for me to find another source of income in order to maintain a modest but always neat and proper wardrobe.

I pondered for a long time what I could do to earn the extra money that seemed so necessary. After many aborted schemes, I found nothing better than some copying for the tax collector. Through the intervention of a friend who was a government employee, I obtained some rolls to copy at home. You are probably unaware of these rolls, and thank God that you and your family were not, as I was, reduced to the harsh necessity of copying them. The rolls were lists of taxpayers, taken from the tax registry of the commune, which I had to copy onto some special printed forms. At that time, all the administrative documents were on paper so rough and shabby that writing on it was very difficult.

Occupied for the great part of the day at M. Cassan's, I could copy the rolls only by getting up early in the morning, going to bed very late, and working on them Sundays and holidays. All that to earn an average of 25 *sous* per day (fr. 1, 25)! It was brutalizing work. Nevertheless, I devoted myself to it with real energy, knowing that in order to reach the goal I had set for myself, I had to have proper attire, and copying these lists was the only way to earn the money I needed. . . .

When I became a travelling salesman for M. Delcros, I had the opportunity to talk with many other merchants and salesmen in Lille. They spoke of it as a city with a great commercial future and as an area full of opportunities for a young man such as I to establish himself by his own efforts. I was taken with the idea because I was already preoccupied with plans for the future. I wrote to my brother about it, and he encouraged me to transfer to Lille, not only because we would have the pleasure of seeing each other often, but also because it would be a step toward the realization of my goals.

Although I was well liked by my employer, the firm offered me no prospects of a partnership. It didn't have enough capital to expand its operations to the point that I might one day acquire a financial interest in it. I was condemned, therefore, to grow old as a salesman and to devote all my energies to [working for] other people. . . .

For a number of years I was a salesman for the Malmazet brothers and M. Vallier. I was with them long enough to ascertain that the associates did not work very well together; besides, there were already too many partners for me to obtain the kind of position I had hoped for in the firm. Once again, I had no other future except as a salesman, well paid but condemned to being constantly on the road. I had accumulated some savings and I hoped to use them to build a future for myself.

Various propositions were made to me, but for one reason or another, they led to nothing. For the most part, these propositions involved the establishment of both a commercial enterprise and a residence in Paris. I had reached the age when I could contemplate marriage, but nothing in the world could induce me to marry a Parisian. Besides, by taste, I had no desire to live in the capital. The customs of Lille agreed with me. My brother had just married a Mademoiselle Comère there and I wanted to live near them. Lacking the necessary capital to start a trading house by myself, I searched for a partner in Lille. . . .

My associate not only failed to provide the capital that he had promised me beyond the sum required by our agreement but also failed to introduce me to any of the bankers in Lille. Thus, I was forced to turn to Messrs. Collon-Bonarme and Sambucy of Clermont, with whom I had regularly deposited my savings. These gentlemen, knowing from long standing my integrity, my diligence, and my desire to succeed, were a great help to me. I deposited all my assets in their new Paris branch and drew on my account to finance all my purchases. Little by little my business practices inspired confidence among the Lille bankers, who now offered me their credit regularly.

The lesson I learned from the imbecile was to take the greatest precautions before contracting even the smallest obligation. I advise you to do the same; prudence dictates it.

My lace business prospered for several years, but gradually a new product began to hurt it. I am speaking of tulle, which replaced lace and was much cheaper. The designs on the tulle, all of which was imported, were nearly all in very bad taste. I thought that if I embroidered on the tulle some attractive French designs, I could sell it easily and make a large profit.

I went to England to learn about this industry and to see if I could bring it into France. I took from England all the information I needed, but I decided against buying the looms used to make plain tulle, for they were too expensive and their purchase would have used funds which I needed in my other commercial ventures. Therefore, I concentrated on information dealing with embroidering tulle, an operation I hoped to start in France. I returned to Lille with some detailed designs and some patterns by which one could determine the number of stitches each design required. Since tulle embroidery work was paid according to the number of stitches in a design, these patterns made it easy for me to determine labor costs and set the final price.

In Saint-Armand I was in contact with two old spinsters who had two very intelligent nieces. The nieces were very good embroiderers but they didn't know how to work with tulle. I showed these ladies some samples of this embroidery and they assured me that if a woman skilled in the technique would give them some lessons, they could easily learn to do it themselves. They also claimed that they would be able to train many other young girls in Saint-Armand to be embroiderers, since there was no other occupation open to them in the region, no matter what their social class. We agreed that if I put my plan into practice my workshop would be in the home of the aunts, who would then be directors, and that the nieces would be foremen, all of them earning a reasonable salary.

When I was sure of being able to establish an embroidery workshop at Saint-Armand on advantageous terms, I left for Paris, where I had a good designer make a number of attractive patterns. I next arranged for an English woman from Nottingham who was very skilled in embroidery work to teach the two nieces of the ladies Dutordoir.

In a short time, the two girls were skilled enough in this new embroidery not only to follow the patterns I gave them but also to teach the technique to some apprentices. What I wanted to create at my Saint-Armand workshop was a sort of mutual school of tulle embroidery that would be capable of filling all the orders I received.

From the start everything succeeded according to my wishes. In a short time I had a factory of more than three hundred embroiderers in the Dutordoir home. The first pieces I put up for sale gave me a profit all the more considerable since labor costs were very low. . . .

In every way possible I tried to speed up production. I was involved with every detail, for the newness of the designs determined their merit and price. But I was unable to rush production as much as I hoped, and the scale of my business remained limited.

Very quickly I had competition, not only at Lille, Douai, and Valenciennes but especially at Saint-Quentin. My competitors stole my designs, and when a design was offered by several houses it lost its novelty, consequently lowering its price and profit. Thus, having taken the trouble to start this operation, having held high hopes of making a fortune from it, I saw that it would be necessary to start over again. Well, it was not my first disappointment, nor would it be the last. . . .

At this time everyone in Lille was talking about the growth of business in linen and overalls. M. Colombier-Batteur, whose father had died some years earlier, had earned what must have been a colossal fortune in this trade, for people called him a millionaire, and there were very few Lille merchants who were that wealthy. The sum seems even more enormous when one recalls that a friend of M. Colombier had ingenuously asked how he had acquired it. M. Colombier allegedly replied: "Nothing could have been easier! I sold a million overalls and I earned one franc on each. And that's how I became a millionaire."

My pretensions were not quite so high, but understanding a little about the linen trade, I decided to try it. It was all the better that I was not dealing in articles of fashion and did not have to worry about the merchandise depreciating in the warehouse.

For a while I was involved in two different kinds of merchandise at the same time. Then, having found an opportunity to liquidate favorably the lace and tulle business, I concentrated entirely on linen and overalls.

In those days there were no mechanical cloth mills. All the linen was made by hand in homes in the countryside by weavers who then sold their product at the markets of Courtrai, Ghent, Roulers, Thielt, Bruges, Remaix, Audemande, Grammont, etc. It was necessary, therefore, to visit all these markets to make purchases. Since at least one market was held every day of the week, a merchant who wanted to make all his own purchases would be traveling constantly. It was advisable to hire some agents to visit this or that market. Then the most important firms had a clerk in charge of purchases and of overseeing the agents.

I began by using agents, whom I checked on from time to time. Then, after my business had grown, I too put an employee in charge of this task.

My cloth trade having grown somewhat, I left the *rue d'Angleterre* and went to live on the *rue de la Piquerie*, where I had some large warehouses. The manufacture of overalls on a large scale required careful attention to minute details, which gave your mother and me a good deal of work. After our employees left, we remained at the office nearly every night until eleven o'clock, and sometimes until midnight, to record what had taken place during the day so that our books would always be up to date.

It was important that all production be linked to the filling of a specific order. Without this precaution one ran the risk of accumulating an inventory that was difficult to sell, for each customer wanted a kind of overall differing in its shade of blue, the nature and width of the linen, the sort of embroidery, etc.

Since large shipments were made only twice during the year, it often happened that at certain times there were no orders. Then I would go on the road, and in a short time I would always find enough orders to keep our workers busy. But God knows the fatigue I endured on those hectic trips! Usually I left Lille and went to Nancy, which was a journey of three days and two nights because there were no railroads then and coaches did not make the trip directly. A carriage took me to Valenciennes, where I waited two hours to take a light cart to Avesnes;

at Avesnes a new carriage to Hirson and from there a ferry for Mé-
zières; from there a large coach carried me to Sedan, and at Sedan another carriage for Verdun; then at last I took a coach to Nancy. Early
the following morning I would see my clients and it was rarely that
the same evening I could not send your mother some good orders,
which she was eagerly awaiting. I would next continue my trip into
Lorraine, Alsace, and Champagne and I would return by way of Bour-
gogne, generally travelling three nights of every five, but saying nothing of it to your mother so as not to alarm her. These trips varied from
twenty-five to forty days, which we both found very long. But an
ordinary salesman would have certainly doubled the time, for he
would not have wanted to subject himself to all the strain that I endured. For several years I had to make two or three of these whirlwind
trips, and God knows all the difficulty that they stirred up for me, no
matter how necessary they were!

My yearly profits did not reflect all the work I put in, but over the
long run my fortune grew slowly. The market was such that one had
to make his decisions with courage. The competition was intense, the
profits small, and one could lose all his customers if he set his prices
higher than his competitors. . . .

In the preceding chapters I have told you of the hard work to which
your mother and I diligently devoted ourselves to make our business
prosper. It is now time to describe for you the order and thrift which
guided our expenditures. Since our annual profits were not very large,
our budget had to be rigorously kept within our income if our savings
were to increase little by little.

Before our marriage, we agreed that your mother would help me in
my business by keeping the records. I explained to her that I wanted
to be near her continually so that she would be completely informed
of all our affairs. I also told her that it was not my intention to put
her on a budget, as had been done in many households, for I had too
much confidence in her to suppose for a single instant that she would
not know how to adjust our expenses to our income.

From the start, your mother performed all her duties marvellously.
Not only was she very quickly conversant in business matters, but she
also promptly became an excellent housewife. She went herself to the
butcher and the fish market, and made all her purchases in cash. Her
account book was an easily understood model of regularity and thrift.
I think that she has saved all the household records and that she could
if necessary give an exact account of all our expenses from the day of
our marriage to the present.

Forty-two years ago, the customs in Lille were not the same as those
of today. The wives of the city's most important merchants themselves

made all the household purchases. In general, the commodities were better chosen, the wives were more conscious of bargains, and the effects were felt in the household expenses. Moreover, their cooking was not the worse for it, but, on the contrary, better. This wise management of the household economy did not prevent many very fashionable wives from helping their husbands in their businesses. Someone has even remarked that the firms which prospered most quickly were precisely those in which the wives participated most. I will cite a few local examples. Madame Wallaert-Desmons, the mother of M. Desmedt, was the major cause of her family's prosperity. Later, Madame Auguste Wallaert-Mille, through her good business sense, was able to direct perfectly the immense activities of that trading house. Madame Crépy, the grandmother of all those whom you know, was responsible for the affluence of that large family.

At the time of my marriage in 1827, there were in Lille only two important banking houses, both directed by women. One, Madame Dutilloy, died a few years ago and left an enormous fortune to M. Bernos. The other was Madame Rouzé-Mathon. I could point to many other wives who, while taking perfect care of their households, greatly helped their husbands, and I deplore the fact that this is no longer the case. I think that everything would be better if there were less luxury. But I will say no more, for I do not want to be included among that group of old men whom Horace described as: "Critics of the present and laudators of times past."

For several years, I carried on my trade in linen and overalls as described above. But at each inventory I found that my income didn't increase as quickly as my small family, and that my profits didn't reflect all the time and effort I put in.

For quite a while I used linen woven in Belgium from machine spun thread, for there were no weavers in Lille capable of imitating the linen made in Belgium.

This product returned a moderate profit, but presented some very severe difficulties. At the time, the English and Belgians sold their cloth according to the numbers of threads in the warp and woof. In order to buy advantageously I had to deal with many parties, and even then I was forced to buy various types of cloth in amounts which were not geared to my sales. I could have sold many articles manufactured with warp numbers of 20, 22, 25, 28, and 30 threads, but it was precisely those numbers that I had difficulty finding. For a number of years I searched for a solution to this problem and several others which I won't take the space to describe. On one of my numerous trips to Belgium I met a very intelligent young man, employed by the Lys spinning mill at Ghent. He was the son of one of my long-time Belgian linen buyers. His goal in life was to build a small spinning mill, but his father, who was fairly well off, was not at all inclined to help him. He hoped that I would be able to help put his plans into operation. We held several meetings and were joined by an English foreman. They supplied me with some information on manufacturing cost, technique, etc. With the aid of these figures and information obtained from other sources, I could compute the production costs of the types of cloth which I had difficulty buying in Belgium.

After studying the matter thoroughly, I concluded that Belgium was not the right place to build a spinning mill designed to supply a cloth mill in France. Thus I began looking for a way to start a small spinning mill in Lille. At the same time, of course, I continued my trade in linen.

To avoid building anything, I was looking for a factory with a suitable power source. My plans became known and one day my brother-in-law, Lepercq, came to see me and asked me, in a timid voice, if it was true that I intended to start a spinning mill. I replied that in fact I was considering it, but that I had not yet reached a decision. Lepercq then took advantage of his knowledge of thread, with which he had been involved for some time in a small business venture. He emphasized his thorough knowledge of flax, with which he had been working for his whole life. Then he proposed that we join in a partnership to start a spinning mill.

The purchase of flax was precisely my weak point. Knowing nothing about it myself, I recognized the importance of having someone make wise purchases. It was unfortunate that I had decided to work with my brother-in-law. Had I been alone, I would have spared myself much trouble and torment, and I would certainly have earned more money. His financial and industrial contribution was infinitely below what I had expected.

With the architect M. Desrousseaux acting as intermediary, M. Boyer offered to build for us, on some land he owned in Wazemmes, a spinning mill equipped with a steam engine and all the necessary power transmission belts. Our rent would be based on Boyer's construction costs. This proposition, which contained some strongly leonine terms, appealed to us as a way to avoid sinking a great deal of capital into construction, while allowing us to start a large number of spindles.

If I had had an associate sharing my views and my ardor for work, and one who was able to contribute capital equal to mine, the conditions imposed by Boyer, although largely favorable to him, would have allowed us to make huge profits. Though limited by the factors mentioned above, the profits exceeded those from my trade in linen and overalls to such a degree that I quickly saw that the spinning factory offered me a much better future than my old business.

JOHANN LEONHARDT VOGEL

In November, 1848, King Maximilian of Bavaria sponsored an essay contest on the question "Through what means can the material distress of the population of Germany and especially of Bavaria be most purposefully and lastingly alleviated?" Johann Leonhardt Vogel, a teacher in Ingolstadt, was one of many in the middle class who entered. The solutions he proposed for the economic ills were unusually outlandish but the tone of his essay and particularly the evils he identified were generally common to the essays.[1] The writers were bitterly hostile not only to industrialization but also to social mobility. So Vogel introduces us to the old middle class, the group that was being left behind by the changing social order. He shares a few values with representatives of the new middle class. His outlook toward the lower classes, for example, deserves careful comparison with Smiles. Vogel's view is distinctly more traditionalist, but there is a common belief in social hierarchy and a related concern that the lower classes not try to defy their lot by spending on inappropriate items. He displays more generally the middle-class reaction to excessive expenditure and lack of restraint. Note also that Vogel writes after two years of deep economic crisis. Many cautious businessmen, men like Faucheur, might return to a more traditionalist outlook when the industrial economy seemed to be going haywire.

But if Vogel suggests some relationship between old and new middle class, his essay reveals the contrast between the two groups far more strikingly. He thinks of the economy as the basis for an unchanging social hierarchy. He can tolerate neither mobility nor technical innovation. Many of the reasons for his position are obvious. He was a small-towner. He was a teacher, not a businessman, and his personal situation had been deteriorating for some time; improving status for the new middle class meant declining status for the old, and on occasion declining earnings as well. Industrialization had only just begun in Bavaria, and Vogel reflects the first shock.

Vogel represented a large segment of middle-class opinion. Views like his helped drive the German middle class to revolution in 1848, which means we must be careful not to oversimplify what a middle-class revolution involved. To be sure, liberals controlled the revolutionary parliaments and some progressive businessmen were included in their ranks. People like Vogel were briefly attracted to liberalism in their search for some means of protesting change. In Bavaria and elsewhere they petitioned and demonstrated. But they quickly realized that liberalism was not the solution, for it supported economic change. So they returned their loyalty to the traditional state, which was not the least of the reasons the revolution failed. The state responded by making some gestures toward the traditionalists. There were some restrictions on new techniques.[2]

1 Edward Shorter, "Middle-Class Anxiety in the German Revolution of 1848," *Journal of Social History* 2 (Spring 1969): 189–216.

2 Theodore Hamerow, *Restoration, Revolution, Reaction: Economics and Politics in Germany, 1815–1871* (Princeton, 1958).

Obviously industrialization advanced rapidly in Germany despite the restrictions. Political institutions changed less rapidly, and the disillusionment with liberalism of the old middle class played no small role in this. The old middle class cannot be dismissed as a mere oddity in the industrialization process. Its very size and social position guaranteed that it would continue to have some impact, even though its basic desire—to halt the industrialization process—could not be realized.

Nor can the old middle class be dismissed as a temporary phenomenon. It might be tempting to assume that Vogel's type would disappear after a generation, as the new middle class progressed. Not so. Particularly in the professions, including teaching, a distrust of modern, industrial society persisted. Some of Vogel's basic arguments were dropped, and of course his solutions to the social problems he saw were highly idiosyncratic anyway. But antagonism to machines, criticism of frivolous spending, some sense that the modern world is immoral—these are themes to be found even in the twentieth century in segments of the middle classes. Fear of overpopulation strikes a familiar chord as well, though it has only recently been taken up again by critics of industrialization. Industrialization thus antagonized a segment of the middle class not only at its inception but recurrently thereafter. A variety of protests well into the twentieth century expressed this tension.

Contest of His Majesty, King Maximilian II of Bavaria

Ingolstadt, in the county of Walt Bibart, governmental area Middle Frankonia, . . . January 1849.

The author of this essay is teacher Johann Leonhardt Vogel.

Question:

"By which means can material hardship of the lower classes in Germany's population, particularly in Bavaria, be alleviated most effectively and permanently?"

Motto:

"If you stand at the spring from which the evils originate you can also dry up the well."

The evil has to be evicted by the same path by which it came.

In accepting the task of answering our test question I sense the difficulty of the solution as well as the importance of it. At the same time my thirty years of experience which I gained in the countryside and the cities demand that I not shy away from a thorough answer to the previous question. I hope to therewith contribute a share to the improvement of our present social conditions.

If we focus clearly on our tasks we find that they are divided into three main components, namely:

This handwritten document, dated 2 January 1849, is essay #156 in the collection numbered MH 9613 in the Bayerisches Hauptstaatsarchiv, Munich. Translated by Gabriela Wettberg.

I. What does this material hardship consist of?

II. How does it come about?

III. How can it be permanently abolished?

I. Under material hardship one would probably understand nothing but the lack of financial means needed to meet the realistic and essential costs of living. In other words, material hardship is nothing else but permanent overexpenditure in relation to income. Where the needed funds are lacking we find that a person or family has difficulties in purchasing those things which are necessary; for instance rent, fire wood, clothing items or land. And where people have to forbear these things there is hardship.

But let us not dwell any longer on this first point which does not actually pertain to the answering of our question. Let us rather proceed to our second objective. It is the search for the cause of material hardship. You will find these reasons only if you answer the following questions:

II. How does material hardship come about? Material hardship will arise

a) if induced by one's own fault. This happens partly due to over-indulgence of the palate, partly due to the purchase of excessively precious clothing and other luxury articles, encouraged by fashion's fancies. But it also occurs because of excessive frequenting of amusement places such as the theater which is connected with financial sacrifices.

b) It is due also to a lack of turnover of the workers' products. This lack is a consequence of the fact that previous buyers of hand-made products are now satiated by the cheaper products of the factories. You may permit yourself to object that it would be advantageous if wares could be sold inexpensively than if they were high in price. But I say "no." This low price has a doubly disastrous effect. For one, the laborers lose their buyers and become unemployed. For another, the middle and lower classes are given the opportunity to spend the little money they need for life necessities on cheap but dispensable items. I may be permitted to cite but one of many thousand examples. Material for a dress costing 6 Taler can be bought by more people than if the same dress were to cost $3 \times 6 = 18$ Taler. In the latter case people not possessing 18 Tl. would save up their six Tl. while in the first case the low cost would induce squander.—As we see, factory manufacturing causes doubly severe hardship. E.g.:

aa) The removal of buyers from the crafts.

bb) Inducement to squander in middle and low classes through cheap wares.

It cannot be denied that machines which produce wares wholesale in a simple, rapid and inexpensive fashion make obsolete many thousand human hands in our beloved fatherland. If all craftsmen were to possess sufficient capital to build their own machines, destruction of these machines would soon be the order of the day. And indeed, this would be the most beautiful way to get the disastrous things off the face of the earth. But since not everyone possesses the required capital to purchase a machine the capital of a few has—machine-like—a devastating effect on entire families.

c) One further reason for the increasing lack of food lies in overpopulation. Because of the latter production has entered an imbalanced relationship with consumption. If only edible items were made in production these objects would face quick dissolution or commutation (consumptive) and the previous demand would reappear. But since metal and wood wares last much longer the demand is satisfied over too long a period. In this the farmer holds an advantage over the urbanite in that his products spoil more quickly. In some businesses production relates to consumption in a ratio of 100:1.

III. How can material hardship be abolished?

This is the main question which we have to answer. Let us first direct our attention to the larger cities. When we propose appropriate measures of aid we find that (as a rule) cities are divided into districts. This division will provide us with the opportunity to find the only workable method to adopt if we are to counteract the previously described financial hardship thoroughly and if, in time, we are to conquer it completely.

These are the measures:

1. In every single city district a commission of 6–8 of the best informed citizens is to be in session on a certain day. (The members are selected by general election).

2. During these sessions the conditions in the families are to be thoroughly researched.

3. Those families whose expenses exceed their resources are brought to a state of despair.

4. The commission will simultaneously research the reasons for the overextended finances in various families.

5. This research is not to be based solely on the information supplied by the people involved but also on the commission's own observations.

6. The causes for any material hardship will be marked down separately in a list for each family.

7. Every individual will be questioned by the commission.

8. If there is a possibility to eliminate the causes for material hardship through one person or a family, which is the case in classes that exceed their budget for the most needed living expenses, the commis-

sion may indicate that they could establish requirements for support by permanently denying themselves any dispensable purchases.

9. A special fund must be established from which will flow cash in the amounts of 6–12 Taler or which will distribute wood or bread.

10. But this aid should not be understood as a prize for denied pleasure seeking.

11. Those persons and families who have experienced a recession in their trade and suffer from the want of bare necessities are to receive particular consideration.

12. The new fund is to be established with a. governmental subsidies b. taxation of factory-produced wares.

13. Through vigorous speeches the commission should effect a diminished indulgence in luxury.

14. Since it is known that every orderly fiscal operation of any community or charity rests on a budget such a budget is to be set up wherever possible.

15. The commission should further effect that those whose existence is seriously endangered decide on emigrating.

16. The expenses of this undertaking would be paid through the fund which I described above.

17. The efficacy of our special commission is to be supervised by special governmental commissions.

In the countryside material hardship will be combatted in the following ways:

1. Strict punishment of those persons who are not working and not prevented from doing so by any handicaps.

2. Single persons with children or physically disabled persons will be permitted a changing shift pattern and they will be given work so that they may earn their bread.

3. Uprooted families should be given lots to cultivate what they most urgently need to eat. That type of land can be found in every community. Many communities have already been freed of debts or will be during the next years. Therefore several of the lots which have been incorporated into the community land can be turned over to financially oppressed families.

4. The setting up of servants' banks in every village. These banks could be supervised by the town teacher.

We hope to have listed the main remedies whereby material hardship could be stamped out *permanently*. The author of this essay could undoubtedly have named other remedies, i.e. the distribution of raw materials for production. But production would merely be increased further by such steps. Therefore this remedy was not listed.

I close with the words with which I opened up this discourse: "The evil can only be driven back on the same road on which it came."

Postscript.

The careful answering of the test question also contributed to the mitigation of my own situation. For eighteen years I have been in a starting position at a salary of 200 Tl. a year which grows smaller every year. I have, through no fault of my own, suffered many a family illness and loss. I trustingly turn to the magnanimous heart of His Majesty with the most humble request that the Royal government may order my promotion soon.

In joyful expectation and with deepest respect
for Your Royal Highness

AUGUSTE MIMEREL

Businessmen, even those on the peripheries of industrialization, could share important elements of the old middle class view. Auguste Mimerel manufactured cloth in Roubaix, a town not far from Lille, during the 1830s and 1840s—the same period Narcisse Faucheur discusses. He was also a vigorous spokesman on behalf of industrialists in his area, particularly in the advocacy of tariff protection against English goods. So some of his views at least had wide currency. As an industrialist, Mimerel was no innovator. Most of his operation was conducted in the countryside, by workers working on simple machines in their own homes, using their own hands and feet to provide the power. Mimerel was not a sponsor of technical changes. And his firm was a small one. Though Mimerel was a man of some substance, his wealth did not increase rapidly. In other words, Mimerel was a far different type from someone like Faucheur.

His views also differed. Mimerel straddled the fence between the old and the new middle class. He could envisage a certain amount of industrialization but he did not want it to go too far. He very definitely did not wish to see British patterns repeated. His view of agriculture, of the proper distribution of wealth, and of the proper conditions of the lower classes have much in common with Vogel's opinions. Rapid industrialization, the proliferation of large companies and large fortunes, would have shocked Mimerel almost as much as they would bother people like Vogel. In Mimerel's own town, though in a different family, a graphic illustration of the contrast in values occurred. A young man named Motte Bossut, who had visited England and was greatly impressed by what he saw, set up a giant spinning plant. His parents, modest industrialists, lent him some money for the operation but refused to enter the factory, which they regarded as immoral. Morality was deeply involved with the differing middle-class reactions to industrialization, and Mimerel indicated some of the key issues. His remedy was simple: high tariffs, so France could produce for her own needs in her own way.[1]

There were many manufacturers who agreed with Mimerel both in attitude and deed. We must remember, in the early decades of industrialization, the thousands of manufacturers who did not adopt new methods. Most of them, in the industries which were mechanizing, would fail; the rate of business bankruptcy was over fifty percent in France and Britain during the first industrial years. Mimerel's own firm collapsed after his death. So, in part, Mimerel represents a transitional generation, the old exposed to the new.

But, as with Vogel, elements of Mimerel's outlook had a longer life. Arguments for tariff protection in France, and, to a certain degree elsewhere, continued to evoke fears of excessive industrialization. And of course such protection often did slow the pressure for further technological change which in turn helped businessmen of Mimerel's type survive at least for a time. In other reaches of business, furthermore, the traditionalist businessman, preoccupied with a family firm and content with stable earnings, flourished for many decades and maintains an existence even today. Shopkeepers, most notably, shared many of Mimerel's values, including a horror of larger economic organizations, and they have played a great numerical and political role in middle-class history. Even in industry itself echoes of the sort of values Mimerel expressed survived in later decades. The textile industry, for example, though of course technologically transformed, never converted to genuinely big business organization as did heavy industry later in the nineteenth century. It avoided cartels and usually even shunned corporations, and the average unit remained relatively small because this was what the manufacturers in the industry wanted.

So Mimerel represents an important position. Possibly we should try to identify a large group between the old and new middle classes, capable of limited innovation but ready to protest too much change. The existence of this group, particularly in the world of small business, helps explain support for anti-industrial protest in bad times, including anti-semitic protest later in the nineteenth century, from people who were capable of some adaptation to new ways when times were good. Mimerel reminds us also of the psychic toll industrialization could take, for even in France some of his dire warnings were soon realized as both industrial firms and economic inequality grew and class struggle intensified. Though he greatly minimizes poverty and the extent to which only rapid industrialization could reduce it, he suggests finally some human values, particularly in dealing with the poor, that the world the new middle class was creating neglected to its detriment.

1 Peter N. Stearns, "British Industry through the Eyes of French Industrialists," *Journal of Modern History* 38 (1966): 50–61, discusses the division in outlook further.

A Comparison of France and England

At a time when you are about to be called upon again to state how wise it is to protect your businesses, it is fitting to prove that this protection can only have great and salutary effects.

Therefore, allow one of your own to place himself under your auspices in order to demonstrate that protection was not instituted in favor of the privileged but particularly for the benefit of the workers and ultimately of the whole nation; and that the country which your labor enriches should not fear, as has been too often asserted, that your doctrines and your actions will infect France with that hideous plague of pauperism which gnaws at and devours England.

In this regard there are two questions to examine:

Is it true that in France industry encourages the encroachment of pauperism?

Is it not true, on the contrary, that the social organization and the economy up to now applied by industry preserve France from this scourge, whereas pauperism and the evils which it carries in its wake are the necessary result of the social organization and the economic condition of England?

First of all, what is pauperism considered in its relationship to industry?

Is it solely and absolutely this state wherein the worker does not find in his work the means to feed himself, to clothe himself, to house himself and his family, so that there results from this destitution a real physical suffering, an alteration of the principles of health and of life?

Is it only this or does it apply when peoples' needs, being always overstimulated, always extended, being no longer satisfied, produces as a result privation, moral poverty more than real destitution; because multiplying the desires to multiply the pleasures often results ultimately in rendering unacceptable a condition which, in another frame of mind, could have been envied because it satisfied all the necessities of life?

Certainly if, according to the first hypothesis, industry could be held responsible, it is assuredly not industry's responsibility according to the second hypothesis. It is not industry which has opened those public courses where people teach that the moderation of the desires is a cause

From *Auguste Mimerel,* Du Pauperisme dans ses Rapports avec l'industrie en France et en Angleterre (*Lille, n.d.*) pp. 5–7, 16–22. *The pamphlet was issued during the late 1830s. Translated by Theresa McBride.*

of poverty and degradation; it is not industry who pretends that the happiness of man depends on the greatest quantity of things that are consumed, and that the most active production possible would always be accepted and matched by consumption.

But has industry, by an excess of work or lowering of salaries, created pauperism, which means in essence the lack of the things necessary to health and to life?

Carry yourselves back, my colleagues, to your farthest memories: consult those who before you provided for and fed the workers, and you will see that the time of actual work has changed almost not at all in France; it has never been below twelve hours a day; it is today almost everywhere thirteen; but since steam has delivered man from bodily fatigue and no longer demands of him the full scope of his attention and his intelligence, one could assert that, in this respect, there has not been an aggravation of the lot of the working class.

Have wages been lowered?

Is it not true that workers in industry today earn from 2 to 5 francs, the women from 1 franc 20 centimes to 2 francs, and the children, according to their age from 40 centimes to 1 franc. The daily rate was almost half as high in 1788; and in any period, even in 1825 when the fever of industrialization stirred everyone, the rewards for work were not as ample.

This state of things bears happy fruits for the proletarian; an increased wage arouses his zeal: thanks to that wage, an inclination toward foresight and order is manifest in more than one manufacturing town; cleanliness of dress, abundance and diversity of food exercise the most fortunate influence on health. But while pointing out this progress, we should also note with regret that the independence, which is the result of a freedom the worker does not always know how to use, combined with the excessive investigation of which he is the object, cause those least advanced in civilization, perhaps more than in any other age, to offer the appearance of a destitution which understandably wounds the eyes. When work is not plentiful, the fear of losing his employment renders exact the most dissipated worker; formerly he almost always had earned more at the end of the year than today because the cabaret takes too significant a part of his time and of his money. . . .

England is in a state of disorder because she needed the work of the whole world: because she successively experiences shocks from Germany, from America, from China and because her thirst for external markets is so voracious that in order to satiate it she sets the world on fire, justifying this motto that she has adopted from necessity. *To sell or die.*

As was said by one of our philanthropists, "for the advantage of providing clothing at a low price to all people, England has reduced her workers to the deepest misery."

Thus the difference between the economic systems adopted by the two countries explains the difference in their industrial position.

Some people say, though in vain, that the scarcity of workers, their insubordination, the frequent debauches which are made possible by the ease or the high level of wages, this charge imposed upon the consumer, this serious blow against public order, are potentially valid criticisms of this economic system that we praise. So we should allow the entry of foreign products. This they say, will be a moderating factor in national industry; it will forestall fluctuations. Supporting the artificial and excessive cost of wages inevitably supports the inordinate growth of the working class and creates a deepseated poverty which today has perhaps not yet developed.

This line of argument neglects the fact that French consumption is abundantly provided for: that the price of things becomes lower every day; that the least crisis induces a glut and ruins the owner; that the wage of the worker has only increased from the share of the owner of the machinery; that the consumer pays nothing of this raise.

The introduction of foreign industry, which would flow in from all sides if the slightest access is opened to it, harms both the industrialist who will have more idle machines and the working class, whose less useful members would be in less demand. Fear of an uncertain evil requires us to be apprehensive lest the progressive state of our population could in the long run cause the dam to be broken which alone holds back the torrent of pauperism.

Apply, if you can, the true remedy to the true evil. Guided by wise instructions and perhaps restrained by wise laws, make the entrepreneurs of industry no longer foolishly cast aside the public welfare in creations which, attracting neither workers nor consumption, languish unproductive, and which inevitably call into the towns a population already too scarce in the countryside; by a revision of the laws of ownership, make savings, which every year seek use, available to agricultural enterprises for which the capital is always lacking, and thus give to the working of the land, so regular by its nature, a new and productive activity; all this would be correct. But for heavens sakes do not sacrifice your country to a principle; and do not, in order to feed the English and the Belgians, close our workshops, throw our population into the market-place, and starve our cities. Do not forget that the stoppage of work causes greater ravage than the cruellest war.

Remember that, in the present nature of things, work and wages made constant by the country's consumption is the lot of France. Frequent interruption of work and of wages as a result of shocks from outside, that is the lot of England.

Let no one say that these positions are optional, that France could become England or England France. With the influence of the economic system is joined the more potent benefits of the social organization and the customs which it has created, in order that dissimilarities between the two peoples are established which do not allow them to imitate one another.

In effect the extent of territory claims in France three-fourths of the population for the cultivation of the land: only the other quarter remains free for industry. The action of the laws ceaselessly divides the land and the capital and thus redistributes the products of work in an equal way.

The population is bound to the soil because many own it and because all can own it: work is united thus to ownership, and is not always and at every instant the only resource. This situation leads to conservation, to economy: hence almost everywhere needs are few in number: hence often families are limited according to their means. Desiring rather a tranquil happiness than an existence ceaselessly agitated for the satisfaction of new desires, the nation, taken as a whole, offers the appearance of mediocrity in fortune; for with a few exceptions, we know about the hideous misery of England only because books have been published about it.

In our France, one does not live to eat, one eats to live; and this way of looking at the utility of products subjects to fewer alternatives human labor, which is exerted only to satisfy real needs in some way and which cannot be appreciably diminished by the slightest circumstance.

The products of the land which agriculture does not consume are exchanged for those of industry, whose abundance is relative to the population which creates them and to that which consumes them and so can never command an excessive price which would long upset the natural order of things.

A good harvest and calm in the state, and the needs of the poor and those of the rich are both satisfied. If these conditions of prosperity come to be altered, industry will suffer without doubt; but as acute as it may be, this suffering will not be fatal. This is the reed which raises itself again after the storm, whose ravages will be lesser to the degree that its unusual causes will have been foreseen and calculated.

Exempt from relying too much on foreign consumption, having no workers unemployed on which employment ought to be imposed, moreover satisfying by work all its needs, would the country gain by ruining the population through forced labor? Will it be happier because everyone would be deprived those hours which education, the family, or nature need? This immolation of man by wealth, if it is admitted into a country, will by competition be imposed on all the others; thus the advantages which were promised by this barbarous creation of capital will vanish. Is that the social goal to be pursued? Is it not in general comfort, fruit of work; in health, in moralization, the fruit of a work wisely regulated!

So, when nature seems to have peopled France so that the machine could only be the auxiliary of man, legislation, whatever are the precepts of science, cannot permit the machines to lead man in their incessant action: it is up to him to command, to them to obey.

In England what an unhappy difference.

The land is not extensive enough, considering the population, and is forever shared between the clergy and several noble families. In order for the country to produce all the cereals necessary for the subsistence of the people, excessive duties are imposed on foreign grains, and the worker supplies the noble proprietors with luxury while paying double the value for his own bread.

There, no equality of sharing in inheritance; great fortunes are preserved intact from century to century: the capitalist, the proletarian, to whom the patrimony is forbidden, remain in eternal dependence upon manufacture, upon the reckless customs which it produces, and upon a wage as ill-assured as those who claim it are numerous.

THE WORKERS

The great debate in the history of the early factory labor force concerns material conditions.[1] Some historians have argued that conditions worsened in the first decades of industrialization, others that they improved. It is not easy to determine trends because factory workers were an entirely new group. Most of them were former peasants, often from the poorest, landless category. To add to the complexity, population increase often forced rural conditions to decline prior to industrialization, so even bad factory wages might seem satisfactory. It is, therefore, important to determine the group to whom workers should be compared. There is also frequent confusion over the types of workers being discussed. Most manufacturing workers still worked at home or in small shops. Their conditions usually did deteriorate. Luddism and other protests from traditional manufacturing labor were a product of this deterioration. But these trends may not have carried over into the factories, where the fantastic productivity of the new machines could allow some slight margin for improved wages even granting the manufacturers' avidity for profits.

Many historians have approached the whole question of material conditions with an ideological bias, seeking to condemn capitalism by proving that living standards declined under its auspices, or to praise it by proving the reverse. Yet the question remains important.

1 T. S. Ashton, "A Revisionist View," in F. A. Hayek, ed., *Capitalism and the Historians* (Chicago, 1954). E. J. Hobsbawm, "The British Standard of Living," *The Economic History Review* (1957); E. P. Thompson, *The Making of the English Working Class* (New York, 1964).

If we are to know what industrialization meant in human terms, we must know what conditions the workers experienced. Conditions in the first decades may have shaped attitudes among workers that persisted long after material standards improved.

Conditions have often been defined in terms of workers' consumption—their food, clothing, housing, and, relatedly, their health. Conditions on the job, however, were probably more significant in defining working-class life, particularly since most workers spent over half their time in the factories. It has been persuasively argued that workers were troubled above all by the tensions factory life imposed on their family life and other values, not by strictly material conditions at all.[2] Yet our evidence on this point is often indirect, for contemporary observers, most of them from the middle class, focused primarily on material standards. They found these sufficiently shocking and could not easily penetrate the problems of psychological adjustment. So, for the first industrial decades, we must examine existing evidence for whatever indirect light it sheds on the question of overall adaptation.

The main problem is, of course, that workers very seldom left written records. Most students of material conditions rely on quantitative evidence above all, statistics on wages, prices, and mortality. These figures are not always reliable and, naturally, they do not tell us how workers perceived conditions. Factory workers protested only rarely in the early industrial decades in western and central Europe. They were not the principal supporters of the kinds of early industrial protest illustrated in the first section of this book. Rarely were they Luddites. Rarely did they form unions; everywhere artisans had a lead of many years in this endeavor. Rarely did they even strike coherently.[3] This could mean that they were contented, or it could mean that they were so confused and impoverished that lack of protest is really proof of their hardship. In either case, lack of protest deprives us of the most obvious way that largely illiterate lower classes "speak" to historians. So we must turn to outside observers for much of our view of the early working class. This raises obvious problems of reliability and bias.

The familiar sources on the early working class come from Britain. Evidence from France and Germany does not fully tally with the British picture. This may suggest that the British sources judge conditions by different criteria from those used on the continent, in which

2 Neil Smelser, *Social Change in the Industrial Revolution: An Application of Theory to the Lancashire Cotton Industry, 1770–1840* (London, 1960).

3 For Germany, see Theodore Hamerow, *Restoration, Revolution, Reaction: Economics and Politics in Germany, 1815–1871;* for France, Peter N. Stearns, "Patterns of Industrial Strike Activity during the July Monarchy," *American Historical Review* (1965), pp. 371–94.

case the question is which set of criteria is more accurate. It is also true that we have a bit more evidence from workers themselves in Britain, thanks to parliamentary investigations of conditions, whereas on the continent outside observers must be used more often. But it is likely that early industrialization for factory labor was harsher in Britain than on the continent. This was due in part to the special difficulties the British inevitably faced as the first industrializers, but we must also ask if human factors, particularly the attitudes of entrepreneurs and government officials, were involved.

Without question conditions on the continent as well as in Britain were appallingly bad—by modern standards, that is. These standards obviously can obscure historical reality. The crucial issue is how workers regarded their own lot and how they got through their lives. Small material improvements, even when seemingly counterbalanced by deterioration in other aspects of life, may have made a great difference to them. They were exposed, unprepared, to a very unfamiliar way of life. But it remains difficult to assess the extent of the shock.

Later in the nineteenth century, sources on working-class life become more abundant. It is possible to discuss the quality of factory life beyond material conditions alone and to gain some insight into the overall outlook of workers. German sources are particularly rich. They reflect a still rather recent industrialization; many German workers were new to factory life even in 1900. They may reflect some peculiarly German longings and introspection.

Though workers in the later nineteenth century were speaking out, it is still not easy to interpret their voice. The problem is that the workers who wrote about their views were atypical. Many of them were convinced socialists, and this included, of course, that minority of socialist leaders with working-class backgrounds. All, by the very fact they wrote extensively, were unusually well educated, though often self-educated. Their situation was unusual in their class. They read widely. In contrast, most workers did not read regularly at all and those who did avoided writings on social problems in favor of diverting novels. But the opinions of the educated workers, though phrased as few workers could have managed, may not be as unrepresentative as their intellectual pretensions suggest. We can even admit that they were unusually sensitive and maintain that the grievances to which they were sensitive were widely felt. But we cannot stop with the articulate workers, however important their views. We must have other evidence. Outside observers can still be used. Their biases must be dealt with, along with the possibility that they asked the wrong questions or received incomplete answers from suspicious workers. For these later industrial decades, the protest of factory workers provides yet another test. The interpretation of industrial protest becomes intertwined with broader questions about the nature and extent of workers' adaptation to industrial life.

Without doubt, for early and later industrialization, the reactions of workers varied widely. Some workers could not accommodate themselves and suffered deep despair. Others adapted fairly readily. Many fell in between. As with the middle class, conventional class labels have concealed great diversity. For workers, too, we must seek explanations for differing outlooks. But the similarity between the two groups ends there. The situation of workers, their lack of property ownership, and generally dependent situation, forced different kinds of adaptations and a different kind of despair. The diverse but distinctive set of attitudes they developed in their early contact with industrialization has persisted in many ways to the present day.

SADLER COMMISSION, *EVIDENCE*

Michael Thomas Sadler was a Tory philanthropist and member of Parliament. He took the lead in fighting for a Ten-Hours Bill to protect all children working in factories, and, in 1832, he chaired the Parliamentary Committee to investigate the actual conditions of factory children. Testimony before the commission is an almost unique source for the first decades of industrialization, because workers were able to speak about themselves. They describe more than the conditions of children; they touch on material conditions more generally. Most important, they give some evidence of outlook, toward family life, factory work, religion, and, even in one instance, toward capitalism. Intermingled testimony from members of the middle class invites comparison with the workers' views. Their sympathy may be surprising, but it is representative of the views of many members of the middle class. It could among other things appeal to more general antipathy toward the world of industry.

Only a bit of the testimony from workers and others bears directly on the question of improving or deteriorating conditions. Again, we must read between the lines to determine whether the conditions described, horrible as they are, were new and if they were recognized as new. Some witnesses complicate the situation by claiming mechanization improved the lot of some types of workers while worsening the lot of others; yet this is probably correct. Witnesses were encouraged to make comparisons with agriculture, and this, of course, may advance our understanding. But the comparisons must be interpreted with caution. There was a pervasive idealization of agriculture in the early industrial decades, particularly, but not exclusively, in the middle and upper classes. Agricultural misery was virtually ignored. Freely-made statements on the superiority of education in agricultural districts were arrant nonsense. Even this unusually direct evidence on working-class life raises complications.

The Testimony

William Cooper, called in; and examined.

1. What is your business?—I follow the cloth-dressing at present.

2. What is your age?—I was eight-and-twenty last Feb.

3. When did you first begin to work in mills or factories?—When I was about 10 years of age.

4. With whom did you first work?—At Mr. Benyon's flax mills, in Meadowlane, Leeds.

5. What were your usual hours of working?—We began at five, and gave over at nine; at five o'clock in the morning.

6. And you gave over at nine o'clock?—At nine at night.

7. At what distance might you have lived from the mill?—About a mile and a half.

8. At what time had you to get up in the morning to attend to your labour?—I had to be upon soon after four o'clock.

10. What intermissions had you for meals?—When we began at five in the morning, we went on until noon, and then we had 40 minutes for dinner.

11. Had you no time for breakfast?—No, we got it as we could, while we were working.

12. Had you any time for an afternoon refreshment, or what is called in Yorkshire "your drinking?"—No; when we began at noon, we went on till night; there was only one stoppage, the 40 minutes for dinner. . . .

21. Did you ever work even later than the time you have mentioned? —I cannot say that I worked later there: I had a sister who worked up stairs, and she worked till 11 at night, . . .

22. At what time in the morning did she begin to work.—At the same time as myself. . . .

28. To keep you at your work for such a length of time, and especially towards the termination of such a day's labour as that, what means were taken to keep you awake and attentive?—They strapped us at times, when we were not quite ready to be doffing the frame when it was full.

29. Were you frequently strapped?—At times we were frequently strapped. . . .

From *British Sessional Papers* 1831–32, House of Commons Vol. XV, pp. 5, 6, 17–19, 50, 52, 72, 87, 105, 129–30, 192, 208–9, 389–401, 483–84, 488.

34. Were any of the female children strapped?—Yes; they were strapped in the same way as the lesser boys.

35. What were your wages at 10 years old at Mr. Benyon's?—I think it was 4 s. a week. . . .

48. When your hours were so long, you had not any time to attend a day-school?—We had no time to go to a day-school, only to a Sunday-school; and then with working such long hours we wanted to have a bit of rest, so that I slept till the afteroon, sometimes till dinner, and sometimes after.

49. Did you attend a place of worship?—I should have gone to a place of worship many times, but I was in the habit of falling asleep, and that kept me away; I did not like to go for fear of being asleep.

50. Do you mean that you could not prevent yourself from falling asleep, in consequence of the fatigue of the preceding week?—Yes . . .

Mr. Abraham Whitehead

431. What is your business?—A clothier.

432. Where do you reside?—At Scholes, near Holmfirth.

433. Is not that in the centre of very considerable woolen mills? Yes, for a space of three or four miles; I live nearly in the centre of thirty or forty woollen mills. . . .

436. Are children and young persons of both sexes employed in these mills?—Yes.

437. At how early an age are children employed?—The youngest age at which children are employed is never under five, but some are employed between five and six in woollen mills at piecing.

438. How early have you observed these young children going to their work, speaking for the present in the summer time?—In the summer time I have frequently seen them going to work between five and six in the morning, and I know the general practice is for them to go as early to all the mills. . . .

439. How late in the evening have you seen them at work, or remarked them returning to their homes?—I have seen them at work in the summer season between nine and ten in the evening; they continue to work as long as they can see, and they can see to work in these mills as long as you could see to read. . . .

441. You say that on your own personal knowledge?—I live near to parents who have been sending their children to mills for a great number of years, and I know positively that these children are every morning in the winter seasons called out of bed between five and six, and in some instances between four and five.

442. Your business as a clothier has often led you into these mills? —Frequently; . . .

460. What has been the treatment which you have observed that these children have received at the mills, to keep them attentive for so many hours at such early ages?—They are generally cruelly treated; so cruelly treated, that they dare not hardly for their lives be too late at their work in a morning. . . . My heart has been ready to bleed for them when I have seen them so fatigued, for they appear in such a state of apathy and insensibility as really not to know whether they are doing their work or not; . . .

461. Do they frequently fall into errors and mistakes in piecing when thus fatigued?—Yes; the errors they make when thus fatigued are, that instead of placing the cording in this way [describing it], they are apt to place them obliquely, and that causes a flying, which makes bad yarn; and when the billy-spinner sees that, he takes his strap or the billy-roller, and says, 'Damn thee, close it-little devil, close it,' and they smite the child with the strap or the billy-roller. . . .

510. You say that the morals of the children are very bad when confined in these mills; what do you consider to be the situation of children who have nothing to do, and are running about such towns as Leeds, with no employment to keep them out of mischief?—Children that are not employed in mills are generally more moral and better behaved than children who are employed in mills.

511. Those in perfect idleness are better behaved than those that are employed?—That is not a common thing; they either employ them in some kind of business at home, or send them to school.

512. Are there no day-schools to which these factory children go?—They have no opportunity of going to school when they are thus employed at the mill.

513. Do not they go to the Sunday-schools?—I do not know; . . .

William Kershaw

1134. What age are you?—Forty-two, . . .

1135. What is your business?—A cloth and operative manufacturer.

1136. Where do you reside at present?—Gomersal.

1137. Are you employed at present?—I have a place, but there is nothing to do . . .

1181. Do you conceive that, circumstanced as you are, you have no alternative but to subject your children to this labour, though it is extremely distressing to your feelings?—Yes; I can that from the very ground of my heart, that it is; I can positively state that my wife and I have been weeks and have had nothing but what the girls have brought in from the mill.

1182. Would you prefer your children to have fewer hours of labour than those which are imposed upon them in what are called brisk

times, than to have better wages and to be thus over-laboured?—I
would; I would submit to almost anything to get the hours of labour
restricted. . . .

1183. Supposing the labour of those children were reduced to ten
hours a day, exclusive of refreshments and necessary intervals, would
there be then some little opportunity left to teach them domestic
duties, and to give them some degree of mental and moral improvement?—Yes, there would.

1184. Would they be able to attend a Sunday-school with advantage?—They would be benefited by learning domestic duties, and
they would be far better qualified to attend to the instructions of the
Sunday-school.

1185. As you are a Sunday-school teacher, will you state your experience respecting the attention and appearance of those children
that are thus kept at long hours of labour?—You see them almost regularly asleep, both in church or chapel and in the school; any person
that goes into the school may at once discern, by looking round, the
difference between the week-day scholars and those who are continually
working long hours at a mill. . . .

William Swithenbank

1777. What is your business?—A cloth-dresser.

1778. Where do you reside?—Park-lane, Leeds.

1779. What age are you?—Thirty-nine.

1780. At what age did you first begin to work in a factory?—Just
turned 8 years of age . . .

1851. Will you state to the Committee whether you had any opportunity of going to a day or a night school?—I had no opportunity.

1852. You mean because of the labour, which is a quite sufficient
reason. But did you go to a Sunday-school, so as to learn the rudiments
of a decent education?—Sometimes I went to a Sunday-school, but being so close confined, we did not like to go; . . .

1853. Can you read and write?—I can do neither. . . .

Mr. John Goodyear

2289. Where do you reside?—At Huddersfield . . .

2443. You have already stated the number of hours that persons are
employed in mills; supposing, then, that there were evening-schools,
is it possible that the children should avail themselves of the opportunity of going to such schools without, at all events, increasing their
sufferings by still lengthening their confinement, and without almost
any chance of their deriving mental or moral improvement from
instruction, when so over-laboured and fatigued?—It would be almost

morally impossible for them to attend evening-schools after working such long hours. . . .

2445. You have stated that some of these children cannot read, and that few can write, all their chance of learning being now confined to their attendance at Sunday-schools?—It is chiefly confined to that. . . .

2447. Perhaps you happen to know, that, from conscientious scruples, the managers of Sunday-schools rarely allow writing to be taught on the Sunday to any of those who wish to derive instruction from these schools, and who have no other means of obtaining it?—At no Sunday-schools with which I am acquainted do they teach writing at all . . .

Benjamin Fox

2720. Where do you live? At Dewsbury. . . .

2722. Have you worked in factories?—Yes, about forty-two years.

2723. You went then at about 14 years of age?—Yes. . . .

2740. What effect has your working in mills had upon you?—It has had a great effect; I can scarcely walk; my knee is crooked and weak.

2742. Do you attribute that to the long hours of labour at the mill? —Yes. . . .

2764. What has been your observation of the conduct of other children who have been little under the instruction of their parents, who have been labouring in the mills; how have they behaved in point of morality and decency?—They talk and act indecently when they have been a length of time in; they encourage one another when they have been any matter of time in the mills; they are impudent enough at last, a deal of them, although when they first come they behave very well.

2765. Are they immodest in their talk?—Yes.

2766. And immoral in their conduct?—Yes, immoral in their conduct; going to the factories is like going to a school, but it is to learn everything that is bad. . . .

2848. Do you think that the abridgment of the hours of labour would be a great benefit to the working classes?—Yes, I do think so.

2849. And that they would be content with less wages, rather than have no mitigation of this labour?—Yes, I am sure I would, for my part.

2850. Are they very anxious for this opportunity?—I have heard my children say, "I would rather go to bed without supper, than I would work till 9 o'clock at night." My little child has cried for his supper, and I have given it to him, and I have found it in his bed in the morning; he was so tired he could not eat it. . . .

2887. From the whole of your experience, you are convinced that the mills and factories, unregulated as they are, are productive of very great mischief to the manufacturing population, and especially to their children?—Yes, they are seminaries of vice. . . .

Mr. Benjamin Bradshaw—near Leeds, a cloth-dresser.

3436. Do you know any other instances of the oppression that is going on in consequence of this system?—Yes, I do; I have been acquainted with it during the principal part of my life. For nearly twenty years I have lived in the factories, ever since the machinery for dressing cloth was introduced; and I have frequently been an eye-witness to the unhappy circumstances under which children have to labour, through the factory system, particularly as it has been lately carried on. . . .

3490. You say that the labour has become more severe of late years than it was formerly?—Yes.

3491. Have there not been great improvements in the machinery?—There have been improvements in the machinery, no doubt, and great improvements.

3492. Is the tendency of improvements in machinery to lessen or increase manual labour?—It is to lessen the manual labour of men, and to increase infant labour.

3493. Are children therefore often at work when their parents are out of work?—I know it to my sorrow. . . .

3509. You state that some years ago they [the factories] were not so bad as they are now?—They were not, because the children were not kept so long at their work.

3510. You stated that their condition was much worse than that of labourers in the agricultural districts, did you not?—I said that the morals of those children were worse than those of children in the agricultural disticts.

3511. How do you know that fact—Because I have travelled much among the agricultural districts. I have travelled in different parts of the north of Yorkshire. . . .

3513. Have you been employed as a preacher for some religious connexion?—Yes, for the Primitive Methodists. . . .

3517. Do you think that the children of the agricultural poor are generally better educated than those who are employed in manufactories?—I do. . . .

Gillett Sharpe—[overseer of poor at Keighley]

5475. Do you believe that the cases of deformity in that town are exceedingly numerous?—Yes; I have had an opportunity of visiting other towns, and it is my opinion, according to my observation, that there is not another town worse, in proportion to the size of it.

5476. Have you always understood that that deformity is attributable to the too early and excessive labour of the children in the factories of that place?—Yes; I consider that labour from too early an age, and long standing, have been the causes of it.

5477. Have you made any observation as to the moral effects of those long hours of labour?—Yes, I have.

5478. What have they been?—I have made these observations; that by being confined so long in the factory, with so little time for relaxation or instruction, they have been prevented from attaining that knowledge which children ought to have in the morning of life, or from learning what is necessary; for the time they are employed in the week is so great that they have no opportunity except on the Sabbath-day, of being instructed; and I have also remarked, that when they have come to school on the Sabbath-day, they have been so fatigued, or so dull, in consequence of the confinement, that it has been very hard work to make any impression upon them, or teach them. . . .

5481. Does it consist, with your observation, that children employed in mills and factories, in that town and neighbourhood, suffer in their health, and also in being deprived of the means of mental and moral improvement, by being so employed?—Yes, with regard to their health; before ever this question was, to my knowledge, agitated, I was in the habit of visiting Sabbath schools, along with others; and one thing struck me when visiting a village where the children did not work in mills; I recollect how healthy they looked, and clean, so different to what they are with us. . . .

Mr. John Hanson-Huddersfield—41

9037. Have you had considerable experience in the manufactures of the West Riding of Yorkshire?—I was brought up in a domestic manufactory in the woollen business. . . .

9066. Do you believe that there is greater distress prevalent amongst the manufacturing labourers, than amongst the agricultural labourers, thoughout the kingdom?—No, I cannot say that in respect to adults.

9067. On what grounds do you think there is an excess of hands dependent on manufactures, as compared with agriculture; does it arise from the different condition of the labourers employed in those two occupations?—I believe that a great many of the labourers in both departments are distressed; but I do not mean to say that it is a question which I can solve mathematically, or state the exact number. . . .

9068. Will you state the grounds of your opinion?—I consider, in the first place, that provisions are too dear for the manufacturing population to purchase them in sufficient quantity by the value of their labour; even those who are fully employed have not an adequate remuneration; and, as agriculture is the source of those articles for which they work, I say that they do not get a sufficient quantity for the labour which they perform, even those who are employed. . . .

10211. With respect to the residences of the agricultural and manufacturing labourers, how would you compare them?—I should say, that in general the residence of the agricultural labourer is incomparably more healthy and more comfortable than that of the manufacturing labourer. There are some cottages in the manufacturing districts which are indeed surprisingly clean and comfortable; but when I have inquired, I have generally found that the wife has not been brought up in a factory; in general the wife has come out of the agricultural districts, or has been brought up in the service. The comfort of the cottage much depends upon the capacity of the wife.

10212. The question did not refer to the internal arrangements, but to the actual state of the cottage itself; in which district are there better houses and more perfect residence, without reference to the conduct of the inmates at all?—As to the residences themselves, it is obvious that in those districts where stone and slate can be obtained, as is the case in many manufacturing districts, more substantial cottages can generally be built than where they consist of lath and plaster walls, or studded walls.

10213. Will you be so good as to inform the Committee what the actual state of things is?—I should say, upon the whole, that I think the agriculturist has quite as comfortable a residence, in respect of the substantiality of the building, as the manufacturer.

10214. In respect of the comparison between the agricultural and the manufacturing cottages, the questions have had, of course, reference to the lowest class of labourers in both pursuits; are not you aware that the cottages in the manufacturing districts of the lowest class of operatives are extremely wretched, and in all respects unfit for human habitations?—There is a great disadvantage in the manufacturing districts with respect to all the worst class of houses; under any circumstances a comfortable and capacious house in the manufacturing districts is far less comfortable than a house of meaner capacities in the agricultural districts, because of having generally no comfortable premises around, and also from having a grade to follow in the house; but there is, I have no hesitation in saying, in the neighbourhood where I live, a large class of operatives' houses of the most miserable description.

10215. Do not the lowest of the manufacturers often reside in cellars; so that in looking at the exterior of the manufacturer's cottage, you are perhaps looking at the cottage that contains many families? —Yes; I know several places in the township of Bowling, where there are dwellings very small indeed; and the cellar occupied by one family;

I have frequently visited, by night, the cottages of the operatives, for the purpose of baptizing a child that was expected to die, and have sometimes found five persons in one bed, three children lying at the feet, with their heads towards the feet of the bed, and their parents at the other end, with a little baby between them.

10216. With respect to fuel in the two cases, and the comfort which the families in the manufacturing and agricultural districts derive from artificial warmth, can you speak?—Undoubtedly in those districts where coals are cheap, very great comfort is derived in the inclement seasons of the year from obtaining artificial warmth; but on the whole, I have observed the cottage of the agricultural labourer to be exceedingly comfortable; although they do not obtain coals so cheap, they obtain a great quantity of wood, a sufficient quantity to answer the purpose. Even in that respect, I should think, on the whole, the manufacturing labourers has very little, if any, advantage over the agricultural; and when the other comforts of the cottage are considered in both cases, I should still say that the agriculturist has incomparably the most comfortable cottage. . . .

10251. With respect to the comparative education of the agricultural and manufacturing poor in the two districts with which you are acquainted, will you be so kind as to compare the children of 15 years of age in the two cases as to their proficiency in reading and writing? —I have no hesitation in replying to that question, by saying that the comparison is incomparably in favour of the agricultural population. . . .

10252. In the agricultural district with which you were acquainted in Essex, what means of instruction were afforded to the poor?—In Essex the parish with which I was most conversant contained, I think I state, somewhere about 400 inhabitants; and the children of the poor, probably up to 8 or 9 years of age, were accustomed to receive instruction in small schools held in cottages . . . ; besides that, their parents often instructed them after the labours of the day were over; and on the Sunday very particular attention was paid to their religious instruction in Sunday-schools.

JAMES KAY

Philanthropic doctors took the lead in directly investigating the conditions of the poor. The following brief passage is typical of what they reported in Britain. James Kay had his practice in Manchester. His report, and the reports of others, contributed to the first factory and sanitary reforms in Britain. Kay noted that conditions in Manchester were unusually bad, so again we have the problem of determining what was typical. Kay gives us a great deal of information, but it is hard to use it to determine whether the new workers had bettered their lot, or the reverse, or how they themselves judged their foul conditions. Kay was, of course, an outside observer. He may have been unduly shocked by the conditions he studied, thus revealing as much about the sensibility of middle-class reformers as about workers' life. If workers were as dulled as he suggests, traditional peasant resignation as well as the shock of transplantation to the horrible conditions of a factory city may have played a role. The image Kay paints of the dissipated, supine worker was a common one. Kay differed from liberal industrialists in placing the blame on conditions rather than on the worker. But again the problem of class bias, in this case quite unwitting, must be raised. Kay gives us part of the picture, and for some workers probably the whole picture; but the implication of uniform demoralization probably plays down some of the more positive adaptation that was also possible. Many workers in Manchester and elsewhere, for example, took increasing care of their appearance and dressed rather fashionably compared to traditional lower-class standards, on Sundays. A minor pleasure, perhaps, but not a sign of complete demoralization. Kay, and many historians since, have seen early factory workers as helpless pawns. However badly one thinks of industrial capitalism, it is doubtful that this is entirely fair to the workers, whose life was indeed highly circumscribed but who were not without some ability to react.

Kay's Report

The township of Manchester chiefly consists of dense masses of houses, inhabited by the population engaged in the great manufactories of the cotton trade. Some of the central divisions are occupied by warehouses and shops, and a few streets by the dwellings of the more wealthy inhabitants; but the opulent merchants chiefly reside in the country, and even the superior servants of their establishments inhabit the suburban townships.

Manchester, properly so called, is chiefly inhabited by shopkeepers and the labouring classes. Those districts where the poor dwell are of very recent origin. The rapid growth of the cotton manufacture has attracted hither operatives from every part of the kingdom, and Ireland has poured forth the most destitute of her hordes to supply the constantly increasing demand for labour.

This immigration has been, in one important respect, a serious evil. The Irish have taught the labouring classes of this country a pernicious lesson. The system of cottier farming, the demoralization and barbarism of the people, and the general use of the potato as the chief article of food, have encouraged the population in Ireland more rapidly

From *James Phillips Kay* (later *Sir James Kay-Shuttleworth*), **The Moral and Physical Condition of the Working Classes Employed in Cotton Manufacture in Manchester** (*Manchester, 1832*), *pp. 6–11.*

than the *available* means of subsistence have been increased. Debased alike by ignorance and pauperism, they have discovered, with the savage, what is the minimum of the means of life, upon which existence may be prolonged. They have taught this fatal secret to the population of this country . . .

When this example is considered in connexion with the unremitted labour of the whole population engaged in the various branches of the cotton manufacture, our wonder will be less excited by their fatal demoralization. Prolonged and exhausting labour, continued from day to day, and from year to year, is not calculated to develop the intellectual or moral faculties of man. The dull routine of a ceaseless drudgery, in which the same mechanical process is incessantly repeated, resembles the torment of Sisyphus—the toil, like the rock, recoils perpetually on the wearied operative. The mind gathers neither stores nor strength from the constant extension and retraction of the same muscles. The intellect slumbers in supine inertness; but the grosser parts of our nature attain a rank development. To condemn man to such severity of toil is, in some measure, to cultivate in him the habits of an animal . . .

Having been subjected to the prolonged labour of an animal—his physical energy wasted—his mind in supine inaction—the artizan has neither moral dignity nor intellectual nor organic strength to resist the seductions of appetite. His wife and children, too frequently subjected to the same process, are unable to cheer his remaining moments of leisure. Domestic economy is neglected, domestic comforts are unknown. A meal of the coarsest food is prepared with heedless haste and devoured with equal precipitation. Home has no other relation to him than that of shelter—few pleasures are there—it chiefly presents to him a scene of physical exhaustion, from which he is glad to escape. Himself impotent of all the distinguishing aims of his species, he sinks into sensual sloth, or revels in more degrading licentiousness. His house is ill furnished, uncleanly, often ill ventilated, perhaps damp; his food, from want of forethought and domestic economy, is meagre and innutritious; he is debilitated and hypochondriacal, and falls the victim of dissipation . . .

LOUIS RENÉ VILLERMÉ

Villermé was a Parisian doctor who conducted an extensive investigation of textile workers under the aegis of the *Académie des sciences morales et politiques*. His report had an impact on the opinion of the upper classes and contributed to the passage of a child labor law in 1841. Villermé was a careful and sympathetic observer. His picture certainly differs from that drawn by comparable observers in Britain. Conditions in France were less harsh. France industrialized more slowly than Britain; French cities grew far less rapidly. City governments were also traditionally more active in functions such as housing inspection and street paving. And French manufacturers may not have been quite so zealous in exploiting their labor as their English counterparts; for example, they were slightly less eager to use and abuse child workers. Even slight differences of this sort could significantly affect workers' situations. Yet, assuming some difference in average conditions, we must ask again whether the British observers were not unduly overwhelmed by the misery they saw, and whether they ignored some types of workers, better paid but not necessarily in the top group of skilled labor, whose standard of living resembled that which Villermé portrays.

For, as Villermé makes clear for just three cities in northern France, all located close to each other and engaged in the same basic industry, diversity was the keynote in early industrial life. Not only individual strength and skill but also the type of industry and the type of city the worker was involved in created huge differences within the labor force. The latter factors remind us also of the role of chance in workers' lives; few factory workers were aware of variations among types of cities, yet the city they happened to move to—usually because it was closest—would be a powerful factor in their existence.

Even as he notes many variations in workers' lives and portrays stark misery, Villermé may be accused of undue optimism, a constant temptation for middle-class people who believed in progress. Note, in comparison to the Sadler commission evidence, that he deals largely with workers as consumers. He is not unaware of factory conditions, particularly the long hours of work. Again, many historians have followed his lead, even some who try to show that conditions deteriorated massively, and who debate formal standard of living alone. Villermé usefully suggests that for some workers improved standard of living might help compensate for unpleasant labor. Presumably, in the long run, worker adaptation to industrial life involved accepting dull or unpleasant work situations in return for greater material rewards. But whether this operated for workers exposed to the first shock of factory work is questionable, particularly when the improvements in living standards were slight. In any case, Villermé's picture of workers' life is not sufficiently complete, for it does not integrate an evaluation of conditions at work into the final interpretation of trends. Note, on the other hand, that Villermé does try to incorporate a judgment of workers' morals into the discussion of whether conditions had improved or deteriorated.

Villermé's approach raises many questions. Again we have a bourgeois account; we can easily identify some of the prejudices that result in the tendency to seek simple explanations for conditions and the readiness to point to workers' moral deficiencies. Yet if we cannot use a careful observer like Villermé as a source for workers' habits and attitudes, we must virtually renounce knowing anything about them at all for this period. We must use him with care, of course, particularly with regard to aspects of life he did not sufficiently study; but his facts seem largely accurate and his own interpretations should not be ignored just because they are "middle-class."

The three manufacturing cities described in these passages were quite different though not far apart. Lille was an old city with much non-mechanical industry, but with a new leaven of modern cotton production. Tourcoing and especially Roubaix had grown up more recently, and their industry depended more completely on new machines. The newer cities were more dynamic than Lille and less beset by problems of archaic methods and the traditional congestion of an old, crowded city.

Villermé's Report

The city of Lille in 1828 numbered 22,281 poor, either aided by charity or qualified to be aided, of the total of 163,453 in the department, and 22,204 of the 171,621 departmental poor in 1833. But in the months of November and December, 1835, when I was in that city, the number had probably increased; it had definitely increased twenty months later, in 1837, when I was there for the second time. As the population of Lille, which does not seem to have grown for several years, is evaluated at approximately 72,000 people, this would mean that 4/13 of the population was indigent!!

It is not surprising, then, that I have seen great misery in Lille. . . . Without education, without foresight, brutalized by debauchery, enervated by manufacturing work, crowded into obscure, damp cellars or into attics where they are exposed to all the rigors of the weather, the workers reach adulthood without having saved anything, and without being able completely to support their families, which are almost always quite large. They are such drunkards that to satisfy their desire for strong liquor fathers and often mothers pawn their furniture and sell the clothing that public or private charity has given them to cover their nakedness. Many are victims of hereditary infirmities. In 1828, there were as many as 3687 housed in narrow, low, underground cellars, deprived of air and light, disgustingly dirty, in which parents, children, and sometimes adult brothers and sisters slept on the same pallet.

This frightful picture may seem exaggerated. The facts which I have observed myself in 1835, a rather prosperous period, prove that it must be believed.

The area of Lille where there are relatively more poor and badly-behaved workers is that of Etaques street, and the alleys and the narrow, winding, but deep courtyards which run into it. It includes a space 200 meters long and 120 meters wide. These measurements are

From L. R. Villermé, Tableau de l'état physique et moral des ouvriers employés dans les manufactures de coton, de laine, et de soie *(Paris, 1840), Vol. I. pp. 78–115, Vol. II, 342–54. Translated by the editor.*

accurate, according to the city map on which I made them. The area in question then is approximately 24,000 square meters in size. A census done in 1826, the detailed results of which have been given to me, proves that the population of the area was then almost 3000 individuals. That means that on the average, each person had eight square meters of space, almost as little as in the two sections of Paris where the people have the least space.

But in these sections of the capitol, the houses are at least four storeys high, and ordinarily five, and sometimes six or even seven; whereas in Lille, in Etaques street and the adjacent courtyards, they are three or four storeys at most, even counting the cellars beneath the houses, which can scarcely be seen from the outside. As a result, the inhabitants there are even closer to each other, even more piled up, if one may use this expression, than in the two most populous sections of Paris.

I have just mentioned Etaques street and its courtyards; here is how the workers are housed there.

The poorest live in the cellars and attics. These cellars have no communication with the inside of the houses; they open onto the streets or courtyards, and one climbs down to them by a stairway, which is very often both the door and the window. They are walled in stone or brick, with a vaulted ceiling and a paved or tiled floor, and all have a fireplace, which proves they were built to serve as housing. Usually their height is six or six and a half feet at the middle of the vault, and they are 10 to 14 or 15 feet wide.

In these dark and sad dwellings a great number of workers eat, sleep, and even work. Dawn comes an hour later for them than for the others, and night comes an hour earlier.

Their ordinary furniture, along with the objects of their trade, is composed of a sort of cabinet or a board on which to place food, a stove, a few pottery dishes, a little table, two or three bad chairs, and a dirty pallet which includes only a straw mattress and some ragged covers. I do not want to add anything to these hideous details, which reveal at a first glance the profound misery of the unfortunate residents; but I should say that in many of the beds of which I have just spoken, I have seen individuals of both sexes and very different ages sleep together, generally horribly dirty and without any nightshirt. Father, mother, old people, children, adults press and crowd together. I stop here . . . the reader will complete the picture, but I warn him that to be accurate his imagination should not recoil before any of the disgusting mysteries which are accomplished on these filthy beds, amid darkness and drunkenness.

And the cellars are not the worst lodgings; they are not nearly as damp as supposed. Every time the oven is lighted in the fireplace, a current of air is created which dries and cleans them. The worst housing is the attics, where nothing prevents the extremes of temperature; for the inhabitants, as miserable as those of the cellars, lack the means to maintain a fire to warm themselves during the winter.

This picture still lacks one feature; the bars of Etaques street and the neighboring streets, observed on Sunday and Monday evenings in 1835, during the cold season.

I wanted to enter these places, where I saw through the doors and windows, through a cloud of tobacco smoke, crowds of the inhabitants of this hideous section; but it was obvious that in spite of my precaution of dressing in such a way as to appear less suspicious to them, my appearance in their midst would have aroused their surprise and especially their distrust. A great number were standing, for want of any place to sit down, and there were many women among them. All drank a detestable grain brandy, or beer. Wine is too highly priced for them to afford. I settled for following all these people in the street, where many stopped at grocery stores to drink some brandy, before entering the bar, and where I heard even children use the most obscene words. I can vow that I have never see so much dirt, misery, and vice, under a more hideous, a more revolting appearance. And these excesses of evil are not displayed by a few hundred individuals alone; in varing degrees, they are part of the behavior of the great majority of the 3000 who inhabit the Etaques street area and a still greater number of others who are scattered in little groups on many streets and perhaps sixty courtyards more or less comparable to those of which I have spoken. . . .

But if there are in Lille a very considerable number of workers such as those of Etaques street and the neighboring courtyards, a greater number still are far from displaying the profound misery and degradation which I have just described only too accurately, although the latter group does not always earn the best wages. But they are clean, economical, and especially sober; they know how to house, clothe, and feed themselves better, in a word to provide more completely for their needs, with the same daily pay. It would be superfluous to speak of these at greater length here. I will add however that many try, in their choice of housing, to live near other well-behaved workers and therefore inhabit the Saint-André section, just as the miserable people whom we were just discussing inhabit especially the Saint-Sauveur section and the Etaques street area.

Finally, in Lille, the mixture of the sexes is the same as in all manufacturing shops; they are separated only when the nature of the operations does not permit their combination.

The long duration of daily work is standard also; with almost all the manufacturers, the day is 15 hours long, of which 13 hours are devoted to real work.

The most numerous workers in Lille belong to the cotton industry, and after them come the thread-twisters, the workers who make sewing thread out of ordinary linen thread. After these come the women who make lace.

All these workers have no support other than their labor and they almost all reside in the city. The workers who come to the city every morning live in the nearest suburbs and hamlets; they belong especially to other branches of manufacturing.

The class of thread-twisters is very remarkable for its cleanliness, its good habits and ordinarily good behavior, especially in comparison with the cotton workers. They receive very low wages, but their sobriety and economy are such that they are usually less miserable than workers of other industries who earn more. . . .

Assuming a family in which the father, the mother, and a ten to twelve year old child receive average salaries, the family could, if the illness of one of its members or a lack of work did not decrease its earnings, bring in the following annual revenue:

The father, paid 1.50 francs per day .... 450 francs
The mother, paid 1.00 francs per day .... 300 francs
a child, paid .55 francs per day .... 165 francs
    in all .... 915 francs

Let us now see what its expenses are.

If it occupies just a room, some kind of attic, cellar, or tiny apartment, its rent, which is payable by the month or by the week, ranges ordinarily in the city from 40 to 80 francs a year. Let us take the average, 60 francs.

Its food: 255 francs a year (.80 a day) for the man, 219 (.60 a day) for the woman, 164 (.45 a day) for the child: a total of 638 francs. But as there are very commonly several younger children, let us say 738 francs a year. So that food and lodging comes to 798 francs. As a result, there remains a sum of 117 francs for the upkeep of furniture, linen, clothing, and for laundry, heat, light, work tools, etc.

Certainly, this is not enough. If an illness, unemployment, or a bit of drunkenness intervene, this family is in great misery. . . .

The usual food of the poorest workers of Lille is composed of potatoes, some vegetables, thin soups, a bit of butter, cheese, buttermilk or pork goods. They eat ordinarily only one of these foods with their bread. Water is their only drink during meals, but many men and even women go each day to the bar to drink beer or, more often, a little glass of their detestable grain brandy. More highly paid workers eat better; they often have a casserole or stew which includes meat, and in the morning have a cup of coffee, usually mixed with chicory, taken with milk and without much sugar. Finally, there are in Lille as in the other manufacturing cities some cheap restaurants in which many workers eat one meal a day. They bring their own bread, and have soup and some other dish there. Among these workers are many whose families live in the city; but the wife, who works in the shops just like her husband, does not have time to cook.

The workers of Lille are very often deprived of a bare subsistence; but they do not complain much about their situation, and almost never riot. In this respect only, they resemble the unfortunate workers of Alsace. Besides, gentleness, patience, and resignation seem to be basic to the Flemish character.

These laborers often have a tubercular condition; this is particularly true of the children, who are discolored and thin. Doctors in the city tell me that various lung diseases kill many more cotton and linen workers than any other inhabitants.

Lille is the city in France where, relatively, the greatest number of workers are enrolled in mutual aid groups, founded to furnish any members who fall ill with compensation proportionate to their regular salary, which they cannot then earn. M. de Villeneuve-Bargemont in 1828 counted no less than 113 such associations, composed of 7667 people; in 1836 there were 106, with 7329 members. But the bad organization of these groups, otherwise so praiseworthy, prevents them from doing any good. In effect, the place where they meet once a month to transact their business is always a bar; and at the end of each year, whatever remains in the bank beyond a certain sum is divided among the members and spent immediately on debauchery. . . .

This example, drawn from associations founded for a very moral purpose, shows that drunkenness is an integral part of the habits of Lille workers. I might add, for those who believe that this deplorable custom is due primarily, as some claim, to the great expansion of cotton production, that 33 years ago, well before this expansion, M. Dieudonné, prefect of the department of the Nord, noted in his statistics of this department that the immoderate use of strong liquors, particularly grain brandy, spread in a frightening way among the people of Lille. . . .

Here is a fact which by itself proves how deeply rooted drunkenness is among the people of Lille. In this city, the custom is to give a dose of theriac, called a sleeper, to children, to put them to sleep. I am told by pharmacists who sell these "sleepers" that the wives of workers buy them especially on Sundays, Mondays, and holidays, when they wish to leave their children at home and spend a long time in the bars.

I have just described the manufacturing workers of Lille as I saw them. I hasten to say that those of Roubaix, Tourcoing, and the rest of the department of the Nord, whose description follows, are much different. . . .

In order to avoid repetitions, I will mention first observations which apply equally to the two cities.

The working population is tending to increase in both cities, mainly by a slow but steady immigration of Belgians and others; but the employers complain of a lack of labor.

Weaving looms work for wool especially during the months of June, August, and September, and the rest of the time is for cotton.

Here as elsewhere the work day in the shops is, depending on the season, 14 to 15 hours, but most often 15, of which two or almost two are granted for meals and rest. Extra work is paid separately; piece workers usually labor for 14 to 15 hours.

A worker family is generally composed of five people, the father, the mother, and three children. It is almost always housed in healthy conditions, in rooms which are well-lighted, large enough, and fairly clean. Many of these families occupy an entire cottage. No one lives in cellars here, as in Lille, and all housing is rented by the year and paid for every trimester.

The weavers who reside in the villages and work at home usually have good habits; whereas workers in the big shops fling themselves into wild expenses and debaucheries which alter their health and ruin their future. Nevertheless, their difficulties are not nearly so great as those of Lille; nothing indicated the excessive misery, dirtiness, vice, and disgusting promiscuity which afflict so many Lille workers. People cite, in Roubaix and Tourcoing, as a particularly bad example of the evil influence of the big shops, the wool combers, who are now noted for their bad conduct, but who twelve or fifteen years ago when they worked at home and lived with their families, saved more than master spinners whose wages were twice as high.

Many workers of Tourcoing and Roubaix live there; but the majority come in each morning from neighboring villages and hamlets. They rarely live more than a couple of miles from their shops.

They are suitably dressed. I noted, early in the winter of 1835–36, that almost all the men wore good trousers of thick cloth, a vest of the same material (often over a shirt), wool socks, wooden shoes, and a cap—and everything was clean, without holes or tears. Women were no less well dressed. Finally, I saw almost no one among them working in bare feet in the spinning plants as is the case in Lille. . . .

Among these workers, everyone, no matter what their sex or age, has each morning one and often two cups of coffee (a mixture of coffee and chicory), with milk and with very little sugar. It is a general custom in the area. In addition, the poorest have thin soups, potatoes or other vegetables, and some milk goods; but bachelors who earn 1.50 to 3 francs, have meat with vegetables every day and drink beer. This diet includes butter and sometimes a bit of salt pork. . . .

A family composed of the father, the mother, and two young children spends 14 francs a week, or 728 francs a year, for food; it is suitably housed in Roubaix for 100 francs, and for less at Tourcoing.

This comes to 828 francs, to which the other expenses must be added.

But let us suppose that this family earns the average wage:

> The father—2.25 francs per day, or per year 675 francs.
> The mother—.90 francs per day, or per year 270 francs.
> In all—3.15 francs per day, or per year 945 francs.

And if a child begins to earn, .30 francs a day, or .90 francs a year, this makes the total 3.45 francs a day, or 1,035 a year.

As a result, this family is rather well off, if illness, accidents, or unemployment do not curtail its earnings, or if, on the other hand, bad conduct does not increase its expenses.

It is true that not all men earn 2.25 francs a day in ordinary times, but there are some who earn more. Many women receive more than 270 francs a year, and a great number of children earn more than 89 francs.

The workers of Roubaix, Tourcoing and the environs seem to marry young. Here as elsewhere, one of the causes of early marriage is the desire of young people to enjoy their whole salary, which they otherwise give almost entirely to their parents for the common needs of the family. By the age of 20 or 21, this desire is particularly great because this is the period of life when the salary reaches its highest point.

The state of health of the workers of Roubaix and Tourcoing seemed to me distinctly better than that of the workers of Lille. . . .

In sum, the manufacturing workers of Roubaix and Tourcoing live in much better conditions and are worth more than those of Lille. In every respect good habits, well-being, cleanliness, clothing, housing, food, health—they generally are much superior.

SUMMARY OF THE CONDITION OF WORKERS

I have now reached the end of this work. I have been careful, while writing it, to avoid all prejudice; my only goal was the truth. Insofar as possible, therefore, I have risen above all individual interests, those of the workers as well as those of the employers. This I shall continue to do in what I have left to say.

There are many factory workers whose earnings are so small that they scarcely suffice to obtain for them the bare minimum of subsistence. Are they today more miserable and relatively more numerous than in former times? Nothing indicates this. Even if we grant, as some people maintain, that the liberty of industry has produced all the good it would produce in France, and that the mutual competition among the workers forces their labor up to the ultimate limits of human strength, and reduces their salary to the lowest possible levels, would this mean that we should set a minimum wage and maximum hours of work for adults, and thus suppress the freedom of conditions between the entrepreneur and those he employs? Certainly, such a measure will never lead to the solution of the great problem which is posed. One can discourse on this subject, one can demand that the government prevent all unhappiness, just as one can demand that doctors cure all illness, but no improvement of the lot of the workers will result. Ordinarily it is harder to do good than people think.

Let us not forget that, except in times of crisis, the great majority of hard-working, economical, prudent workers can maintain themselves and their families, even if they cannot save. Unfortunately those whom drunkenness and other debaucheries ruin, or who are capable of living only on a day to day basis, are extremely numerous.

These latter seem to ignore that they are at the mercy of all the vicissitudes of commerce and manufacture, and that for them every day can be a day before loss of a job, and in consequence loss of bread. They seem to forget completely that the remedy for their poverty is in good behavior, in a persevering care never to spend all that they earn, and of course not to spend more. Let us repeat to them the belief of Mr. Charles Dunoyer: that nothing truly effective can be done for them except by themselves—by their efforts, their patient activity, their gradual savings, and their care in not increasing their burdens more rapidly than their fortune.

These are truths which must be tirelessly spread among manufacturing workers. They must know that the 8 billion francs estimated (on what basis I admit I do not know) to be the total yearly revenue of

France allow on the average only 240 francs per person; that anyone of them who works three hundred days a year for just 16 sous (3/4 of a franc) earns that much; that he triples this if he receives 48 sous (about 2-1/2 francs); and that agricultural workers, in general, earn far less than factory labor does.

In calculating the approximate average salary of workers, regardless of age or sex, we find that for workers in the cotton industry it perhaps equals, in spinning and weaving, about one and a third times the average earnings of a Frenchman (and it is much more in calico manufacturing), and for workers in the wool industry, it comes to twice these same earnings. But if we consider only adults, again regardless of sex, the ratio is double in cotton spinning and weaving, and almost triple in wool manufacturing. As to silk workers, I lack all the information needed to solve the problem; but in France they almost all earn more than 240 francs a year, especially at Lyons, where their earnings commonly reach a level two to four and a half or even almost five times that sum.

It is very true that an average share in the revenue of France, allocated to each inhabitant whatever his age, could never suffice for the upkeep of an adult male in the big cities, such as Lyons, Rouen, Lille, etc. But all adult male workers receive in these cities a much higher salary, which would suffice for all their needs, if they behaved better and if, on the other hand, there was never an industrial crisis. As to young children employed in such great number in the factories everywhere in our country, the average revenue of 240 francs is much higher than is necessary for their upkeep.

It is also good for workers to know that their condition is today better than it has ever been; the documents from which one can deduce a knowledge of the lot of the common people in different eras prove this. I have been struck, moreover, stopping in places which I had visited formerly, to see workers there eating better bread, wearing shoes instead of going baefoot, owning leather shoes instead of wooden ones, living in better lighted, cleaner, more comfortable houses, with better furniture than before; in sum, to find them in all these places not as I would have wanted to see them in every case, but in a *generally less bad* situation than twenty or thirty years earlier.

Many people deny these facts. Touched by the misery of so many workers, they maintain that their condition has never been more deplorable, but they ignore the fact that the improvement of the workers' lot depends almost always on their own will, their good behavior, and that workers can in their turn, although perhaps less often than formerly, rise to the rank of manufacturer and acquire and possess the advantages thereof. I might note, in favor of my opinion, that every day agricultural workers leave the countryside to compete with urban labor, without ever returning to agriculture, and, moreover, cite the results of the research of M. Charles Dupin. But a very simple argument puts my opinion beyond doubt; bread and clothes, the essential bases of the well-being of the people, and the two most important articles to which all others are subordinate, have never been cheaper, or rather, have not been sold at such low prices for many years; and nevertheless wages have increased just as the prices of other things. The current high price of bread (December, 1839) is too recent to constitute a real exception.

This improvement, on which oldtimers almost unanimously agree, has created among the people, including the workers, tastes and needs which do not allow most of those who experience them to appreciate their better conditions. What was only luxury and superfluity for them thirty years ago has now become a necessity. These new needs increase their desires and prevent the less well paid from saving any money; or if some savings are achieved they are so small that they feel that they would have to wait too long to find a good use for them—and so they frequently do not bother with them. This belief that no good use can easily be found for savings is one of the main causes of the bad conduct and indigence of the working classes; savings banks, by destroying this belief, render them a great service.

I have just spoken of improvement. I should remind the reader that simple weavers do not share in it or at most are very little affected by it. . . .

However, we must stipulate here that the present industrial workers not be compared with the *master workers* of the period before 1789. Certainly, the advantage would not lie with the former: the old master workers were all really manufacturers or entrepreneurs and were often limited in numbers, having purchased their position and being alone entitled, within limits guaranteed by the statutes of their professions or guilds and to the exclusion of all others, to fill orders, maintain a shop, receive apprentices and give work to journeymen. However, if one compares these latter to our present workers, and this is what must be done to be consistent, the difference would be entirely to the advantage of modern labor.

I do not want to reproduce here the declamations of those who not only deny the improvement, but also picture industry and commerce —these two great sources of liberty, well-being, and civilization—as causes of misery, brutalization, and all sorts of evils. To listen to them, industry, developed as it is in our country, can not advance without worsening the conditions of all those whom it employs; and their oppression, slavery, and torture are already the results of this. Thus whoever works in a wool or cotton spinning plant struggles continuously against the machines which he surveys or directs, and has no more rest than the wheels and levers of which these are composed; each blow of the piston, each blast of the steam pump, stimulates his movements like those of the machines; they push him ceaselessly, and only when they themselves stop in the evening do they let him go, exhausted, broken with fatigue.

This picture which I have seen drawn in many writings is singularly exaggerated. Without doubt, it has been done from imagination.

Everywhere, moreover, a man condemned to work earns his bread by the sweat of his brow; but everywhere also, idleness, lack of foresight, debauchery, and corruption inevitably produce misery.

We are not interested in knowing if these evils result from manufacturing, but if their frequency among our workers results from the great development of industry, if they are the inevitable consequence of it.

Once the problem is posed this way, its solution follows: The workers in our factories do not have (with the exception of the children) more difficult labor than others, especially in comparison with agricultural labor; moreover, they generally, I can even say almost always, receive higher salaries, and in areas deprived of industry, the creation of an industrial establishment is always a great benefit, in absolutely every respect. But very commonly also, in France in the present state of things, manufacturing workers lack sobriety, economy, foresight, and good habits; very often, they are miserable by their own fault alone.

This evil is not new, but it is greater than ever; it results mainly from the habitual agglomeration of workers in huge shops, which are like caravansaries where different sexes and ages are mixed, and from their residence in the cities, especially in the big cities, which factories multiply by bringing huge numbers of people together. It results also from free competition, the very cause of the rise and the prodigious development of industry, but a cause also of often overabundant production of manufactured goods, of the glutting of shops, of the depreciation of merchandise, of the ruination of a great number of manufacturers, and of many crises, many variations in the wage rate, which are so harmful to workers. Today, under the regime of this competition, we are struck by its disadvantages, as people were struck in 1789 by the more serious drawbacks of the guilds and the privileges which some manufacturers possessed, by the exclusion of all the others, to produce certain articles.

It would be very desirable to remedy the unfortunate consequences of free competition, and prevent the imprudent establishment of factories which subsequently must be closed, after having called in hundreds or thousands of workers, from near and far, often at the expense of agriculture, who, suddenly reduced to the most awful misery, become burdens on the communes and departments where these factories are located. "From another point of view," M. de Villeneuve-Bargemont has said, "what strikes any man animated by a spirit of justice and humanity in the examination of the situation of the working class, is the dependent and abandoned positions in which society entrusts workers to the owners and managers of factories; it is the unlimited opportunity, given to speculative capitalists, to assemble around them whole populations to utilize according to their interest, to dispose of, in a way, at will, without giving any guarantee of existence, of a future, or of physical or moral improvement to the people involved, or to society, which should protect them." [1]

In spite of all these facts, the improvement of which I spoke a bit earlier remains nonetheless a fact. But will this situation endure? This is a question which one dare not answer affirmatively, especially when we know how harmful the centers of industry are to habits of economy on the part of workers, and how increasingly difficult it is for labor to rise to the class of employers, because of the huge capital which the creation of the factory now requires.

SHOP RULES

In their zeal to explore material conditions, historians have unduly neglected the temper of work in the factory.[2] Workers in their rare protests seldom raised questions about factory organization, so again we have little knowledge of their own reactions. But factory organization may have been one of the most unpleasant and novel aspects of their lives. Factory rules seldom departed much from the pattern suggested in the following example, from the Benck textile company in Bühl (Alsace), in 1842.

The rules give us some insight into employer policies. Manufacturers had to remake workers' mentalities to a significant degree. They had to impose a new sense of time. Peasants had known seasons and days, but the new workers had to know hours and minutes. Shop rules convey this and other aspects of the new mentality factories tried to "teach." At the same time, they suggest some of the ways workers reacted to the new situation, long retaining some traditions including the desire for more leisure time and days off. Employers were not immediately successful in reshaping workers' behavior, and workers were not always mindless, demoralized automatons. This was why rules were needed. Yet gradually, particularly after the first generation of factory labor, employers had their way. Some of the rules of factory

1 A. de Villeneuve-Bargemont, *Economie politique chrétienne*, v. III, pp. 161–62.

2 See Reinhard Bendix, *Work and Authority in Industry: Ideologies of Management in the Course of Industrialization* (New York, 1956).

life were internalized. The question then is how painful this adaptation was for workers and what compensations, if any they could find for it.

Rules for Workers in the Factory of Benck and Co. in Bühl

Article 1. Every worker who accepts employment in any work-site is obligated to read these rules and to submit to them. No one should be unfamiliar with them. If the rules are violated in any work-site, the offenders must pay fines according to the disorder or damage they have caused.

Art. 2. All workers without exception are obligated, after they have worked in the factory for fourteen days, to give a month's notice when they wish to quit. This provision can be waived only for important reasons.

Art. 3. The work day will consist of twelve hours, without counting rest periods. Children twelve are excepted; they have to work only eight hours a day.

Art. 4. The bell denotes the hours of entry and departure in the factory when it first rings. At the second ring every worker should be at his work. At quitting time the bell will also be sounded when each worker should clean his workplace and his machine (if he has one). It is forbidden under penalty of fines to abandon the workplace before the bell indicates that the work-side is closed.

Art. 5. It is forbidden to smoke tobacco inside the factory. Whoever violates this prohibition is subjected to a heavy fine and can be dismissed. It is also forbidden under penalty of fines to bring beer or brandy into the factory. Any worker who comes to the factory drunk will be sent away and fined.

Art. 6. The porter, whoever he may be, is forbidden to admit anyone after the workday begins. If someone asks for a worker he will make him wait and have the worker called. All workers are forbidden to bring anyone into the factory and the porter is forbidden to admit anyone. The porter is also forbidden to let any workers in or out without the foreman's permission during the hours of work.

Art. 7. Any worker who misses a day without the Director's permission must pay a fine of two francs.[3] The fine is doubled for a second offense. Any worker who is absent several times is dismissed, and if he is a weaver he is not paid for any piece he may have begun unless he can prove he missed work because of illness and should therefore be paid for work he has already done.

From the Archives du Haut Rhin 1M123c¹. Translated by the editor.
3 The average daily wage for men was approximately two francs.

Art. 8. All workers in the factory are obligated to be members of the Sickness Fund, to pay their dues, and conduct themselves according to its statutes.

Art. 9. The foreman and the porter are empowered to retain any worker leaving the factory and to search him, as often as the interests of the Director may require. It is also recommended to the foreman to close the work-site himself, give the key to the porter, and to allow no worker inside during meal periods.

Art. 10. Workers should only go in and out of doors where a porter resides, else they will be fined, brought under suspicion, and dismissed. They cannot refuse to surrender any of their belongings at work, for which they will be reimbursed according to the valuation of the Director and the foreman. Workers are also ordered to be obedient to the foreman, who is fully empowered by the Director. Any disobedience will be punished by fines according to the importance of the case. Any offender is responsible for the consequences of his action. It is also forbidden for any worker to seek work in any of the company's work-sites other than the one in which he is employed; anyone encountered in another work-site will be punished.

Art. 11. Every worker is personally responsible for the objects entrusted to him. Any object that cannot be produced at the first request must be paid for. Weavers are obligated to pay careful attention to their cloth when they dry it. They will be fined and held responsible for any damage.

Art. 12. In return for the protection and care which all workers can expect from the Director, they pledge to him loyalty and attachment. They promise immediately to call to his attention anything that threatens good order or the Director's interests. Workers are also put on notice that any unfortunate who commits a theft, however small it may be, will be taken to court and abandoned to his fate.

Bühl, Haut Rhin, July 1, 1942.
Benck & Co.

Seen and approved by us Mayor of the Community of Bühl
Bühl, July 1, 1842.

The Mayor
Harenlop.

MAX LOTZ

The following passages come from lengthy letters written in the early twentieth century by Max Lotz, an otherwise unknown miner in the Ruhr Valley, to Adolf Levenstein. Lotz, who had little formal education, was

born about 1876. Levenstein was a socialist who conducted a rather elaborate poll of workers in several industries concerning their conditions and
outlook. Lotz's letters were an outgrowth of this poll. The poll itself was
almost certainly biased toward responses from socialist workers. Lotz's own
views may be less than fully representative because of the same bias. He himself seems to recognize that many of his fellows are different and he scorns
them for this. Note, in fact, his vacillations on the character of "the masses."
The thoroughness of his discussion of a miner's life and the meaning of socialism is unusual.

Lotz raises the question of how much had changed in the worker's lot
since the early industrial period. Wages were better, unquestionably, but
how much difference did this make? Lotz is a truly alienated worker. He
finds no joy in his work and no satisfactory relationship to the established
order around him. Only socialism tempers his isolation. Perhaps the labor
movement, even when committed to revolution in theory, served to modify
workers' alienation by giving them something to belong to, a separate society to identify with.[1] This process had only begun with someone like Lotz.
Again, he seems to be articulating an alienation that workers earlier in industrialization may have experienced even more often, though they were
unable to express themselves.

One point particularly must be noted in judging what Lotz's alienation
consists of. Lotz stresses the evils of the job itself. Most outside observers
and most historians have paid most attention to life outside the job, to consumption standards, and even more to formal labor movements. We tend
to assume that workers managed to switch their own focus in the same way,
abandoning pleasure in work for pleasure in outside life, most particularly
for material rewards.[2] Lotz tells us that one kind of worker, at least, did not
easily make this adjustment, for he specifically says that no amount of pay
could compensate for his degrading toil. He may, of course, be an exception,
not because his job conditions were unusual but because he paid so much
attention to them. Note that he worries not only about the material conditions at work but also about the degrading human relationships involved.
Again, perhaps some workers could tune these problems out, but few could
do so altogether. This is one area where formal protest through strikes is an
inadequate measure of workers' grievances, for strikes rarely conveyed the
depth of unhappiness with the job. A recent study reminds us that even in
the 1960s as workers' consumption standards approached middle-class levels,
workers continued to have a distinctive life style because of the type of work
they did and because, unlike the middle classes, they usually found no pleasure on the job.[3]

Lotz, therefore, helps us to examine one vital aspect of workers' life. Yet
one cannot escape the impression that he was an unusual type—a blue collar

1 For one approach to this problem see Guenther Roth, *The Social Democrats in
Imperial Germany; a Study in Working Class Isolation and National Integration*
(Totowa, N.J., 1963).

2 Eric Hobsbawm, *Labouring Men* (New York, 1967), pp. 405–36.

3 John H. Goldthorpe and others, *The Affluent Worker in the Class Structure*
(Cambridge, 1969).

intellectual. He was widely read, though self-taught. Again, this immediately differentiates him from most of his peers. His concern for the meaning of life, his analysis of religion, and his rejection of it, were not common, though Lotz talks of other workers with similar concerns. Most Ruhr Valley miners, relatively recent arrivals from the countryside, were in fact still at least nominally religious. They, like most European factory workers, would lose their religious attachment, but it is doubtful that they agonized over the process as Lotz did. Their religion had been more ritualistic than theological, so in losing it they did not lose their sense of what the world meant. Similarly their socialism, when as was usually the case they turned to it, was not a substitute theology. In these matters Lotz was part of a small minority. But it was a vital one, for it provided the loyal nucleus of socialist movements, the nucleus that clung to socialism with religious-like intensity. Most workers took socialism less seriously, but in years when socialism had to battle government and employer resistance just to stay alive the devout minority was essential.

There is still, as with other working-class documents dealt with in the section on protest, the question of the exact contribution Lotz makes to an understanding of his class. Granted that few workers shared his more elaborate intellectual concerns or his ability to express them. Lotz may nonetheless reveal something of the quality of ordinary workers' life and outlook simply because of his unusual perceptiveness.

A Miner's Letter

. . . [Y]ou are right when you write that thinking is a cause for suffering in my class. And why? Because by thinking I learn how miserable and unhappy I am. If the veil of ignorance lay over my spiritual eye my heart would truly feel but half the pain of earthly suffering. And if you consider it worth while to discuss the above fleeting autobiography in your book *Workers' Fates* than do not forget to mention that there are still workers and human beings who try to escape the sticky air of plebeian way of thinking with the courage of desperation. They do this in spite of the warning sign *chemin defendue* [*sic*.] which was affixed to the road of life of our workers by the Christian-capitalistic fiends of morality. You should further mention how my sensual instinct hammered powerfully at the portals of the earthly temple of lust. But no doorman appeared. But my dialectic eye sees no bridge over which my feet can step in order to reach the isle of the saved. Why all this now? You know, of course, that the economic

From Adolf Levenstein, Aus der Tiefe, Arbeiterbriefe *(Berlin, 1905),* *pp. 21–22, 35–36, 48, 57, 59, 60–73. Translated by Gabriela Wettberg.* *The translator has attempted to preserve something of the ungainliness of Lotz' style.*

development demands these sacrifices. And I know it, too. And the further this process matures the closer the goal approaches.

But one more thing. You were wondering why there was no place for me [as a leader] in the workers' movement. Why? Do I not fill my place? If of course, you understand by this that I desire to remove myself from the manual labor that ruins me, then you are right. I truly abhor engaging my mind daily for the rough chores of the miners. But the political party makes high demands on her agitators. I lack the practical ability to express my views, namely the captivating eloquence and ready wit. I rather believe that the thought remaining locked up in the brain does not possess invigorating significance and therefore does not even exist visibly. That is the cause. Could training help me? I do not know. My weapon is the lonely working pen. Up to the present it was still asleep in my desk. I wonder if it will ever grow wings . . .

If those so called men-of-order always speak of the fact that free trade unions turn the workers away from religion because they are based on socialistic principles, than I will always think of Rheinhold Prüfer in order to point out the fallacy of their Philistine words. Because this is a man thoroughly infused with genuine religious piety. He belongs to one of the sects which is composed primarily of Poles. It is spread out over the entire Rhineland Westphalian industrial region. He left the Protestant denomination about eight years ago as a consequence of its basic religious concepts. He is probably a Baptist because he never consumes alcoholic beverages and believes in the return of Christ to this world. Jesus would then erect a thousand year *Reich,* though it would remain invisible. But all people therein should adhere to the same faith. The wild beasts would then lose their predatory nature and lion and tiger would eat grass. (How naive.) The happiest harmony would prevail everywhere. A particular type of missionary effort would be reserved to the Jews. After a time span of about a thousand years the world would come to an end and eternal paradise would beckon to all humanity. A beautiful utopia. But he, too, places his hope in socialism even though through this purely religious aberration. At any rate, the changing game of eternal longing for man's salvation from the earthly and economic misery exercises its influence here. He never curses, which many a Christian should note as example. (I myself have taken to this bad habit.) And if he becomes disheartened by the haste with which the work in the mine has to be accomplished then his favorite exclamations are: "It just isn't possible," or "a thousand, a thousand." The latter exclamation probably refers to the thousand year kingdom which will come while he indicates his own belief in this illusion of his world view by the first one. Up to the present he has always avoided polemics when discussing his principles with me. He may have feared that he would not be able to cope with my satirism. He actually fears me groundlessly. I let him know that, too, because I respect a genuine conviction. My law is not the ridiculing of other people's convictions but rather the enlightening of their errors. Besides he possesses a sense of humor in spite of the ascetic principle underlying his religious concepts. If, during working hours, a joke is not absurd he joins heartily in the laughter. That is what I had to say about the mining foreman.

I have to give a somewhat lengthier description of the second miner, Bruno Bittner. He is currently 33 years old. About one and a half years ago he was persuaded to migrate to the Ruhr region with his family by a Silesian recruiting agent. He was to mine for the "German Emperor" which belongs to the coal baron Thyssen. He arrived in the Ruhr paradise with about fifty others who had also been taken in. He did not last long in the original shaft. After a stay of six months he changed from "German Emperor" to "United Gladbeck." There I was ordered to be his fellow coal-miner. Whenever he gets to speak of his original recruitment (at the time the supervising miner N.N. of shaft 4 acted as the receiver of workers) he usually mentions a delicate episode involving the supervisor and a miner's wife to which he had been a witness. But stop, I go beyond my task here because I merely intended to relate how Bittner acted in our working relationship. He is generally a conscientious worker equipped with a fair amount of skills as is common among workers. He works quietly which is a consequence of his phlegmatic nature. But he is capable of becoming quite angry and then he will curse. But his rage generally lasts but a short while. One gets used to cursing in the mines. Higher employees as well as laborers indulge in this bad habit. Unlike Prüfer he likes to talk and does not reject the pleasurable consumption of *Schnaps* and other alcoholic beverages. If he has become angered by family quarrels the amount of spirits exceeds his regular measure considerably. His religious beliefs are rather muddled. He can no longer get enthusiastic over the Christian lullaby of spiritual perspective nor about the song of forbearance of earthly pleasures which pertains to it. On the one side he sees the increasing wealth, on the other he observes how the priestly class condones such "God-willed order." He cannot grasp that the completely benevolent and loving "creator of world and men" has intended this screaming disharmony and still does will it. . . .

But we cannot let it go at that. The capitalistic titan, the coupon man, demands more. If he is not successful in seeing the miner cut up in the swamp, crushed under rocks, destroyed and corroded by misery or waning away as a cripple, then the master seeks revenge through the eyes of his slaves. The visual nerve becomes overly strained because of the flickering of the gasoline lamp, that eternal flickering of the small light in front of his eyes. The lamp always has to be quite close to the work and many miners consequently look into the flame of the weather lamp as they sit or stand, while not at work. It is the nature of the thing. One always seeks light. A trembling of the pupils forms in the eyes of many miners. At first it is not noticeable but it gradually becomes stronger. Where this eye ailment reaches a certain stage the stricken person becomes unable to work in the pit any longer. The stricken man becomes unsure of his grip, he often misses the desired object by one foot. He has particular difficulties in directing his glance upward. If he fixes but barely on an object his eyes begin to tremble immediately. But this calamity only appears in the mine or in artificial light. Above ground and in daylight it is never present. I know a laborer working quite close to me who takes a quart of liquor daily into the shaft. As soon as the trembling begins he takes a sip and the pupil becomes calm for a short while—so he states. Thus one can become a habitual drunk, too.

But this is not all. Almost all miners are anemic. I do not know what causes this pathological diminution of blood corpuscles in miners, whether this results from a general lack of protein in the blood. I suppose that it is caused mainly by the long, daily stay in bad air combined with the absence of sun or day light. I reason that if one places a potted plant in a warm but dark cellar for a long time it will grow significantly more pale and sickly than her beautifully scenting sisters in the rose-colored sunlight. It must be like this for the drudges down there. Anemia renders the miner characteristically pale. . . .

Let's go, shouted Prüfer, who had already picked up a shovel. Four more wagons have to fall. It is almost 12:30 now. [p.m.] All right, I agreed, and we swung the shovels.

Away it goes, commanded Bittner when the wagons were fully loaded. Jump to it, there is plenty of coal. Well, if I were a pickman, mumbled the chief pickman then I'd have myself a drink. And he breathed heavily behind the wagon.

Let's set up the planking until Rheinhold comes back so that things don't look so scruffy, I said to Bittner even though we would rather have stretched out on the pile of coal because we were so tired.

He replied: I don't care, but first I want to wring out my trousers. And standing there naked he started to squeeze the water from the garment. I followed his example. When we had finished it looked around us as though a bucket full of water had been spilled. I do not exaggerate. In other locations where it was warmer yet, the workers were forced to undergo this procedure several times during their working hours. But let us remain here.

We put our undergarments back on and did not pay attention to the unpleasant feeling which we had doing so. We placed the wooden planks and cleared aside the debris in order to establish good working conditions for the other third which usually did not do the same for us—because they were too fatigued.

The work is becoming increasingly mechanical. No more incentive, no more haste, we muddle along wearily, we are worn out and mindless. There was sufficient coal, Rheinhold could come at any time. My forehead burned like fire. As a consequence of the anemia from which I suffer I occasionally experience a slight dizzy spell. Bittner does not know about it. But in my head it rages and paralyzes me beyond control or without my being able to think. When it becomes unbearable I stop my slow, phlegmatic and energyless working. I then sit on the side wall of the mountain in order to slurp the last remaining coffee. Since Bittner has nothing left in his coffee container he sparingly drinks from Prüfer's bottle in order not to take everything away from him. . . .

For the eight waggons which we mined we received a salary of M 9.60. Of this sum M 0.60 goes for dynamite expenses and 5 Pfennig were yet deducted for lamp gasoline. For us M 8.85 remained which we were to divide among the three of us.

The shift today consequently brought each of us a salary of M 2.85. Is that proper compensation for a human being who climbs down into the polluted, dark and dangerous shaft? Is such an "assembly line" system dignified for a modern, civilized worker? Does such a procedure render honor to a liberal, free-thinking capitalist from the standpoint of humanity? etc. etc. . . .

This is a brief description of one shift in the pit. And this torture, this inhuman haste repeats itself day after day only that the various states of exhaustion express themselves mildly or very pronouncedly in the physical state of the individuals. And that is not all; the spirit, too, the conscience of the individual degenerates. And one drudge, grown vacuous through his work, is put beside another one, and another one and finally this "modern" circle has closed in on the entire working force. And he who says that primarily the professional group of the miners is the rudest, least educated and spiritually lowest class of men does not lie. Of course, there are exceptions here, too. But these exceptions are supposed to validate the rule according to a simple type of logic. In any event, it truly takes spiritual magnitude to occupy still oneself with belletristic, scientific and thought-provoking materials after a completed shift. When I come home in that condition I still have to cope with other necessary heavy work around the house. And finally there only remain the evening hours for the writing tasks which I deem noble. I then sit at my table, oblivious to the world, thinking and writing and straining—to satisfy you.

And now I still have to tell you about the behavior of my professional colleagues on pay day. But I do not wish to transmit a deep, moralistic contemplation but merely wish to sketch some general types which have evolved from my observations. I will therefore limit myself. Please forgive me, my worthy friend, I know you just wanted to know the ones I omitted. But let us leave it at that for the time being.

It is still well known that particularly among miners the level of education is deplorably low inside as well as outside. This fact is probably mainly connected with the confining of this kind of occupation below the ground and the rough and slavish side effects of the miners' working there. The miners are commonly made of thick, grainy wood. If this changes slowly but markedly (with the exception of an upright character which, astonishingly enough, preserves its stable form) if gradually a conscious type of man evolves who is certainly not bad at the core, one can attribute this to the eminent cultural work of the union and the party. One of the main evils from which the miner suffers is his great penchant for alcohol. One can of course understand how such a capitalistic chain-bearer comes from his pit into day light, receives his hunger salary and spends a part on the intoxicating scents of alcoholic poisons. Here he has an effective remedy that makes him forget his misery, a misery rooted in his material impotence. In general, the reflexes of bitterness function as follows:

In the wash room a deafening noise prevails. Here you hear a group quarreling and cursing. It is about an employee of the mine taking advantage of a miner with his salary. . . . Liquor, which a miner or a friend carries along does not fail its effect in this hot house sultriness. The defrauded man yells and carries on, and in his drunken furor he throws his misery into everyone's face. He then stumbles to the cashier's counter and rudely demands the missing money. Of course this is never within the competence of a cashier. In the end he becomes penitent and is therefore thrown out by the mining police. Everyone laughs at this comical interlude. But my heart contracts with pain at the brutality with which a man, maybe a family father, is trampled on simply because he insisted on his rights in a state of indignation at the wrong time.

There you see vexed, haggard and embittered physiognomies. Family fathers with livid, hollow faces, you see their secret rage, their inner resentment pulsating in each man's temples because the salary which he receives does not suffice in order to buy the necessities for his family. In the back of his eyes there is spontaneous flickering. He thinks of booze all of a sudden. Afterwards he will drink until he breaks down unconsciously. Then he sees nothing anymore and does not want to see anymore—that is in fact why he drinks. The atrocious misery in his family lies behind him—at least for one day. And his family? His wife? The children? My hand trembles when I think about the scenes I already saw. But I can and will not write about them here.

Furthermore you observe a number of young boys to whom life is a halfway secret enigma. They have received money. And they go to the bars with organ music and the sound of card games. Youth wants to live it up. I know this urge since I myself once succumbed to it. The money is rolling and there will be a hangover and a slow shift yawning at you in the morning. And a punitive notice at the black board again brings their foolishness to mind.

But another image yet. The habitual drunk. On pay day he does not even go to the mine. After he throws down his salary booklet he counts the money with trembling fingers. His eyes shine. And usually he does not return to the pit until the last penny has been spent on liquor. The Ruhr region possesses many such figures. They drown unnoticed in the current of our hasty existence. . . .

POST SCRIPTUM

. . . I herewith hope to provide you with insight into the psychological make-up of my thinking about the shameful position of my ego. I will give you as much as I can. I am afraid of this step well knowing that I cannot find sufficient words to express the internal and external slavery under which I clearly groan. But I know that my entire thinking and feeling in relation to the riddles of life rest in this work.

. . . At this point I feel the need for a personal remark. I urgently ask of you, in connection with the thoughts we previously discussed, which I even regarded necessary for discussion, that you draw no conclusions which might resemble a tapping of you on my part. This would provoke repulsion in me. I want nothing of you but that which I can rightly demand. And up to now that is nothing. I concede one exception to you in respect to the mailing of books which possibly appears indispensable to you since this bears cultural significance, at least to you and me. . . . The recognition that things are as they are and that I should see my salvation merely in the stupidity of the masses, that is the scorpion of my hopelessness. You will object that I could enter the labyrinth of world knowledge inspite of all this and that I could feel happy in this knowledge. This is relatively true, yes. But knowledge is followed by thinking. And what good is a thought to me—no matter how appropriate or successful—if it is only locked up in my mind. It must escape the narrow constricts of my head. It must come alive, must be transferred to as many other brains as possible if it is to be of any practical use at all. In order to achieve this I have to write books, become a writer. But, as you know, this costs money, much money, and, above all, it is time consuming. I could only write at the expense of my own spare time and the money which I badly need for other things. And when need oppresses me daily I stand brooding before the riddle of hope; I am then overcome by an insurmountable weariness and this state of mind snuffs out everything I have been attempting to construct.— —

You will ask in astonishment what these dashes signify. For a moment I am perplexed. And suddenly I discover with horror that I am unable to think methodically, yet. Even though I sense with all my faculties that which I intended to describe to you. But I do not find the proper form into which I can clothe the thoughts I wanted to transmit. Now that fear arises of which I spoke to you at the beginning of this chapter. It is a feeling which always befalls me and restricts me when I wish palpably to modify powerful thoughts which move me, for the outside world. I admit with bitterness that it is a sign of lack of education, not being able to do that. But it is of no avail, I want to be capable of doing it even if I have to begin anew. All of a sudden it titillates me tremendously to be drawn into a new process of thinking. I instinctively sense that great tasks await me yet.

If I again and again return to economic and historical contexts in the following, it is because I realize the need to do so since it is the invasion into the structure of the natural economy upon which I base my world view.

When I think how the noise underground envelops and buries me, a slavish worker, how it is possible that the curse of work hovers over me iron-like, how the struggle of life oppresses me brutally then I would like to scream out loud, wildly and shrill with rage and internal furor. But I have to remain silent within myself and my heart. There, deep in my breast, a mortally weary soul sighs. How mindless, how insensitive and rude are the people of my own *milieu* because of their shameful condition. They are not guilty of their misery because the systematic suppression of their personality is the guilt of those gentlemen of miniscule morals which scream to heaven. . . .

. . . I merely refer you to the shattering fact that a two thousand year reign of Christianity sufficed to brand the psychology of the peo-

ple unspeakably. We still feel the atrocious mass hysteria of the middle
ages right into the beginning of the twentieth century. The fool's
cap still sits on the head of many a would-be learned and educated
man. The health restoring faculty of prayers in fashionable circles
and complete belief in witchcraft in rural areas of our modern industrial state are proofs for my contention. But not the spirit alone
has been demeaned by the historical process of ridicule to a lowly
state of misery caused by religion. But the entire organism of the human race has suffered. The modern industrial proletariat as well as
rural servants and the small farmers sigh under the masterly system
of *latifundiae* which has been sanctioned by religion. . . .

And the coal production of the Saar, the central German charcoal
industry are characteristic for the position of the mass man today in
a Christian state. The mining depot of Wendel which had received
special mention by the Pope has affixed burning candles to the en-
trance shaft of Saint Barbara, one of its mines. And all the while the
drudges and earners of their wealth drown in hunger and misery.
These conditions were brought to my attention primarily through
socialistic reading material. They induced me to revise my thinking.
I became an observer of the situation. At first my concern was external
because it is natural that my attention would be focused on the surface
of the human condition. So I turned my attention to the distribution
of salaries. It seemed unjust to me. There was still the animal impulse
in me but it was nevertheless my first step in the search for human
value. Egotism is of course the resonance of economic sensitivity. A
gigantic inner evolution was necessary in order to find dignity, great-
ness and value which I possess in this universal organism and to which
I have a right. If I held any ethical views at which I had arrived
by myself when I was young then there were two incentives for my
morality. One was the spiritualistic nature of religion with its inner
contradictions and attempts at synthesizing theory and practice har-
moniously. On the other hand there was capitalism which led me on
vigorously in my struggle. I need not define the developmental factors
of corruption and usurpation in this capitalistic society. "Capital" by
Karl Marx characterized this world calamity well. I therefore desist re-
peating it for you. But I would like to tell you of the effect the capitalistic system has on my emotions. First there is the entire soul, the
gold. The demoralizing peculiarity of gold is learned, not inborn, I
believe. But I cannot understand that it was capable of exercising such
disastrously forceful influence on the entire human race. It is incomprehensible in the sense that only a minute minority is concentrated
opposite an overwhelming majority. Long time ago the egotistical
trait of the mass man should have implemented sweeping measures.

But it did not do so because it was opposed by the radical force of individual wealth, religion. The incomprehensibility lies herein, namely that the unconscious, ideational happiness of the utopic pseudo world would be stronger in the minds of men than the conscious tangible wish for a realistic improvement of life. Is capitalism with its concubine, religion, truly the cause for the degeneration of the human race? If so these factors should be destroyed. Let us deal with the direct and indirect capitalistic mass murderer of men. I particularly abhor that audacious frivolity with which he corrupts men. He robs men of any self confidence and forces them into positions of dependency with their "bread giver." He prescribes their political, sometimes their religious convictions. In short, he deprives them of their right to self-determination. . . . It undoubtedly requires a premonition of the low intelligence of the masses to rule them for the egotistical motive of amassing wealth. And yet preconditions for an uprising are given in the mass with its egotistical character. But the "outrage of the human spirit," the revolt of the collective soul of the human race against the minority clique of the gold owners (Henrik Ibsen's theory) does not come until after a social change and not before, as the Norwegian had thought. I am therefore particularly enraged that so many intelligent men in the masses are depraved by the pressure of capitalistic working conditions. The cultural and artistic treasures thereby lose some of their significance and spirit. And I myself? I feel my impotency too clearly. What am I? What is my meaning in this great world plan where brutal physical and psychological forces feast themselves in orgies? Nothing! Nothing at all! Zero! But why should I be a zero if I do not wish to be one? And I absolutely do not want to be one. I want to go high up; yes, I want to be the highest in the pantheon of human spirits. But the present social order, which they call mockingly the divine and best one, beats me back brutally. I became a social democrat, because I wanted to force it. I had to become one to prepare my way. Only social democratic activities could give me goals and offer me economic security, too, so that I may attempt my plans. I therefore adhere to socialism with every fiber of courage and idealism. But I do not wish to ascend alone. I want to see all of them up there in the light circle of conscious human happiness, all those who still suffer shamefully with me. Their fate fills me with bitterness because I am supposed to perish with them and they with me.

If I wanted or were able to be servile or corruptible, I would not have to worry about my daily bread. But I have to suffer because I am unable to do so. This vile order does not allow us to be noble and magnanimous. I know that many have been physically destroyed, crushed, pulverized, smashed, and harmed, branded, and sold out. They all have attempted to escape the repulsive mephitis as I have. But nobody can poison the spirit, the consciousness of being a human being in the most noble sense. Before all it cannot be this false deity whom almost everyone worships, and who is presumptuous enough to insult humanity so disgracefully. Nobody can set up spiritual barricades for me, not even democracy, because to me democracy means to venerate the general spiritual indolence and psychological brutality. I wish to be alone in the paradise of thinking. I tolerate no soothing council there except dialectics. I walk to the altar of the party program to collect my thoughts. But no one sees me kneeling there.

PAUL GÖHRE

Again a middle-class observer. Paul Göhre was a student at an evangelical theological school when he interrupted his studies to work for three months in a machine tools factory in Saxony in 1890. Do three months make any outsider an expert? (Göhre spent years rehashing his experiences.) Middle-class bias may be detected at several points, as in the interpretation of workers' family life. And a new problem of bias, much more specific than the general issue of bourgeois prejudice. By this time, the socialist movement was well underway and most members of the middle class were frightened by it. Göhre seeks to understand socialism and he had some sympathy with it, but he was not a socialist and his effort to analyze it and to qualify workers' acceptance of socialist theory reflects this. Again, we have to ask how much the combination of middle-classness, Christianity, and non-socialism warps his comprehension not only of the labor movement but of workers' life in general.

Yet, for all their problems, accounts such as Göhre's are essential. It is not only that they deal with aspects of life that more intellectual workers like Lotz tended to neglect. There are worker autobiographies less ethereal than Lotz' statements, that discuss family relationships, sexual experience, and the like. What Göhre really contributes is a picture of types of workers not sufficiently articulate and, in some cases, not sufficiently aggrieved to describe their vile lot. It is possible to conclude that, despite his position as outsider, Göhre conveys more typical worker sentiments than an alienated socialist was able to do.

The contrast between Göhre's picture and that of Lotz is by no means total. He differs on the meaning of socialism to workers, but his colleagues were thorough-going socialists in their own way. His colleagues did not agonize over work conditions as much as Lotz did, but they were sensitive to personal relations on the job, and they too resented undignified, degrading treatment. Conversely, they are more attuned to possible pressures outside the job, not only as consumers but as family men, than Lotz was. Relatedly, their socialism was often linked to dissatisfactions as consumers. These workers were not completely alienated. Their expectations for their children reveal some relationship to middle-class aspirations, though this could be a source of discontent as workers realized their hopes were unfounded amid the existing class barriers to advancement. Their socialism expressed more a desire to remedy specific problems than to remake the world; in some cases it coexisted with a rather traditional view of the proper social hierarchy. This seems to represent a pragmatism more typical than the anguished statements of Lotz. It corresponds with the conclusions of other contemporary sociological studies of workers in Germany—also by middle-class outsiders, to be sure. It is reinforced by the relative mildness of the German strike movement during these same years and by the fact that German socialism itself became increasingly reformist and bent on practical gains within the existing system.

This does not mean that Lotz should be forgotten. The key point is that workers varied. Socialists varied, and different types of socialists brought different contributions to the movement. Different industries produced different kinds of workers. Mining was far more arduous than machine building and so might more easily drive a sensitive personality to despair. Without much question, in any single industry, sensitivity varied with the person. And again, Göhre's description is in no sense completely incompatible with that of Lotz. The conditions he portrays could produce profound dismay. Again, we must ask how much the physical and moral setting of working-class life had changed from the earlier years of industry. Wages were higher but factory work had become more intense and the factory itself far larger and more impersonal. It is questionable whether there was much net gain. Within Göhre's own account there are contradictions, possibly stemming from his role as outsider, but also suggesting the different experiences and outlooks individual workers could develop. He talks of a decay of family life but cites many examples of close family ties and affection. One can use Göhre to portray workers as downtrodden and downcast or to see their adjustments to the industrial setting as they built their own social and familial structure and derived some contentment from it. Most workers probably shared elements of both roles—as did Lotz himself, in his own way, as he found refuge in his ideas. If disruption and confusion form one theme in working-class history, positive efforts to adjust form another, equally important one.

Göhre's Account

But back to our factory. Several of those who limited themselves to cold lunch customarily found warm compensation in the evenings at home. Then, at least if the entire family consisted of only adults or older children, the situation was not so serious. Sometimes the whole family consumed the delayed supper with the workers. But where there were small children a second evil followed the first. As we know warm meals in the evening are never conducive to or healthy for children.

From Paul Göhre, Drei Monate Fabrikarbeiter (*Leipzig, 1890*) *pp.* *37–40, 108–15, 205–207. Translated by Gabriela Wettberg.*

For most of my other fellow workers supper consisted of potatoes, or bread and butter, shortening or linseed-oil, sometimes supplementary foods. The quantity and quality of those meals were always determined by the amount of income, thrift and the current expenses of each family. But coffee was never lacking. The boarders, too, received several free cups. But commonly, they kept bread and butter for themselves.

These are the remarks which I am able to transmit from my coworkers about living, clothing and dietary conditions. Already these fragmentary bits of information, I think, prove my previous contention right, namely the necessity of crowded conditions and the modesty of their way of living. But they also explain another fact one learns daily anew in living with these people which is infinitely more significant and more fateful than the first one; namely the fact that as a consequence of these conditions among our urban industrial population the family doesn't exist anymore—already today. The familiar organism, based on blood-relationship of parents and children and composed of only such related members which, among the higher social strata, was merely loosely or more closely joined by few servants, has today more or less given way to a circle of relatives and friends. The basis of this new community builds purely on economic needs of shared dwelling and living expenses. It is now composed of blood relatives and strangers joining by chance. Family ties clearly take second place to economic obligations. The mother assumes the position as head of the household. She receives a certain fixed sum from her husband, the grown children and the strangers and is therewith obligated to pay the expenses for monthly rent, food, laundry and similar items while each one will take care of his own clothing expenses.

Therefore it is not the social democrats and their agitation who bear the main responsibility [for the disintegration of the family unit.] Rather it is those very conditions which result from our whole economic situation. They make it impossible for working families to consume common breakfasts and lunches. They force them to move into barely adequate houses and the most crowded apartments. In addition, the families are compelled to accommodate frequently changing strangers and associate with them on a most intimate level which is customarily reserved to family members. One must think how closely joined and without separation the rooms and apartments lie, beside and above one another, in barracks for workers or in formerly rural residences remodelled after the above fashion. How thin are the walls of rooms in houses constructed flimsily, so thin that every loud word can be clearly understood by the neighboring family. The three or four "chambers" of one floor only possess one hallway. Its use must be shared as are the water supply, the toilet and other facilities. All this leads to a mutuality of daily activities which is frightening if one looks into it and which must necessarily result in the death of family life. There simply is nothing else possible but that the children of such families continuously live almost as siblings with each other whereby the hallway is their favorite place for common games and chit chats. The young men and girls come into most intimate contact with one another, men into confidential exchange of thoughts, but often they quarrel and fight, too. Women must exactly know each corner, each shortcoming, each item of clothing and household appliance of the neighboring family. The shared use of such items as kitchen appliances through loaning and borrowing brings about a communistic trait for the household of a family since it is poorly equipped with such appliances. There are, in addition, the cramped conditions of the single dwelling units which forcibly drive people out of doors. At night, whenever possible, they escape into the streets, the yard, into the better, more spacious rooms of the neighbors, the taverns or meetings. One should further consider that their lack of space is still augmented by the presence of boarders who bring along strange and often enough not exactly pious or better customs, a different way of life, a new *Weltanschauung*, other needs which they seek to express in an uninhibited fashion, just as at home. One may take into account that these unfamiliar guests leave the house simultaneously with the husband and grown children and that they return at the same time as they do. They sit at the same table with the others and until bedtime they read, smoke, converse with one another or play cards. In fact, in many families parents and children can only be alone without disturbance during the night when everyone sleeps, because even the last opportunity for private togetherness, the morning and noon meal, is spoiled, as can be deduced from the above account, that is by the working conditions which prevent the father, son and daughter from going home to eat. But where it is possible, the one-hour break barely suffices, in my estimation, to go both ways, to and from the home, to consume the meal without comfortable rest but rather in haste. It is impossible in cases of long distances which are common among workers in large factories.

I will speak in a different place of the effect these conditions produce on the morality, the character, the disposition of the workers. I merely intended to state the fact of a change already under way, and despite the causes which brought about such change. I repeat again, they are, above all, the result of our present economic situation. Therefore *it* must be accused as the main culprit and not social democracy which, as it has done so often, only drew the ultimate consequences from the effects of the prevailing conditions and integrated them into a system. The sad conditions which exist are merely basis and cause for the spreading social democratic family ideal of the future. One should not be deceived about this fact (this is especially true for certain clerical circles). Instead of bemoaning the disintegration of the traditional Christian family ideal which does indeed exist and instead of accusing social democracy, they should rather cooperate in this case so that the fateful economic causes of these conditions will be finally and permanently eradicated . . .

SOCIAL AND POLITICAL CONVICTIONS OF
MY FELLOW WORKERS

The first and most important effect of this agitation is the fact that the entire working force of Chemnitz and surroundings, which I got to know, is somehow widely tied to the social democratic party with few exceptions, so that the workers live more or less in the current of their ideas and regard this, their workers' party *par excellence*, their sole appointed and strong representative. The workers with whom I have associated are filled—consciously or by instinct—with the awareness of an existing hostile contradiction of their interests and those of the entrepreneur; they desire a unified, energetic organization of the masses to which they belong. The worker yearns for great progress, for an uprising of the fourth class which is composed of the masses. He also has—being a child of these new fermenting times abounding with ideas, some new interests like his other contemporaries, physical as well as spiritual desires the fulfillment of which he demands. And he knows, sees, senses that this elementary want and yearning, this striving and needing will be satisfied by no one else but the social democratic party, without reservation and selfishness, energetically and with far reaching consequences.

It is for this reason that he has joined the party in spite of the fact that many things may separate him from it or repulse him. And I am quite certain that no presently existing power nor spiritual force will divert him from this party easily. They will not be able to extinguish the thoughts which the party has awakened and from which it is also being reborn. And therefore adhere to it without exception the young and the old, the ones who are well off and the ones badly off, married and single people, skilled and unskilled, thrifty and improvident people, industrious and lazy men, the wise and the ignorant, successful social climbers and those who have lost social prestige, natives and immigrants, all groups, classes and categories of the productive process, except for a very small minority. They consider themselves social democrats, follow the leaders and believe in them, their words and writings just like a new gospel. More than once have they spoken to my face in the factory: "What Jesus Christ was until now someday Bebel and

Liebknecht[1] will be." This expresses the consciousness that today the working community is social democracy; that the two coincide and will do so ever more strongly and that they all belong together in their sufferings, joys and ideals no matter how many differences and contradictions exist that will always be divisive forces among them.

To prove this I cite a number of quite spontaneous remarks made by different working comrades. They all have the same meaning: "All of us up to the last man voted the social democratic ticket," "Every worker is a social democrat," "I vote for my own," and most poignantly "Here everything is social democratic, even the machines." What expresses itself here is always the same idea, simply the opinion—in a general sense—that social democracy and the working class have to be one and the same thing. However, a number of the other quotes by different workers seem to contradict these directly, because some people occasionally stated that "only about half of the 400 or 500 laborers of our factory are social democrats." But this is only seemingly a contradiction. With that they only meant such people who expressed their social democratic orientation somehow particularly noticeably, in particular those belonging to social democratic election committees, topical or financial aid or recreational clubs affiliated with the party. In that sense of course not even half of the workers could be called social democrats. Social democrats by definite orientation but only in the widest sense of the word, this held true for the overwhelming majority of my working comrades, as I have stated.

In our department during the course of time I have only been able to find three conscious and self-professed non-social democrats of all the 120 men. Two of them were in the Hirsch-Dunker union consisting of about 70 members which also exists in Chemnitz. The third one was a good, faithful soul who was still too deeply motivated by faith, and he also came from an overly conservative and wealthy rural background. He could not have had any social democratic inclinations with good conscience and from inner necessity. They said of him that he only worked in the factory for his own pleasure, he did not have to do so. Beside these three there were actually a few others, as far as I was able to observe, who had indeed nothing in common with social democracy. But they kept this to themselves and preferred to keep their colleagues in the dark about their convictions. Sometimes an inborn great shyness rather than mere speculation was the cause. Even though their number cannot be estimated I do not believe that there were really too many of them. In any event, these neutral people even together with those three frank courageous dissenters against social democracy formed only the smallest minority of the working class. The

1 Auguste Bebel (1840–1913) and Karl Liebknecht (1826–1900) were founders and initial leaders of the German Social Democratic Party.

latter considered itself naturally social democratic or openly professed to be so.

That, of course, does not mean that each of these was a consciously aiming social democrat clearly oriented to the principles and the program of the party. That holds true for barely three, at the most four percent of all: the small group of those leaders and instigators of agitation, their closest friends and pupils. They alone knew and understood the entire official program, its interim demands no less than its ultimate, most radical goals. They had, often in glowing fanaticism, forcefully suppressed and silenced their own contradictory practical experiences, the spiritual heritage of the past and the critique of their common sense. They had worked themselves into this program often with indescribable pains and at financial sacrifices of all kinds until they were completely consumed by its thought process and only lived in it and for it, until they were only able to see and judge people, things, conditions and events through the eyes of the party. This circle of workers was mostly composed of genuine, honest German fanatics and idealists. Some of them were also filled with great ambition and thirst for action. But according to all my observations only few among them were of the genre of full-fledged egotists who clandestinely seek and find personal advantages. Here, in this small group, and in it alone, one truly found represented and expressed the views and principles of the social democracy clearly and purely. Principle and goal were firmly recognized and aimed at. But workers give expression to them more rarely than we could have suspected and expected.

But we cannot speak of equal, unified and clear political and social conscience among the remaining overwhelming majority of the social democratic working class. The most different, diverging and confused views were represented here in a colorful mixture of all nuances and shades. Here their own practical experiences were not suppressed or effaced—what everyone had done in his life and profession up to that time, the personal wishes and expectations they presently nursed and strove for, the peculiar impressions they had perceived in their homes and elsewhere in earlier, non-social democratic times. On the contrary, they were frequently especially active and lively, and everything together, personal experience and wishes and previous influences, was combined into an often only very loose and limited connection with the social democratic views. Even those were not complete, lucid or in order. Only few of this great, vast circle had studied the party writings anywhere nearly as stubbornly and seriously as had that other group which I described initially. What they possessed in the way of political and economic views of social democratic origin was what had remained from short, semi-digested articles of the social democratic local press which they read irregularly. Partly it stemmed from lectures and talks of social democratic gatherings and finally also from personal association with devoted and ambitious comrades. Depending on one or several of the above named factors gaining predominance and the decisive influence in this amalgamation, depending, also, on the intellectual abilities of a given man and his greater or lesser degree of initiative there arose a complete or incomplete, clear or contradictory, rational or irrational but always colorful mixture of political and social thought. This confluence was never synonymous with the true and programmatically accurate socio-political view of the normal or elite social democrat. It could not fit into any party pattern. It was expressed now amiably, friendly, quietly and devoid of passion, then rudely, in a repulsive, stinging or noisy fashion, once skilfully or clumsily, another time rarely or frequently. And even though almost every one of these people, by necessity, held a particular position toward the social democratic program, different from that of another one's, and while each one subsumed often the most diverse, even most conservative views under that program, they all felt and knew themselves to be social democrats. Many firmly believed that their very scanty fragments of thought were those of the party, his own peculiar ideals also that all-encompassing ideal of social democracy. Under such circumstances it is virtually impossible to give an exhaustive description of these confused, varying views which have never been clearly expressed. I myself have naturally not been able to learn about them all and must limit myself to reproducing certain traits which appeared particularly blatant to me.

Initially they all agree with one another on one of several very important points. That is the relationship to the ultimate radical goals of the social democratic party program. I do not contend that they openly rejected them or opposed them with any consistency. But neither the official democratic republicanism nor economic communism were actually very popular with the majority of these average social democrats, particularly not with the wiser, reflective, practical, experienced and mature men among them. These were factors for which most of their minds had no inner understanding and equally many hearts could feel no enthusiasm or warmth. But they accepted them—like so many other things of the social democracy—as something which necessarily belonged to it and had to be this way. They left it with indifference up to the leaders so that those might cope with the incomprehensible problems. Many of them were secretly convinced or expected that these prophecies would never come true. In reference to that, a rather well-off, childless and therefore carefree-living driller, an elderly, good-natured, polite man but also an enthusiastic adherent of social democracy said to me exactly this, "The way Bebel wishes our future things will never be. He has already changed much and will continue to do so." Another one, as equally wise, deliberative and devoted social democrat told me in a lengthy conversation among other things the following: "You know, I never read a social democratic book and rarely a newspaper. I used to not occupy myself with politics at all. But since I got married and have five eaters at home I have to do it. But I think my own thoughts. I do not go in for red ties, big round hats and other similar things. All that does not amount to much. We really do not want to become like the rich and refined people. There will always have to be rich and poor. We would not think of altering that. But we want a better and more just organization at the factory and in the state. I openly express what I think about that, even though it might not be pleasant. But I do nothing illegal." In general men who were wiser and more self-confident did not fear to take a particular stand on current questions of their party. Such did a mechanic, the eldest, most experienced in the entire department. He considered himself a social democrat just like the comrade whom I quoted above. He explained to me that he by no means expected or even wished for the realization of all their demands. He was not in agreement with the official party position on the question of woman and child labor, as were many others. As we all know party leaders have urged up to the present that the entire social democratic agitation be directed towards its elimination and that the workers insist upon its abolition. "But that is nonsense. If a man earns a sufficient salary he will automatically not let his wife and children work in the factory. But if the money is needed then they have to help earning it, as unfortunate as that may be. In that case one should not limit their salary. It is wrong to maintain that salaries would go up as a consequence. Maybe somewhat, but not very much. Should a compensation really be created salaries would have to be doubled on the average. Then no man would have to send his wife or child to work. But who can expect this of the factory owners? I don't even believe they would financially be able to do that if they wanted to." In this expression of opinion it does not matter whether the arguments are factually or economically sound or wrong—in the case of the latter we would judge them to be unsound —but what matters is that we prove that intellectually capable, skilled and thinking workers do not only preserve their own views but also express them among their comrades without feeling ashamed, in spite of their allegiance to the social democratic party. They should have the desire to ponder over problems within themselves without being sidetracked by the slogans of a republican-communistic order of society. Current and future questions of principles (for the ones aiming higher and being more farsighted) of their own organization in which they have a share occupy a large and broad group of the best workers most strongly. They are familiar with those matters, they understand them and possess experience and judgment in them. Many a man was unable to find peace of mind over the relatively harmless problem of the bi-weekly pay days. They urgently wished for a weekly pay day. I thought that this matter was rather unimportant. But they strongly disagreed. They felt that their needs for one week could be predetermined in advance. They would then be able to keep their money together for that period and appropriate it accordingly. This would not be feasible with a bi-weekly pay day. Greater expenses which came up during that time by necessity would consume much. And at the end of the two weeks ends would barely meet or they would even have to borrow money. That in itself was not exactly a convincing argument but rather another proof for the financial inefficiency of our workers. For others again a more just salary was the main diving force in their political and social views. And rightly so. . . .

Our working youth of today does not only lose the salary which it has earned under such hardship on the dance floor and during the nights from Sunday to Monday but it also loses its most valuable strength, its ideals, its virtue and its chastity. But it is really not surprising. It would be a miracle were it not so. Let us stop and think for a moment. During the week our young people are in an ugly factory, day-in, day-out, at monotonous, often boring work, in dirt and sweat and without proper relaxation at lunch. They spend the evenings of their working days in the street, in front of their house or in a small, narrow room of their boarding host with the noise of children and kitchen smells. Their sleeping quarters are pitiful. And all this while they earn comparatively decent wages, while they are without control, without parental love and care. In short, they are without the beneficial influence of a strong family union while possessing youthfully strong limbs and youthful desire in heart and mind. Then comes Sunday with its sleeping late, its rest and freedom which is denied to them by no one and the proper use of which they are not taught. There lures the sound of music. There are young, fresh faces of smiling girls. There are the glittering lights, the high and wide ceiling of the beautifully painted dance hall before them. Yes, here they find compensation for the ugly monotony of the week—all in one evening, one night, a thousandfold compensation for the hundred ugly impressions of the entire week. It is actually understandable that the young, unattached people throw themselves into this fantastic current, that it enchants their souls and that they finally lose their best to it. I do not accuse, I do not excuse, either, I merely describe what is truthfully happening and explain what is yet to come for sure.

I contend that as a consequence hardly any young man or girl over 17 is chaste among the working population of Chemnitz. Sexual intercourse is prevalent among the youth of today that has been reared on the dance floor. It is simply considered the most natural self-evident fact. There is rarely a trace of consciousness that this means to commit a sin. Down there the sixth Commandment in that sense does not exist. But the worker hardly ever associates with prostitutes who charge money. That is considered a disgrace. The prostitutes themselves are held in contempt. But almost every boy or girl has his or her lover who perform this service quite naturally. Besides that the young man seeks to frequent other girls as well who are willing. And in fact this is neither rare nor difficult. But at the same time those girls (who let themselves be used by the first acquaintance) are looked down upon by many. One does not go steady with such a girl. If a girl becomes pregnant she usually gets married, regardless of whether she has been with the man for a long time or just a few weeks. It is not important that they know each other well, that one of them may be a good-for-nothing, that they may or may not be suited for one another. The young people are thus driven into marriage by chance or sexual indulgence and its possible consequences. It is rarely true love, inner need or rational deliberation.

Here we find the most valid explanation for the misery in the workers' marriages and for the hope of all those, including the social democrats, who mean well for the people, to bring about a new state of affairs, emancipation for women and the new social democratic ideal for marriages. I refer here to the remarks in the conclusion of the second chapter. Indeed, for many men women merely exist as a means to satisfy their sexual drive, a general impediment to his advancement or, at best, with things working out favorably, a capable household manager who keeps the man energetically at a leash. According to the remarks of several of my working colleagues marriage is the "ultimate and greatest stupidity a man can commit." Actually things are a bit better in some families. Gradually a mutual sympathy and respect grow between many partners. Despite the generally deplorable conditions I found a number of truly beautiful marriages, deepened by genuine love. But over all the fact stands that down there women are much less appreciated by men. They are less respected and treated worse than in other classes. They are kept strictly and not infrequently beaten. At the same time a husband demands conjugal faithfulness without feeling bound by this himself. Also in other matters a great lack of consciousness in mutual ethical obligations which are prescribed for marriage prevails.

One ray of hope for both parents in this dingy and at best indifferent and monotonous married life are their children. The tenderness which they withhold from one another is often transferred to the children, in fact so much so that this sometimes results in a lack of manners. They become spoiled. The parents do for them whatever they are capable of. They take care of them as best as they can. They spend much time with them and take them along on their customary walks in the evening and on Sundays. They invest their utmost strength and ambition in them in order to enable the son to become something halfway "decent." This means that he may at least learn a little more and achieve a higher position than his father did—circumstances permitting. The manual laborer likes to see his son as a turner, a plumber his as a carpenter, in short, as a skilled worker. The skilled worker in turn would most like to see his son become a merchant, lower civil servant or something similar. The children in the families of my working colleagues were not overworked. If occasionally they were able to earn some money, all right. But as far as I could observe they were only rarely strained or abused as bread winners. No one begrudged them their freedom but granted it as long as possible to the children. And if one became ill they were greatly concerned and did everything to keep the child alive. Then even the strictest social democrats who were of course inimical to customary medicine and occasionally played doctor themselves gave up their obstinate viewpoint. They let themselves be persuaded by their wives to fetch an expensive doctor. Their love for the child was still greater than the prejudice of a pseudo-education which knows all the answers.

ROBERT TRESSELL

Still another picture of workers, this time construction craftsmen and laborers in southern England, is to be presented. Southern England, it must immediately be noted, was not an industrial center and these workers were definitely not factory workers. Here is the cause of many of the differences in view between these workers and factory labor in Germany and elsewhere. It could also be argued that there is something typically English about their undogmatic political views. Certainly, compared with Germany, English socialism was slow to develop and quite pragmatic and untheoretical. The possibility of national differences in the working as well as in the middle classes cannot be discounted.

But the more important point is that workers of this sort could be found in all the industrial countries and their views do not derive solely from the fact that they worked outside factories. Indeed despite their resistance to socialism the opinions of these workers do not completely differ from those of Göhre's workmates. It is true that these workers recall some of the sense of rights and dignity that can be found in artisanal protest in the early industrial decades. But many factory workers, as former artisans or peasants, could do the same; in the passage from Göhre, their evocation of traditional social hierarchy suggested this. And at the same time construction workers were, by 1900, subjected to a fully capitalist system of work, even if they avoided the complete mechanization and the rapidity of work of a factory setting. This makes their resignation and the reasons for it all the more interesting.

Robert Tressell was the penname of Robert Noonan, a housepainter of Irish extraction who worked for builders in Hastings. His novel, *The Ragged-Trousered Philanthropists,* was first published in 1914, in a partial version. Novels can be a fruitful source for the social historian, and a novel by a workingman about workers may be given particular credit. Yet one would obviously hope for independent evidence, for even the most realistic novelist might indulge his fancy in describing social types.[1] Tressell was an oddity among his colleagues, and not simply because he wrote a novel. He bitterly resented the capitalist system; Owen, a character in his novel, was clearly an alter ego. Yet his propaganda, like that of Owen, fell on deaf ears. There is more than a slight analogy with the situation of Max Lotz. But while Lotz did not try to characterize his fellow workers in great detail, Tressell does. The question is whether, in his situation, he could accurately do so. For example, he has colleagues spout a surprising array of "middle-class" opinions about poverty and its causes. Doubtless, middle-class ideas were shared by many workers, but one wonders if Tressell is not to some extent mixing his dislike of benighted workers with his hatred for the propertied classes.

Still, Tressell's work is significant beyond its illustrations of the values and limitations of even an unusual novel as historical evidence. He completes the picture of the major types of workers in the later nineteenth century and of adaptations to industrial (albeit in this case not factory) life. His workers would be hard to stir to protest, but not because they lacked grievances. They mixed resignation—a sense that poverty was irremediable—with humor and beer and, in a peculiar way, a belief in their own dignity, and got through life. These were the workers—a majority even in Britain, where unionization had gone furthest—who did not join unions or vote in protest, if they voted at all.

Divisions in the working class are not as sharp as those in the middle class. Among other things, workers could not long afford the luxury of protesting industrialization itself. But large numbers did retain a fundamentally traditional outlook, within—though more commonly outside—the factories. Others were alienated. Still others managed considerable adaptation to industrial life while seeking some new rights to complete the process. Even in 1900, the working class in any modern sense was only fifty to a hundred years old in the leading industrial countries. Small wonder that it was still in the process of becoming. Class unity would increase subsequently, but it is questionable even in the later twentieth century whether the diversity of reactions to industrial life has disappeared.

1 For a study that builds a picture of social classes (though not workers) entirely on novels and illustrates the uses and dangers of the approach, see Ernest K. Bramsted, *Aristocracy and the Middle Classes in Germany* (London, 1937).

The Ragged-Trousered Philanthropists

Sawkins was not popular with any of the others. When, about twelve months previously, he first came to work for Rushton & Co., he was a simple labourer, but since then he had 'picked up' a slight knowledge of the trade, and having armed himself with a putty-knife and put on a white jacket, regarded himself as a fully qualified painter. The others did not perhaps object to him trying to better his condition, but his wages—fivepence an hour—were twopence an hour less than the standard rate, and the result was that in slack times often a better workman was "stood off" when Sawkins was kept on. Moreover, he was generally regarded as a sneak who carried tales to the foreman and the 'Bloke.' Every new hand who was taken on was usually warned by his new mates "not to let that b———r Sawkins see anything."

The unpleasant silence which now ensued was at length broken by one of the men, who told a dirty story, and in the laughter and applause that followed, the incident of the tea was forgotten.

"How did you get on yesterday?" asked Crass, addressing Bundy, the plasterer, who was intently studying the sporting columns of the *Daily Obscurer*.

"No luck," replied Bundy, gloomily. "I had a bob each way on Stockwell, in the first race, but it was scratched before the start."

This gave rise to a conversation between Crass, Bundy, and one or two others concerning the chances of different horses in the morrow's races. It was Friday, and no one had much money, so at the suggestion of Bundy, a Syndicate was formed, each member contributing threepence, for the purpose of backing a dead certainty given by the renowned Captain Kiddem of the *Obscurer*. One of those who did not join the syndicate was Frank Owen, who was as usual absorbed in a newspaper. He was generally regarded as a bit of a crank: for it was felt that there must be something wrong about a man who took no interest in racing or football and was always talking a lot of rot about religion and politics. If it had not been for the fact that he was generally admitted to be an exceptionally good workman, they would have had but little hesitation about thinking that he was mad. This man was about thirty-two years of age, and of medium height, but so slightly built that he appeared taller. There was a suggestion of refinement in his clean-shaven face, but his complexion was ominously clear, and an unnatural colour flushed the thin cheeks.

These selections are taken from a 1955 edition, published in London; pp. 33–34, 37–38, 44–50.

There was a certain amount of justification for the attitude of his fellow workmen, for Owen held the most unusual and unorthodox opinions on the subjects mentioned.

The affairs of the world are ordered in accordance with orthodox opinions. If anyone did not think in accordance with these he soon discovered this fact for himself. Owen saw that in the world a small class of people were possessed of a great abundance and superfluity of the things that are produced by work. He saw also that a very great number—in fact, the majority of the people—lived on the verge of want; and that a smaller but still very large number lived lives of semi-starvation from the cradle to the grave; while a yet smaller but still very great number actually died of hunger, or, maddened by privation, killed themselves and their children in order to put a period to their misery. And strangest of all—in his opinion—he saw that the people who enjoyed abundance of the things that are made by work, were the people who did Nothing: and that the others, who lived in want or died of hunger, were the people who worked. And seeing all this he thought that it was wrong, that the system that produced such results was rotten and should be altered. And he had sought out and eagerly read the writings of those who thought they knew how it might be done.

It was because he was in the habit of speaking of these subjects that his fellow workmen came to the conclusion that there was probably something wrong with his mind. . . .

Easton was still reading the *Obscurer*: he was not able to understand exactly what the compiler of the figures was driving at—probably the latter never intended that anyone should understand—but he was conscious of a growing feeling of indignation and hatred against foreigners of every description, who were ruining this country, and he began to think that it was about time we did something to protect ourselves. Still, it was a very difficult question: to tell the truth, he himself could not make head or tail of it. At length he said aloud, addressing himself to Crass:

"Wot do you think of this 'ere fissical policy, Bob?"

"Ain't thought much about it," replied Crass. "I don't never worry my 'ed about politics."

"Much better left alone," chimed in old Jack Linden sagely, "argy-fying about politics generally ends up with a bloody row an' does no good to nobody."

At this there was a murmur of approval from several of the others. Most of them were averse from arguing or disputing about politics. If two or three men of similar opinions happened to be together they might discuss such things in a friendly and superficial way, but in a mixed company it was better left alone. The "Fissical Policy" emanated from the Tory party. That was the reason why some of them were strongly in favour of it, and for the same reason others were opposed to it. Some of them were under the delusion that they were Conservatives: similarly, others imagined themselves to be Liberals. As a matter of fact, most of them were nothing. They knew as much about the public affairs of their own country as they did of the condition of affairs in the planet Jupiter.

Easton began to regret that he had broached so objectionable a subject, when, looking up from his paper, Owen said:

"Does the fact that you never 'trouble your heads about politics' prevent you from voting at election times?"

No one answered, and there ensued a brief silence. Easton, however, in spite of the snub he had received, could not refrain from talking.

"Well, I don't go in for politics much, either, but if what's in this 'ere paper is true, it seems to me as we oughter take some interest in it, when the country is being ruined by foreigners."

"If you're goin' to believe all that's in that bloody rag you'll want some salt," said Harlow.

The *Obscurer* was a Tory paper and Harlow was a member of the local Liberal club. Harlow's remark roused Crass.

"Wot's the use of talkin' like that?" he said, "you know very well that the country *is* being ruined by foreigners. Just go to a shop to buy something; look round the place an' you'll see that more than 'arf the damn stuff comes from abroad. They're able to sell their goods 'ere because they don't 'ave to pay no dooty, but they takes care to put 'eavy dooties on our goods to keep 'em out of their countries: and I say it's about time it was stopped." . . .

"The greatest cause of poverty is hover-population," remarked Harlow.

"Yes," said old Joe Philpot. "If a boss wants two men, twenty goes after the job: ther's too many people and not enough work."

"Over-population!" cried Owen, "when there's thousands of acres of uncultivated land in England without a house or human being to be seen. Is overpopulation the cause of poverty in France? Is overpopulation the cause of poverty in Ireland? Within the last fifty years the population of Ireland has been reduced by more than half. Four millions of people have been exterminated by famine or got rid of by emigration, but they haven't got rid of poverty. P'raps you think that half the people in this country ought to be exterminated as well."

Here Owen was seized with a violent fit of coughing, and resumed his seat. When the cough had ceased he sat wiping his mouth with his handkerchief and listening to the talk that ensued.

"Drink is the cause of most of the poverty," said Slyme.

This young man had been through some strange process that he called "conversion." He had had a 'change of 'art' and looked down with pious pity upon those he called 'worldly' people. He was not 'worldly', he did not smoke or drink and never went to the theatre. He had an extraordinary notion that total abstinence was one of the fundamental principles of the Christian religion. It never occurred to what he called his mind, that this doctrine is an insult to the Founder of Christianity.

"Yes," said Crass, agreeing with Slyme, "an' thers plenty of 'em wot's too lazy to work when they can get it. Some of the b———s who go about pleading poverty 'ave never done a fair day's work in all their bloody lives. Then thers all this new fangled machinery," continued Crass. "That's wot's ruinin' everything. Even in our trade ther's them machines for trimmin' wallpaper, an' now they've brought out a paintin' machine. Ther's a pump an' a 'ose pipe, an' they reckon two men can do as much with this 'ere machine as twenty could without it."

"Another thing is women," said Harlow, "there's thousands of 'em nowadays doin' work wot oughter be done by men."

"In my opinion ther's too much of this 'ere eddication, nowadays," remarked old Linden. "Wot the 'ell's the good of eddication to the likes of us?"

"None whatever," said Crass, "it just puts foolish idears into people's 'eds and makes 'em too lazy to work."

Barrington, who took no part in the conversation, still sat silently smoking. Owen was listening to this pitiable farrago with feelings of contempt and wonder. Were they all hopelessly stupid? Had their intelligence never developed beyond the childhood stage? Or was he mad himself?

"Early marriages is another thing," said Slyme: "no man oughtn't to be allowed to get married unless he's in a position to keep a family."

"How can marriage be a cause of poverty?" said Owen, contemptuously. "A man who is not married is living an unnatural life. Why don't you continue your argument a little further and say that the practice of eating and drinking is the cause of poverty or that if people were to go barefoot and naked there would be no poverty? The man who is so poor that he cannot marry is in a condition of poverty already."

"Wot I mean," said Slyme, "is that no man oughtn't to marry till he's saved up enough so as to 'ave some money in the bank; an' another thing, I reckon a man oughtn't to get married till 'e's got a 'ouse of 'is own. It's easy enough to buy one in a building society if you're in reg'lar work."

At this there was a general laugh.

"Why, you bloody fool," said Harlow, scornfully, "most of us is walkin' about 'arf our time. It's all very well for you to talk; you've got almost a constant job on this firm. If they're doin' anything at all you're one of the few wot gets a show in. And another thing," he added with a sneer, "we don't all go to the same chapel as old Misery."

"Old Misery" was Rushton & Co.'s manager or walking foreman. "Misery" was only one of the nicknames bestowed upon him by the hands: he was also known as "Nimrod" and "Pontius Pilate."

"And even if it's not possible," Harlow continued, winking at the others, "what's a man to do during the years he's savin' up?"

"Well, he must conquer hisself," said Slyme, getting red.

"Conquer hisself is right!" said Harlow and the others laughed again.

"Of course if a man tried to conquer hisself by his own strength," replied Slyme, " 'e would be sure to fail, but when you've got the Grace of God in you it's different."

"Chuck it, fer Christ's sake!" said Harlow in a tone of disgust. "We've only just 'ad our dinner!"

"And wot about drink?" demanded old Joe Philpot, suddenly.

" 'Ear, 'ear," cried Harlow. "That's the bleedin' talk. I wouldn't mind 'avin' 'arf a pint now, if somebody else will pay for it."

Joe Philpot—or as he was usually called, "Old Joe"—was in the habit of indulging rather freely in the cup that inebriates. He was not very old, being only a little over fifty, but he looked much older. He had lost his wife some five years ago and was now alone in the world, for his three children had died in their infancy. Slyme's reference to drink had roused Philpot's indignation; he felt that it was directed against himself. The muddled condition of his brain did not permit him to take up the cudgels in his own behalf, but he knew that although Owen was a teetotaller himself, he disliked Slyme.

"There's no need for us to talk about drink or laziness," returned Owen, impatiently, "because they have nothing to do with the matter. The question is, what is the cause of the lifelong poverty of the majority of those who are not drunkards and who do work? Why, if all the drunkards and won't-works and unskilled or inefficient workers could be by some miracle transformed into sober, industrious and skilled workers tomorrow, it would, under the present conditions, be so much the worse for us, because there isn't enough work for all now and those people by increasing the competition for what work there is, would inevitably cause a reduction of wages and a greater scarcity of employment. The theories that drunkenness, laziness or inefficiency are the causes of poverty are so many devices invented and fostered by those who are selfishly interested in maintaining the present state of affairs, for the purpose of preventing us from discovering the real causes of our present condition."

"Well, if we're all wrong," said Crass, with a sneer, "p'raps you can tell us what the real cause is?"

"An' p'raps you think you know how it's to be altered," remarked Harlow, winking at the others.

"Yes; I do think I know the cause," declared Owen, "and I do think I know how it could be altered————"

"It can't never be haltered," interrupted old Linden. "I don't see no sense in all this 'ere talk. There's always been rich and poor in the world, and there always will be."

"Wot I always say is this 'ere," remarked Philpot, whose principal characteristic—apart from thirst—was a desire to see everyone comfortable, and who hated rows of any kind. "There ain't no use in the likes of us trubblin our 'eds or quarrellin' about politics. It don't make a dam bit of difference who you votes for or who gets in. They're hall the same; workin' the horicle for their own benefit. You can talk till you're black in the face, but you won't never be able to alter it. It's no use worrying. The sensible thing is to try and make the best of things as we find 'em: enjoy ourselves, and do the best we can for each other. Life's too short to quarrel and we'll hall soon be dead!"

At the end of this lengthy speech, the philosophic Philpot abstractedly grasped a jam-jar and raised it to his lips; but suddenly remembering that it contained stewed tea and not beer, set it down again without drinking.

"Let us begin at the beginning," continued Owen, taking no notice of these interruptions. "First of all, what do you mean by Poverty?"

"Why, if you've got no money, of course," said Crass impatiently.

The others laughed disdainfully. It seemed to them such a foolish question.

"Well, that's true enough as far as it goes," returned Owen, "that is, as things are arranged in the world at present. But money itself is not wealth: it's of no use whatever."

At this there was another outburst of jeering laughter.

"Supposing for example that you and Harlow were shipwrecked on a desolate island, and *you* had saved nothing from the wreck but a bag containing a thousand sovereigns, and he had a tin of biscuits and a bottle of water."

"Make it beer!" cried Harlow appealingly.

"Who would be the richer man, you or Harlow?"

"But then you see we ain't shipwrecked on no dissolute island at all," sneered Crass. "That's the worst of your arguments. You can't never get very far without supposing some bloody ridiclus thing or other. Never mind about supposing things wot ain't true; let's 'ave facts and common sense."

" 'Ear, 'ear," said old Linden. "That's wot we want—a little common sense."

"What do *you* mean by poverty, then?" asked Easton.

"What I call poverty is when people are not able to secure for themselves all the benefits of civilisation; the necessaries, comforts, pleasures and refinements of life, leisure, books, theatres, pictures, music, holidays, travel, good and beautiful homes, good clothes, good and pleasant food."

Everybody laughed. It was so ridiculous. The idea of the likes of *them* wanting or having such things! Any doubts that any of them had entertained as to Owen's sanity disappeared. The man was as mad as a March hare.

"If a man is only able to provide himself and his family with the bare necessaries of existence, that man's family is living in poverty. Since he cannot enjoy the advantages of civilisation he might just as well be a savage: better, in fact, for a savage knows nothing of what he is deprived. What we call civilisation—the accumulation of knowledge which has come down to us from our forefathers—is the fruit of thousands of years of human thought and toil. It is not the result of the labour of the ancestors of any separate class of people who exist today, and therefore it is by right the common heritage of all. Every little child that is born into the world, no matter whether he is clever or dull, whether he is physically perfect or lame, or blind; no matter how much he may excel or fall short of his fellows in other respects, in one thing at least he is their equal—he is one of the heirs of all the ages that have gone before."

Some of them began to wonder whether Owen was not sane after all. He certainly must be a clever sort of chap to be able to talk like this. It sounded almost like something out of a book, and most of them could not understand one half of it.

"Why is it," continued Owen, "that we are not only deprived of our inheritance—we are not only deprived of nearly all the benefits of civilisation, but we and our children are also often unable to obtain even the bare necessaries of existence?"

No one answered.

"All these things," Owen proceeded, "are produced by those who work. We do our full share of the work, therefore we should have a full share of the things that are made by work."

The others continued silent. Harlow thought of the overpopulation theory, but decided not to mention it. Crass, who could not have given an intelligent answer to save his life, for once had sufficient sense to remain silent. He did think of calling out the patent paint-pumping machine and bringing the hosepipe to bear on the subject, but abandoned the idea; after all; he thought, what was the use of arguing with such a fool as Owen?

Sawkins pretended to be asleep.

Philpot, however, had suddenly grown very serious.

"As things are now," went on Owen, "instead of enjoying the advantages of civilisation we are really worse off than slaves, for if we were slaves our owners in their own interest would see to it that we always had food and———"

"Oh, I don't see that," roughly interrupted old Linden, who had been listening with evident anger and impatience. "You can speak for yourself, but I can tell yer I don't put *myself* down as a slave."

"Nor me neither," said Crass sturdily. "Let them call theirselves slaves as wants to."

330.94 S   CIRC = 3 day

STEARNS   GENERAL
                 COLLECTION
The Impact of the
Industrial Revolution   17644

replace ded 12/85

DATE DUE	BORROWER'S NAME	ROOM NUMBER
	Chris Cattle	M-36
	Eric M'Cathy	M-81
out 10/15/86	J McCoy	